SHADOW OF THE PLANTATION

"SEEM LAK' I AIN'T NEVER BREAK EVEN"

SHADOW OF
THE PLANTATION

By
CHARLES S. JOHNSON

PHOENIX BOOKS

THE UNIVERSITY OF CHICAGO PRESS
CHICAGO & LONDON

THE UNIVERSITY OF CHICAGO PRESS, CHICAGO & LONDON
The University of Toronto Press, Toronto 5, Canada

TABLE OF CONTENTS

ACKNOWLEDGMENTS

THE method and objective of this study demanded long hours with each of the six hundred families who form the basis for these observations. Without the aid of the skilled services of several field assistants and their complete and enthusiastic co-operation, it would have been impossible to satisfy the requirement of representative volume and of an intimate record of family life. In this connection the work of Miss Ophelia Settle, Mr. Lewis Wade Jones, Miss Josie Sellers, and Miss Ann Savage proved invaluable. Besides, there have been others of the staff of the Social Science Department whose work in checking and rechecking the statistical data of the study merits fullest acknowledgment.

The study itself was made possible by the Julius Rosenwald Fund, through Dr. Michael M. Davis, who has been interested and in turn has interested the United States Public Health Service in certain of the health problems of this and several other similar counties of the South. To this Fund and to Dr. O. C. Wenger of the United States Public Health Service grateful acknowledgments are made.

The willingness of a number of scholars in this field to give attention to the data and to the author's interpretation of them has been as gratifying as their suggestions have been helpful. I wish to acknowledge a debt of gratitude for the valuable criticism and counsel of Dr. Louis Wirth, Dr. Ulrich B. Phillips, Mr. E. R. Embree, Professor Monroe N. Work, Dr. W. F. Ogburn, Dr. Howard W. Odum, and of my colleagues Professor Horace M. Bond and Dr. E. Franklin Frazier. I reserve for special mention the vital contribution to this volume of Dr. Robert E. Park, whose insight and long acquaintance with this field have provided a constant illumination for the whole development of the study.

C. S. J.

INTRODUCTION

SOME time during the winter of 1898 and the spring of 1899 William James read to his students in philosophy a notable paper he had then just finished writing, to which he later gave the quaint and intriguing title, "A Certain Blindness in Human Beings."

The "blindness" to which James here refers is a kind of blindness to which we are all subject, by the very limitation of our human nature and of our individual experience, our blindness, namely, "to the feelings of creatures and peoples other than ourselves."

"We are," as James says, "practical beings each with limitations and duties to perform. Each is bound to feel intensely the importance of duties and the significance of the situations that call these forth. But this feeling in each of us is a vital secret for sympathy with which we vainly look to others. The others are too much absorbed in their own vital secrets to take an interest in ours."[1]

It is not possible to suggest in a word the significance which this fact of the isolation and loneliness of the individual—each in his own little world, hugging his own personal secret—assumes in James's interpretation of it. Suffice to say that the fact connects up directly with a definite philosophy to which James subscribed and to a theory of knowledge to which—if he did not first formulate it—he lent a powerful support.

I

My reason for referring to this essay here and to the conception of human relations and of knowledge, which it so persuasively sets forth, is that it seems to shed light, from an unexpected source,

[1] William James, *Talks to Teachers on Psychology; and to Students on Some of Life's Ideals.*

ix

upon the problem and method of this present study and of social studies generally, particularly when they are concerned with the customs and institutions of isolated and provincial peoples; peoples who, though they live close to, and dependent upon us, as we upon them, are still outside the orbit of our ordinary life and understanding.

This volume is concerned with the Negro peasants of the southern plantations, but the Negroes of the "black belts" are not the only peoples in America who live on the outer margins of our understanding and to whose vital secrets we must confess a certain blindness. There are other peoples, white peoples, like the Acadians of southwestern Louisiana; the Mennonites and so-called Pennsylvania Dutch of Lancaster County, Pennsylvania, and vicinity. There are also the mountain whites of the Appalachians and the peoples of mixed racial ancestry like the Mexicans of New Mexico and the little isolated communities of Indian, Negro, and white mixtures, scattered about in remote parts of Virginia, North Carolina, Alabama, and Louisiana. All of these are peoples who live, to be sure, within the political boundaries of the United States but live nevertheless on the margins of our culture. In this sense, and for the further reason that they occupy a place somewhere between the more primitive and tribally organized and the urban populations of our modern cities, they may be called "marginal peoples." The distinction between them and the peoples by whom they are surrounded is that they are not merely people, but folk people, and their culture, in so far as it differs from that of the majority of us in the United States, is a folk culture.

What is a folk culture and what is the folk? A very simple way to state the matter is to say that the "folk" is a people whose current history is recorded, if at all, by the ethnologist rather than by the historian or the newspaper. Not that folk peoples do not have history, but it exists for the most part in the form of unrecorded ballads and legends which, with its folk lore, constitutes a tradition that is handed down from generation to generation by word of mouth rather than through the medium of the printed page.

It is characteristic of the folk that it has a habitat and that its culture is local. Gypsies are folk, too, but they are the exception. Though they wander, they manage somehow to preserve a cultural isolation and a tribal solidarity as complete as that of any other preliterate people. In all our various attempts to study human nature we invariably encounter these exceptions. They constitute, in fact, the most valuable data that an investigation ordinarily turns up: first, because they are the starting-points for fresh observation and further reflection; and, second, because in the long run the exceptions always prove the rule.

Redfield in his volume *Tepoztlán*, which is a study of one of the marginal peoples of Mexico, similar in some respects to those in the United States, is at some pains to define what he conceives the folk to be. He says:

> Such peoples enjoy a common stock of tradition; they are the carriers of a culture. This culture preserves its continuity from generation to generation without depending upon the printed page. Moreover, such a culture is local; the folk has a habitat. And finally, the folk peoples are country peoples. If folk lore is encountered in the cities it is never in a robust condition, but always diminishing, always a vestige.[2]

And then he adds:

> The southern Negro is our one principal folk. He has a local tradition orally transmitted; he makes folk songs. Except for him we have to search for folk peoples in the United States. In the mountains of the south and southeast we have a sort of vestigal folk. And here and there, in such occupations as involve long periods of isolation and a relative independence of the printed page—as, for example, among lumbermen or cowboys—a sort of quasi-folk develop, who write anonymous folk songs and sometimes build up, around campfires, folk sagas of the Paul Bunyan variety.

On the other hand, the folk are not to be confused and identified with the peasant who has left the soil to live and work in the city. Such peoples constitute what might be described as the "populus" or, better still, the "proletariat."

So the Negro of the plantation—though the two are closely related and the history of the one goes far to explain the existence

[2] Robert Redfield, *Tepoztlán, A Mexican Village* (University of Chicago Press, 1930), pp. 1–6.

of the other—is not to be identified with the mobile and migratory Negro laborers who crowd the slums of southern cities, or, like the hero of Howard Odum's *Rainbow round My Shoulder*, go wandering about the country celebrating their freedom and their loneliness by singing "blues."

These blues, which, by the way, first gained recognition as a form of popular ballad in night clubs of Beale Street, Memphis, are the natural idiom of the Negro proletarian, just as the "spirituals" have been, and to a very considerable extent still are, the natural expression of the mind and the mood of the plantation Negro. The distinction between the folk of the villages and the open country and the proletarians or populus of the city is expressed and symbolized in the difference between the folk song and the popular ballad, the spirituals and the blues.

II

Marginal peoples, peoples in transit between simpler and primitive and more sophisticated and complex cultures, such as characterize our modern industrial and urban civilization, constitute, as I have suggested, a special problem in method, but one which is after all fundamental to studies of society and human nature everywhere.

There are no special difficulties in describing the external forms and the obvious expressions of a local culture. The difficulty consists in making that culture intelligible; in discovering the meaning and the function of usages, customs, and institutions.

Anthropologists, in their studies of primitive peoples, have distinguished between (1) material and (2) non-material elements of a culture. Material culture is represented by the tools, artifacts, and in general the technical devices employed by a people in their dealings with the external world. Non-material culture, on the other hand, includes all those institutions, ceremonial customs, ritual dances, and what not by which a people maintains its morale and is enabled to act collectively.

Institutions are, generally speaking, devices which come into existence in the effort to act collectively and exist in order to make collective action more effective.

But customs persist and preserve their external forms after they have lost their original meaning and functions. Institutions are borrowed or imposed upon peoples to whose traditions, instincts, and actual needs they are quite foreign, or have not yet been fully assimilated. Fashions change, and with the change institutions, though they still persist, are looked upon with profoundly changed attitudes.

Considerations of this sort have led anthropologists in studying culture to distinguish between form and function, and to emphasize the subjective and less obvious aspects of the cultural complex. The study of a society or of a people turns out under these circumstances to be the study not merely of its institutions but of its mentality.

What is meant by mentality in this sense is stated impressively by Redfield in the concluding chapter of his volume *Tepoztlán*. "If by mentality is understood," he says, "a complex of habits employed in meeting unfamiliar problems," then mentality, too, is an aspect of culture. "If the individual undergoes experiences of a very different sort from those undergone before, he develops a correspondingly new organ, a new mind."

But there is a less obvious aspect of social institutions in which they appear in even more intimate and vital association with the people whose life they serve. It has been observed that as long as their social institutions are functioning normally, primitive peoples ordinarily exhibit an extraordinary zest in the life they lead, even when that life, like that of the Eskimo in the frozen North or the pigmies in the steaming forest of Central Africa, seems to be one of constant privation and hardship.

On the other hand, when some catastrophe occurs which undermines the traditional structure of their society, they sometimes lose their natural lust for life, and that euphoria which enabled them to support the hardships of their primitive existence frequently deserts them. That catastrophe may be, and frequently is, the sudden advent of a more highly civilized people intent upon their improvement and uplift by incorporating them in a more highly organized industrial society.

Under such circumstances, a people may be so completely obsessed by a sense of their own inferiority that they no longer desire to live as a people; and if they live as individuals, they will prefer to identify themselves, as far as they are permitted to do so, with the invading or dominant people.

It is in some such way as this, i.e., by the incorporation of defeated or merely disheartened people into some larger and more complex social unit, that castes are formed.

It is evident, in spite of all that has been written of human nature and of human behavior, that the sources of joy and sorrow are still obscure. It is evident also that, as Stevenson says, in a passage in *Lantern Bearers* quoted by James, "to miss the joy is to miss all." That is to say, if you miss the joy you miss the one aspect of a people's life which more than anything else gives vitality to cultural forms and ensures their persistence, possibly in some new and modified form, under changed conditions. For this reason, the most subjective and least obvious aspect of the life of peoples and cultures is nevertheless one that cannot be neglected, particularly in the case of peoples who, as I have said, are in process of transit and subject to all the vicissitudes of profound cultural change.

This zest for life is just that personal and vital secret which, for each one of us, gives meaning and significance not merely to the life of the individual but of the society, of whatever sort it be, of which he is a member and a part.

III

Although it describes itself as a study of "social and cultural change," the materials on which this study is based are not those with which anthropologists are familiar or are likely to approve. As a matter of fact, the study starts with a different tradition— the tradition, namely, of the rural sociologist, who conceives his community rather as a statistical aggregate than as a cultural complex. One reason for this is the convenience and the necessity of making use of the available statistics, which have been collected and classified on the basis of existing administrative units rather than of the region or of any other sort of natural area.

Thus the investigation assumed at the outset the character of a survey and study of a population rather than of a people, and the plan, as originally conceived, was, by a process of sampling, to describe and characterize statistically a population area.

The area chosen for this survey was a slice of one of the familiar "black belts," historically the region of cotton culture in the South. Macon County, of which Tuskegee is the county seat, is the seat also of Booker Washington's famous industrial school for Negroes and the county which, during his lifetime, was, so to speak, the rural laboratory in which he carried on his experiments in rural education—experiments which graduates of his school and others, with the assistance of the Rosenwald Fund, have extended to most other parts of the South.

It was assumed, no doubt, that Macon County offered a fair sample of Negro rural population, and that a study of its population would indicate what Negro education—unaccompanied, to be sure, by any special or systematic effort to reorganize on any considerable scale the plantation system—had been able to do to keep the Negro on the soil and, by raising the general level of his intelligence and encouraging him to take the initiative in improving his own condition, to improve the condition of the country as a whole.

There were other reasons why a study of Negro culture should assume the technical form of a survey beside the desirability of starting with the available information in regard to the region. One was the character of the Negro community itself, and of the very tenuous lines of connections which hold the rural population into any sort of solidarity that could be described as communal. Another was the fact that the Negro community is so completely interpenetrated and dependent upon the dominant white community that it is difficult to conceive it as having any independent existence.

Outside of the plantation the only centers of Negro life are the rural churches and rural schools. The social situation is reflected in the human geography of the county.

A bird's-eye view of Macon County discloses a country of softly rolling uplands and interspersed with fragrant, wooded swamps.

Plantation, hamlet, and town, still rather widely dispersed, are connected by a network of rural roads which, except for a few stretches of recently constructed thoroughfare, wind their way leisurely along rolling ridges in order to escape as far as possible the perils of the sometimes heavy spring rains. Closer observation of this same countryside discloses the existence of another, narrower, and less obvious network of footpaths which—unplanned, unplotted, and without official recognition—intersect, connect, and supplement but never compete with the public highways.

These two systems of transportation—the public highways connecting the towns and the plantations and the footpaths connecting the humbler habitations of the Negro tenant farmers—suggest and symbolize the complicated interrelations and divisions between the races in Macon County and in the South generally, suggest also some of the complexities and some of the difficulties of studying one section of a population without taking some account at the same time of the other.

IV

If the study of culture is to reveal what makes life for individuals or peoples either significant and exciting or merely dull, what are the kinds of facts most likely to disclose this vital secret?

Undoubtedly the most revealing portions of the present study are the candid comments of the peoples studied on their own lives. As recorded here, in the language and accents in which they were uttered, most of these statements have the character of a human document.

The value of a human document as a datum is that it brings the object that is under investigation closer to the observer. Like a magnifying glass, it brings into view aspects of the object that were before that time not visible or only partially so. It sometimes happens that a casual remark, like a ray of light through a keyhole, will illuminate a whole interior, the character of which could only be guessed at as long as one's observations were confined to the exterior of the structure.

A good many of the remarks recorded in this study are so concrete, so pregnant with human interest, that they might have been written by Julia Peterkin or Du Bose Heyward, whose stories of Negro life exhibit an insight and "acquaintance with" the life they are describing that is unusual even in writers of realistic fiction.

As a rule, the individuals whose conversation and comments are here recorded are not in any sense a selected group of outstanding personalities in the community; rather they are just the ordinary mine-run of the population. A good many of them are old women, grandmothers, who with the freedom traditionally accorded to "old mammies" on the plantation are accustomed to express themselves more vigorously and more volubly than other members of the family. Besides, grandmothers, partly because they are less mobile than other members of the families and therefore more likely to be at home, are in a position to speak with authority in regard to marriages, births, deaths, and all the other facts that the investigators' schedules called for.

The statements recorded, while they do not represent a selected group of individuals, do exhibit an interesting diversity of types such as one would expect the intimate associations of an isolated community would inevitably produce. It is true that every kind of cultural association produces a certain degree of cultural homogeneity, but it invariably produces at the same time characteristic personality types. Among these an occasional individual is sufficiently outstanding to achieve a recognition in this record that is not accorded to the others. This was the case of Zach Ivey, who was clear and convinced that he had had a better time when he was a slave than he had ever had since; and by way of contrast to Zach Ivey there was Riny Biggers, who had early been impressed with the high value of literacy and differed profoundly from the views on slavery which Zach Ivey professed.

It is interesting to know that the relative merits of slavery and freedom are still a matter in regard to which there are differences of opinion among the Negroes on the plantations in the South. It is indicative of the immense weight of the tradition which still supports the plantation system. It makes significant and intelligible a remark made to me years ago by an old Negro farmer in Macon County who, though he could neither read nor write, owned and conducted successfully a plantation of eleven hundred acres. He said, with the peculiar quizzical expression of a man who would like more light on an obscure problem: "You know we'se jus' so ign'rint down heah we don' see much dif'rence 'tween freedom an' slavery, 'cep' den we wuz workin' fer ole marster an' now we'se workin' fer oursel's."

V

One can hardly escape the impression in viewing the facts of this survey that it is the inheritance of a tradition, embodied in the present plantation system, which more than anything else inhibits the progress, not merely of the black tenant but the white land-lord, and that with the persistence of that tradition the small and independent farmer cannot make headway.

Under these conditions the Negro rural school, instead of creating a settled class of Negro peasant proprietors, seems, particularly since the World War, to have conspired with other tendencies to hasten the movement from the rural South to the northern cities. On the whole, the plantation, as at present organized, seems to be a sick and dying institution. It still remains, however, what it was before the Civil War, the focus and center of the Negro life in the rural community; but it is no longer able to maintain either the discipline or the morale of an efficiently functioning institution; and plantation life has apparently lost whatever zest it may ever have had for the generations of white folk and black that it once nourished.

The plight of the cotton plantation is probably due not entirely to its inability to shake off its ancient heritage, which involves among other things the tradition of Negro racial inferiority. The prosperity of the cotton plantation in the southern states is dependent, finally, upon its ability to compete with other cotton-raising areas in the world-market.

Most that is still problematic in the condition of the Negro peasant seems to focus about two quite different institutions: (1) the plantation and (2) the Negro peasant family. What is the future of either or both, since the fate of the one seems to be bound up in that of the other?

The Negro peasant family, as it exists today, is certainly a rather amorphous social organism. In slavery, parents had little or no personal responsibility for the provision and care of their children, since that office was early taken over by the planter or his overseer, who assigned some older and experienced woman to the task. The consequence was that natural maternal affection, rather than any common economic interest, constituted the tie that held the family together. The male member of the family did not count for much in this arrangement. The family was, and still is, matriarchal in character.

It was not until freedom imposed upon the Negro tenant the necessity of making his farm pay that the Negro farmer began to reckon his children as a personal asset. The effect of this was that parents began to discourage the early marriage of their children, the consequence of which would be to deprive them of their children's services.

When a Negro farmer reached the position where he owned property of his own, he had a new incentive and found a new means for maintaining the permanence of the family, since he was eager to transmit this property to his children, who in turn looked forward to inheriting it. The permanence of the property interest became the basis for a continuing family tradition, and for a more consistent life-program for both the family as a whole and its individual members.

As long, however, as the freedman continued to live under the shadow of the plantation, these changes made but slow progress. With the advent of emancipation the status of the Negro on the plantation had been suddenly transformed from that of a field hand to tenant farmer. But the actual change was not as great as might have been expected. The freedman was not able at once to enter into the spirit and tradition of a free competition and industrial society. He had no conception, for example, of the secret terror that haunts the free laborer; the fear, namely, of losing his job and of being out of work. On the contrary, his first conception of freedom was that of a condition in which he would be permanently out of work. So far, therefore, from being possessed by that mania for owning things which is the characteristic, as the communists tell us, of a capitalistic society, his first impulse and aim were to get as deeply in debt as possible. If, therefore, the agents of the "Third International" find that such Negroes are as yet not ripe for communism, it is undoubtedly because they have not had as yet the opportunity to realize the evils of a free and competitive society.

What the findings of this survey suggest, then, is: (1) the necessity of a wider—in fact, a world-wide—and comparative study of the cotton plantation not merely as an economic and industrial but as a cultural unit; and (2) a comparative study of the actual conditions of the world in which the people on the plantation live.

VI

One thing that complicates any attempt to study Negro peasant institutions and culture is the fact that, though the white man and the Negro have lived and worked together in the United States for three hundred years and more, the two races are still in a certain sense strangers to one another. One way in which this fact finds expression is in the statement that the Negro has not yet been, and perhaps never can be, assimilated. Another and more drastic expression of the same conviction is the familiar statement, repeated in most every part of the world in which Europeans have settled: "This is a white man's country."

It is very curious that anyone in America should still think of the Negro, even the Negro peasant of the "black belts," as in any sense an alien or stranger, since he has lived here longer than most of us, has interbred to a greater extent than the white man with the native Indian, and is more completely a product than anyone of European origin is likely to be of the local conditions under which he was born and bred.

There is, nevertheless, a sense in which the Negro, even though culturally he be a purely native product, is not assimilated, though in just what sense this is true it is difficult to say.

One is reminded of the old lady who, visiting the Indian village at the World's Fair, was moved to speak a friendly word to one of these aborigines. What she said was: "How do you like our country?"

It was her view that, this being a white man's country, an Indian would naturally feel a little strange in it. It did not occur to her that an Indian might not share this common-sense assumption.

It is just these naïve assumptions, which are matters of common sense in one class, caste, sect, or ethnic group but not in others, that seem to constitute the final obstacle to the assimilation of peoples. They reveal social distances between individuals and peoples otherwise unsuspected.

William Graham Sumner has invented a word to describe the state of mind that these innocent and generally unconscious prejudices betray. He calls it "ethnocentrism." In savage people ethnocentrism betrays itself in the disposition to call themselves "men" or "human beings." Others are something else not defined. They are, perhaps, like the flora and fauna, part of the landscape but not human.

This trait is not confined to nature people. We are all disposed to assume that other peoples, with other customs, are not quite human in the sense that we feel this is true of ourselves. This is part of that blindness to which James refers.

The incurable ethnocentrism of peoples makes it difficult to communicate freely and candidly with strangers, particularly when the purpose of the inquirer is to go behind exteriors and discover what is behind their faces, namely, their attitudes.

The great value and the great vogue of psychoanalysis is due to the fact that it has developed a technique for getting behind visible forms and the external expressions of the people to discover the subjective aspect of personal behavior and culture, the thing which at once intrigues and baffles the student of personality and of culture.

If this ethnocentrism makes it difficult, on the one hand, to discover the subjective aspect of a people's culture, it makes it difficult, on the other hand, to describe realistically their customs and usages when one knows that such descriptions are likely to be misinterpreted. One is often tempted under such circumstances to state things in a manner to meet and correct in advance the expected misinterpretation. But that, too, is impracticable and no solution of the difficulty. Realistic descriptions of manners and customs are always likely to be a little shocking. In the final analysis, however, it is undoubtedly true that if anything, at least anything customary and accepted in any human society, seems shocking or merely quaint, it is because that custom or usage is not quite intelligible.

There is an old French adage to the effect that "to comprehend all is to forgive all," and not merely forgive but accept as something not alien but indubitably human, like ourselves.

Only so far as this is anywhere achieved can such studies of human nature as this be said to have wholly achieved their purpose.

ROBERT E. PARK

Chapter I

THE BACKGROUND

THE PATTERN OF THE PLANTATION

THE plantation as represented in tradition and popular fancy is so far removed from the existing institution as to be but slightly related to the character of the folk that it bred. In the romantic fiction, which has so largely supported the concept, it is a far-flung, comfortably self-contained agricultural unit, crested by a spacious white mansion with imposing colonnades supporting cool and spacious verandas, and surrounded in ample and flower-laden grounds. In the background are the cotton fields stretching far and white into the distance. There are long rows of white-washed Negro cabins; sleek, contented slaves, laughing and singing as they work; little pickaninnies capering with the abandonment of irresponsible fledglings in the clearings of the cabins or on the smoothly clipped lawns. As further evidence of opulence and self-sufficiency there are the smokehouse, the sawmill, the blacksmith and carpenter shops, and the commissary.

Phillips gives an account, written in 1860 by a visitor to Oak Grove, in Alabama, on the Cocoa River.[1] Four hundred acres of rich land were in cultivation. Behind the mansion, which commanded a broad valley view from its verandas, were the dairy, the smokehouse (containing thirty thousand pounds of pork), the barn, the corn cribs, the wagon sheds, and, somewhat removed, the inevitable group of Negro cabins. On a stream bank stood a gristmill and sawmill, and in another part of the tract a second slave quarter and the overseer's home.

Such a plantation as Oak Grove came nearer to the popular con-

[1] Ulrich B. Phillips, *Life and Labor in the Old South.*

ception than the preponderant majority. The stage, and particularly the minstrel, a long literary tradition, beginning no doubt with *Swallow Barn*, and warm memories of the past have helped build up the conception most familiar to the present generation. Economic factors have very largely been lost in the pictures handed down. Francis Pendleton Gaines, who has studied and discussed the southern plantation at some length, observed that

the feudalistic structure of society is probably the foremost large fact reflected in the tradition. The tradition . . . . manifests little interest in the number that composed a gang, or the labor that made a task, cares nothing for the difference between a full and a three quarters hand, or for the amount of furlough granted pregnant women; instead, the romancer seizes upon a bandana glistening in the sun, upon a coon hunt, a breakdown, a mammy's lullaby, and multiplies these things indefinitely.[2]

British travelers in America during the heyday of the plantation consistently pointed out the similarity of the southern plantation in social ideal to the historic English manor, and this fact has significance. For, whether or not the ideal was ever actually achieved in point of luxury or of social brilliance or in universality of fact, the tradition registers a rough conformity to the feudalistic patterns, and, as Gaines so pointedly observes, the inferences easily included a magnificence and medieval splendor which were, in reality, lacking.[3]

The actual plantation devoted to cotton was based on a rigorous and dull routine, with strict diversification of labor: house servants, field hands, cooks, blacksmiths, carpenters, the midwife "for white and black of the neighborhood, as well as a doctress of the plantation," overseers, and, when they could be afforded, drivers to maintain discipline and order on the place, and be responsible for the quiet of the Negro houses and for the proper performance of tasks. In January there was ginning, sorting, and moting of cotton; in February more ginning and moting, ground-cleaning, fence-mending, and ditching. In March there was bedding of cotton ground; in April planting, fencing, ditching, picking joint grass, working cotton—the eternal hoe industry. In May, June,

---

[2] *The Southern Plantation.*   [3] *Ibid.,* p. 153.

2

July, and August more hoeing and working and some picking; in September, October, and November more picking, clearing new ground; in December moting and ginning. There were tasks and punishments for falling short. Every detail of life was regulated not by any internal compulsions but by a system of physical punishments and rewards. Once established, custom and routine gave permanence to the structure of relations. Life, on the whole, was a grim business. Such were the imperatives of the economic system.

The Negro of the plantation came into the picture with a completely broken cultural heritage. He came directly from Africa or indirectly from Africa through the West Indies. There had been for him no preparation for, and no organized exposure to, the dominant and approved patterns of American culture. What he knew of life was what he could learn from other slaves or from the examples set by the white planters themselves. In the towns where this contact was close there was some effect, such as has many times been noted in the cultural differences between the early Negro house servants and the plantation hands. On the plantation, however, their contact was a distant one, regulated by the strict "etiquette" of slavery and the code of the plantation.

The present Negro population of these old plantation areas can best be understood by viewing it in the light of this plantation tradition, with its almost complete dependence upon the immediate landowner for guidance and control in virtually all those phases of life which are related to the moving world outside. The Negro families retain, through the older members of the community, a distinct memory of this early society. They take their cues from it; they are seriously affected when the relationship fails. Such families as escape from the prevailing economy of dependence into the new responsibilities which go with independence find economic complications and shades of social conflict which manifest themselves in various ways, sometimes prompting them to migration, but as often leading to resignation and relapse from the ownership status to tenantry. The gradual decline in Negro ownership and the increase in the tenant class are evidences of this struggle.

3

In things economic there is everywhere now this dull, sometimes fatalistic, and unquestioning dependence upon the landowners and the soil, both of which are at times capricious. Toward this situation with its uncertainties the Negro families have adopted an attitude of easy-going trustfulness, reinforced by religion and adjustable in an amazing degree to the frequent discouragements of crop failures. In things social the group turns inward, finding its satisfactions in expressions of social life which are often elemental, but under certain traditional controls which are distinguishably a heritage of the plantation system under the institution of slavery.

In a sense the southern rural Negro population has tended to represent the surviving traditions of an earlier period. They have been the repositories of certain folk ways which, in the changing pattern of American life, are being discarded. Puckett has pointed out that the unlettered rural folk, and especially the Negroes who have had fewer educational advantages on the whole than have the rural whites, are of a "very conservative nature and often cling to outworn usages and customs, many of which were practiced by the populace at large but later discarded and forgotten by the more educated elements."[4] Their dialect is in part a survival of the English of the colonists, their superstitions most often are borrowed from whites, their religious beliefs are in large part the same as those held by isolated whites, their folk lore is scarcely distinguishable from that brought over from Europe by the early colonists, their religious emotionalism is similar to that commonly demonstrated in white Methodist camp meetings until very recently.

When these early patterns were imperfectly copied, as would be expected from the nature of their relationship to their white masters, it is not difficult to understand how imperfectly they would be reflected later in behavior as well as in beliefs. Viewed in this light, such matters as "illegitimacy," relations of parents to children, divorce, extra-marital relations, food habits, the uses of leisure, behavior in emotional crises involving love, death, reli-

[4] Newbell N. Puckett, "Religious Folk-Beliefs of Whites and Negroes," *Journal of Negro History*, January, 1931, pp. 9–35.

gion, become more intelligible. The patterns of social behavior to which the Negroes were exposed, whether set by planters or poor whites, cannot be said to have been ideal, from the point of view of current standards. Many crudities of manners, now largely abandoned by the white population, were at one time accepted rules of conduct and still survive deeply imbedded in the modes of social life of the Negroes, modified only as they have been able to escape their cultural isolation.

An important aspect of the feudal ideal was provincialism, "the splendid isolation," which in itself has given a certain flavor to the white former master as well as to the Negro former slave in the present survivals of the plantation. The plantation itself operated against anything like widespread culture.[5] The high vogue of drinking, gambling, and dueling would perhaps be expected to be carried over to the slaves as part of their conception of the privileges of freedom. Limited as they were by the exigencies of slave marriage and slave family life, it is not unnatural that standards of morality would be imperfectly understood. Moreover, despite the strength of specific moral standards current during slavery, it was impossible for them to escape observing the broad lapses at times from these ideals, on the part of the gentlemen of the plantation themselves. The poorer whites were largely illiterate and frequently accused by the master-class of a complete lack of culture as well as of morals. Here again, though perhaps not as close as in the former case, was an influence which could prove of little value to the maturing of the Negro plantation slave's social concepts and ideals.

One characteristic of folk groups is isolation. Rural areas in general exhibit a measure of isolation, but it is of the nature of rural life in America to destroy itself through increase of communication with the outside. There are indeed few rural areas which aspire ultimately to be self-contained and exclusive. Natural barriers are only temporary obstructions to communication, and with the rapid increase in transportation, literacy and reading, the radio and the motion picture, and the mail-order catalogue, distance—physical and social—is being steadily dissolved.

[5] Gaines, *op. cit.*

Of the possibilities and consequences of isolation in our own culture the American Negroes present an excellent example—an example all the more interesting because Negroes now represent virtually every stage of the acculturation process in America, and have found a place somewhere in every occupation from the most backward to the most forward.

Actually, distance from the centers of larger activity plays only a minor rôle in an isolation which is for them fundamentally cultural. According to accepted social theory, there is no American "folk" because there is no American peasantry. But everyone knows that this is less a fact than an ideal. There are persistent social blocs which for one reason or the other defy prompt incorporation into the approved general pattern.

The Negroes in areas of the South, notably in the cotton and cane belts, represent an American type which can most nearly be described as "folk," and so far as their lives are rooted in the soil, they are, perhaps, the closest approach to an American peasantry. "To be shaped in mind and social reaction, to some extent in character and finally in expression," says Mary Austin, "is to be folk." The marks of such an encircled life may be observed in their fixed accommodation, to the prevailing economic system, an accommodation so complete as to be commonplace. It may be observed in the characteristic folk ways associated with this life; in the characteristic forms of its thought and expression; in the illiteracy which shields them from the contacts and influences by which social changes are introduced, and which limits the range of their interests; restricts the development of thought and speculation beyond the requirements of their simple routine of life. It may be observed in the survival, with but small modifications, of the tradition of slavery; in the survival of the tradition of the plantation, which in turn embodies an economic system affecting the proprietors as well as the tenants. If these folk groups have a social life, it is unique and is due in large measure to the fact that they are cut off from the most direct channel of communication with the outside world and its interests through the economic system itself,

6

which restricts economic negotiations virtually to their immediate white landlords.

Given the setting of a high degree of Negro tenantry in the familiar cotton economy, and similar measure of isolation, differences between these Negro folk groups are not great. In the area studied in Macon County, Alabama, the group was a fairly homogeneous one, and was adjusted, both physically and mentally, to the tradition of cotton cultivation inherited from the period in which it reached its nadir as a system, before the Civil War.

THE TRADITION OF THE PLANTATION

The state of Alabama is a country of extremes, from the rich Black Belt area, superbly adapted to cotton cultivation, to the wretched pine barrens where impoverished whites were driven before the Civil War by the richer and stronger slave-owning proprietors. Three belts of the Appalachian Mountains terminate in the state, merging with one another and with the gulf coastal plains. The northern portion of the state, transected by the Tennessee River, is a part of the Allegheny-Cumberland Plateau. It is fertile land, but not so richly fertile as other sections. To the south is the convulsive irregularity of the Appalachians, which became at a late period in the development of the state the center of the mining industry around Birmingham. These were sparsely populated as late as 1850.[6] Across the center of the state, extending from Randolph County on the Georgia border to Fayette County near the Mississippi line, is another area of barely fertile territory but with occasional patches of rich fertility.

The Black Belt begins along the line marked by Montgomery and includes eleven counties, among which is Macon, the focal point of these observations. This section has been historically the home of the planters. South of the Black Belt is the sandy stretch which has resisted cultivation and was little known throughout the early history of the state except to be dismissed with the designation of "Piney Woods."

[6] Boyd, *Alabama in the Fifties*.

As an important cotton-growing state Alabama utilized the plantation system to the fullest. It has always been even more agricultural than Virginia or Carolina. Importance as a cotton state was manifested for years in the state's larger balance of exports of cotton over the southern states, and the dominance of the plantation system is marked historically in the fact that a bare 7 per cent of the population in 1860 owned 333,000 slaves.

The cotton counties were the chief slave counties and are, consequently, the plantation counties. They are Dallas, Marengo, Greene, Sumter, Lowndes, Macon, and Montgomery. Sections of the state, poorer as well as less adapted to cotton cultivation, had an average of 1.4 slaves to the household. Madison County, in the northern part of the state, actually had over two families to each slave. The average number of slaves per plantation for the state was 4.5. However, in the cotton counties the large plantations set the prevailing patterns. In 1850 there were 790 owners of from 30 to 70 slaves; 550 owners with from 70 to 100 slaves; 312 with from 100 to 200; 24 with from 200 to 300; and 10 with from 300 to 500. Thus some 150,000 of the slaves were on plantations of 50 or more, even though only a third of the white people were directly interested in slavery.[7]

On the one hand were the poor planters still living in their rude log houses, with unglazed windows and lacking most of the refinements, but obsessed with the urge for more land on which to plant more slaves. On the other hand were the wealthy proprietors who stretched huge plantations over a country so unhealthy and undeveloped that they could not themselves live in it, and settled themselves in such luxury as their means would allow in Montgomery, Tuscaloosa, and Tuskegee. Around these latter a society developed. But with few exceptions there was on the plantations a complete absence of those touches of light and civilization to temper the lot of the slaves.

Macon County was a part of the territory ceded by the Muscogee Indians, established by an act in 1832, and took its name from a North Carolina statesman. When General Macon died, Thomas

[7] *Ibid.*

8

Jefferson referred to him as "the last of the Romans." The county covers about 600 square miles, devoted zealously to cotton cultivation from the beginning of the English and American occupation. It was the birthplace of Osceola, the mixed-blood Seminole chief who for many years resisted the invasion of the whites with unparalleled ferocity. From the earliest period of the Indian wars, Tuskegee, the county seat, was a garrison of one sort or the other. Many of the best known of the early founders of the county were from Georgia: Dougherty, Logan, Battle, Perry, Mason, and Echols. They came at the beginning of the nineteenth century just as the state emerged as a new territory.

When Olmstead passed through Macon County before the Civil War, going from Columbus, Georgia, to Montgomery, he was appalled and depressed by the dreary aspect of things. He labored for one full day "through a hilly wilderness, with a few dreary villages, and many isolated cotton farms, with comfortless habitations for blacks and whites upon them."

Early foreign travelers in America always noted this dismal stretch in covering the highlights of the new republic. They would land in New York, move southward through Philadelphia, Washington, Richmond, and Norfolk to Charleston. These all were new, separate, and unique attractions, evidences of youthful statehood. From Charleston the next point was Savannah, and then on to Macon, Georgia. From Macon the route led through Columbus across the dirty Chattahoochee into Alabama, through Macon County to Montgomery, the capital of the state, and at one time the capital of the Confederacy. Russell, of the *London Times*, found himself on this trail ten years after Olmstead, and it was still uninteresting country, to him, with nothing to recommend it but the natural fertility of the soil. The people were rawer, ruder, and bigger; chewed more tobacco, squirted it farther; and swore more earnestly. The towns, then as now, consisted of a huddle of small houses and cabins, an inn, a blacksmith shop, and a post station, and rearing up occasionally in the midst of these the more pretentious dwelling of a proprietor, gleaming white.

In 1850 Tuskegee was not only a thriving town but laid claims to being something of an agricultural center. It had a population of 3,000, two female colleges, a male high school, two schools for boys and girls, three churches with nine ministers, two hotels, six dry-goods stores, three drug stores, three groceries, three confectionery stores, one ice-cream saloon, two jewelers and watchmakers, three tailor shops, three furniture stores, two carriage establishments, a steam mill, millinery and mantua-making places, three printing offices, four editors, and seventeen lawyers.[8] It was the heart of a powerful plantation area.

In 1840 there were just 5,369 whites and 5,878 blacks in Macon County. In twenty years the whites added 3,000 to their numbers, but to the blacks were added 13,000 more slaves. In the back country, moving toward Montgomery, the vast plantations began. At La Place lived Dr. N. B. Cloud, described as "the giant of antebellum agriculture." Mount Meigs was one but not the only sprawling village. To the west and south the traveler might stumble upon other clusters of dwellings, or stage-coach stations, with their characteristic indications of frontier life.

Tuskegee is better known now for the Tuskegee Normal and Industrial Institute, founded by Booker T. Washington, and for the United States Veterans Hospital (for Negro veterans of the World War). Three railroad lines cross the county, two of the Western Route and one of the Atlantic Coast Line. In addition there are three main automobile highways, a most important one being that from Atlanta to Montgomery.

Once a section of large plantations, Macon County, as many others, has gradually been broken up into smaller areas, developed by tenants. There has been some landownership by Negroes, but this, in recent years, has followed the general decline, only a bit more rapidly. In 1930 there were 3,714 farms and farm operators, 242 less than in 1920. Of these, 3,114 were Negroes and 600 whites. The whites lost 7 during that decade while the Negroes lost 235. The 600 white operators had 71,855 acres in farms, or an average of 103 acres per operator; the 3,114 Negroes had 145,173 acres, or 46 acres per Negro operator. That it is a tenant area is attested in

[8] *Ibid.*

the fact that 43 per cent of the white owners control 43,376 acres, the remaining 57 per cent of Negroes only 32,899 acres, while there are 140,753 acres in farms which are developed by tenants and owned, for the most part, by absentee landlords of either this state or other states. There are, to be exact, 21,688 acres developed by white tenants and 104,417 by Negro tenants.

Although the entire county is regarded roughly as a part of the Black Belt, the northern and southern sections show important differences. In the northern section, where trading is done about the town of Notasulga, are to be found many small farms operated by whites. Over many years these small proprietors, or poor whites, have filtered into the northern section as an alternative to emigration farther west, in order to escape the consequences of the plantation system. The southwestern section of the county is, and always has been, characterized by large plantations with Negro tenants.

Throughout the area are scattered the homes of Negroes which date back, for the most part, to a period of forty years and more. The small unpainted or whitewashed cabins, surrounded by a disordered array of outhouses, are spaced at distances convenient for plantation development. Most of the buildings have the worn and sagging aspect of age, with their invariable "dog run" providing a cooling shade; vagrant and inclosed patches of garden, growing close to the house, their newspaper wall covering, and, piled in some spare corner, a dirty heap of cotton seed.

In the early summer there are wide areas of cotton, except for patches of undeveloped woods, sandy areas, where nothing will grow, and the essential stretches of corn and sorghum. Here and there is a house of different design, with weatherboarding. These are the homes of white residents, and occasionally of Negro owners. The villages are small concentrations around a general store or commissary, gin, post-office, a church, and the homes of the proprietorial white landowners and residents. Roughly, the present arrangement is a survival of the earlier plantation system under the old parish division.

The old blacksmith shop and stable of the early days of the

county have given place to an automobile repair shop. The inn is a grocery store. The houses are the same, only generations older. The white of the mansion house has gone, symbolizing, it would almost seem, the inevitable abandonment by the lords of the manor to the Negroes who still hang on, trying to nurse a living out of the earth. Foxtail and broomsedge, harbingers of senility, and the ubiquitous boll weevil, a new pestilence, keep this black labor alive, vainly fighting against the approaching final desolation. Everywhere there are the sad evidences of an artless and exhausting culture of cotton.

The hard white highways of Alabama have drawn a ring as distinct as the color line around these decaying plantations—each with its little settlement of black peasantry. Here they live almost within sight of the passing world, dully alive, in an intricate alliance with a tradition which has survived the plantation itself. The plantation of olden times has gone, leaving them a twin partner of the earth, and upon these two—black man and the earth—the proprietor himself, growing ever poorer, depends for the mutual preservation of all. The machine has not entered here yet, for the routine of cotton cultivation, and especially weeding and picking, demands a discrimination which can be taught the dullest peasant, but which no machine as yet has mastered. As a consequence, the system has continued to breed its own labor support in the thousands of Negroes whose lives and only hopes are bound up with its fate.

THE COMMUNITY

The area of Macon County covered by this study extends over 200 square miles and is virtually the total lower third of the county. There are the small village concentrations, but over four-fifths of the population live out in the open country on and around the farms which they own or rent, or the plantations on which they are employed. The village communities are, as a rule, so loosely identified by the names that confusion exists even among the residents as to where one begins and the other ends. Since the towns are so largely built for the convenience of the white folks and there is so little advantage to the Negro farming population in living in the towns, these locations are scarcely more than post-office addresses and occasional market places for Negroes.

The center of this population is about ten miles down the highway from Tuskegee and from four to ten miles in the country back of the highway. Tuskegee, if reached by horse and wagon, which is a popular method of travel, despite the vogue of the automobile, is a full day's journey away. The school is known, but visits there are rare. Occasionally produce or chickens are carried to the village to be marketed. Jerry Wilson, living in Shorter, admitted a certain interest in the place. He said: "If I had some money I'd hire somebody to take me to Tuskegee. I went up dere once to commencement." In Sambo a group of cabins had been whitewashed eighteen years before in anticipation of a visit from Booker T. Washington. That was the last coating they had had, and to all appearances the last effective contact with the institution. The nearest large city of the state is Montgomery; there has been some migration back and forth from this city and across the Georgia line.

The distribution of these families conforms to the physical arrangement of the plantations. The most frequent layout is the cabin, or small cluster of cabins, for each convenient agricultural unit suitable for renting or tenant-farmer use. The very large plantations have close-set rows of cabins on the edge of vast stretches of cotton land. Occasionally some fortuitous division of land throws a group of cabins or frame dwellings together. Traveling through the country, one may observe, standing stark and alone at the crossroads, a church or a store, with no dwelling in sight. It is a part of the character of this community, it would seem, to be bound together over a wide area by crooked little footpaths which serve as the threads of neighborliness. Such loose physical association must, of necessity, foreclose certain advantages of co-operation for social improvement and protection; and make difficult, if not impossible, the development of a sense of community such as might be found in more closely knit villages or in town life.

Here live almost hidden in the fields, or at wide intervals along

13

the country road, over 11,000 Negroes. There is, however, scarcely a stretch of this territory which does not give some sign of life. Along the dusty roads men in the universal garb of blue-denim overalls are forever trudging, casually going somewhere. They are interested in every happening that crosses their vision. Around the cabins or small frame dwellings, visible from the roadway, children are at play, old folks are puttering about or chatting idly in the cooling shade of the dog-run. Pots of soiled clothing are boiling in the yard, attended with a stick by women too old for the fields. Old men tinker with rickety plows or the intricate disrepair of a mule's harness. A loud laugh from out the cluttered spaces calls attention to another cabin set far back from the road. Slinking, hungry dogs infest the region of the houses. Adolescent girls, their hair twisted and held in thin stiff braids by tough threads, sit idly, dangling bare legs, scaly with pellagra. A wagon in which chairs have been placed, and occasionally an excessively noisy and antiquated Ford, carry teeming families to town. Shorters, Hardaway, Sambo, Chesson, Liverpool, are only political divisions. Negroes of this area neither know nor are bound by these artificial boundaries.

According to the 1930 census there were 22,320 Negroes in the total population of 27,103 persons in Macon County. The Negro population was only slightly more than that for 1910, but considerably greater than in 1920, when it was 19,614. The decrease between 1910 and 1920 may be attributed primarily to the migrations during the war period. In spite of the recent gains during the past decade, the proportion of Negroes in the total population has steadily decreased, being 84.6, 83.3, and 82.3 per cent for the three decennial censuses of 1910, 1920, and 1930. The effects of the migration are still apparent in the present age composition of the population, although it is manifest that many apparent irregularities in the age distribution as represented by the census should be attributed to ignorance on the part of the people concerning their ages.

The 612 families on which this study is based are located in eight settlements. These settlements as indicated do not conform to political or administrative divisions. Although in some cases they have the same name as the precincts for the county, they represent more nearly the community to which the people feel they belong. Table I shows the number of families in each subcommunity included in this study.

In the 612 families there were 2,432 persons, or slightly more than a tenth of the Negro population in the county in 1930. The age distribution of the Negro population in this county showed the deviations from the normal distribution which have been attribut-

TABLE I

Location	Shorter	Hardeway	Millstead	Chesson	Liverpool	Tuskegee	Sambo	Cecil	Total
Number....	276	187	33	60	21	23	5	7	612

ed to migration.[9] It has also been recognized that these deviations from the normal distribution are due to errors in estimating ages.[10] In addition to the smallness of the group between twenty and forty, there is also a smaller group of children under one than appears in the age distribution of the native white population.[11] The 612 families included in this study show the same abnormalities,

[9] See *U.S. Census*, II (1920), 150, for the following comment: "The age distribution of Negroes in urban and in rural areas is affected by the very considerable country-to-city migration of persons of this race in the active-age periods, and probably also by differences in birth and death rates between the two classes of communities."

[10] "The age distribution of males and females among the Negroes, as reported, presents a peculiar condition. According to the returns there was in 1920 a slight excess of females below the age of 15, a much larger excess of the age period from 15 to 34, and a small excess in the 35–44 period. From the ages of 45 to 69, however, there was a very great excess of men, followed by a moderate excess in the 70–79 periods and an excess of women in the ages above 79. The ratio of males to females for the Negroes in the period 45–49 (138.7 to 100) was higher than the foreign born white ratio for any age period. The number of Negro men enumerated as in this age period in 1920 (320,506) was almost exactly the same as the number reported for the age period 35–39 in 1910 (320,450). This, of course, is an impossibility, for the reason that, disregarding the slight effect of immigration, the group of Negro men 45 to 49 years of age in 1920 would be made up solely of the survivors of those in the 35–39 age period in 1910. Inconsistencies of this character are due, wholly or in large part, to errors in estimating ages which cannot be ascertained exactly by the enumerators" (*ibid.*, pp. 147–48).

[11] "The age distribution of the Negroes and Indians, which is practically unaffected by immigration, is roughly similar to that of native whites. Among the Negroes, however,

with the exception that the deficiency of males is noticeable at an earlier age period and the preponderance of females is greater. In the Negro population for the county there were, in 1930, 98 more males than females, while in our families the difference was much greater, being 146 for the 612 families. The deficiency of males in the population surveyed was almost entirely among those between the ages of fifteen and forty. The percentage of the population composed of boys between fifteen and nineteen was 1.4 per cent smaller than for the girls. This disproportion was even greater for men between twenty and thirty, and thirty and forty. The percentage in favor of the women amounted to 2.9 and 2.5, respectively, for these two age groups.

Survivals

The essential observation of this study is that the Negro population of this section of Macon County has its own social heritage which, in a relatively complete isolation, has had little chance for modification from without or within. Patterns of life, social codes, as well as social attitudes, were set in the economy of slavery. The political and economic revolution through which they have passed has affected only slightly the social relationships of the community or the mores upon which these relations have been based. The strength and apparent permanence of this early cultural set have made it virtually impossible for newer generations to escape the influence of the patterns of work and general social behavior transmitted by their elders.

Macon County has a Negro population with a tradition much older than that of a Negro population in any city of either the North or the South. It offers little encouragement to new blood. The strength of tradition thus is magnified because of the low level of literacy and consequent imperviousness of the area to the modifying influence of news and the experiences of other communities.

----

the proportion of children under 5 is considerably smaller than in any of the native white classes, while the proportions in the age periods from 10–29 years are smaller than the corresponding ones for either the native whites of native parentage or those of foreign parentage" (*ibid.*, p. 146).

Together these factors tend, naturally, to give unwonted prestige and authority to the older families, who have at least the factual argument of survival to bolster their claims to importance.

A useful clue to the character of the present population is to be found in the character of the elders themselves, and their active memories of the past. Much of this study will be concerned with the social tradition of this group and how it is being modified, even though slowly, by various new outside influences. One of the first circumstances encountered in dealing with this older population is the confusion about ages. Only with their presumed independent status have they found it necessary to reckon their own ages. It is only natural, thus, that ages are calculated from the coming of freedom, but even with such a point of reference there is a wide range of speculation. Georgiana Jackson explained: "I don't know how old I am. I was born in slavery. I remember when the Yankees first come and say dere want no more slavery." Liza Cloud, now blind, decrepit, and extremely dirty in her neglect, said: "Slavery I know all about, looks like. I was sixteen years old when the Yankees come through. I can't tell about the year I was born but I know the month. I was born the first of May. You know back there colored folks didn't know nothing about the years." Still another, a male family head reckoned his age, with no qualms of uncertainty, from the fact that he was "a half-hour old when freedom come." Even this type of record lends itself more satisfactorily to calculation than some other speculations based, for example, upon the type of clothing worn, or the amount of work one was able to do, or the condition of the plank road running through the county at the time of their first age consciousness.

The most common method of keeping reasonably accurate ages is through their "white folks," who made and kept this record for the Negroes. Those who lacked the continuing relationship with a single white family would have them set down the most likely age or date of birth in a Bible. If the white folks died, or the Bible was lost, their ages were also lost and this was counted as irrevocable, not to be troubled about further. After all, ages are only needed at rare intervals, when a census is being taken or for the even less exacting requirement of an obituary and death certificate. With the utmost casualness the matter of ages could thus be dismissed: "I had all our ages in the Bible and one of my boys what got married tuk it and when I got it back so many of the leaves was tore out I didn't know it was a Bible and all the ages was gone." Or: "I don't know my age. My Bible got burnt up and hit was in it."

The importance attached by the younger people to the keeping of one's own age was one of the faint but important symbols of independent status. A young woman who had been reared by her grandmother from an infant said with some feeling: "The only thing I hate about my grandma is she wouldn't tell me my age." The old folks would observe that "people didn't tell ages in dem days lak dey do now," and make no effort to alter the easier arrangement of relying upon their white folks to supply this information when necessary. This continued reliance was only one of the numerous points of their dependent relationship. Occasionally there would be exhibited courage sufficient to doubt the estimate, even though made by their white folks, as in the case of Jennie Smith who gave this account of her age: "I am about seventy-seven years old this last gone February. I am satisfied I'm older'n this but that's what the white folks gied me when I was freed, but if I don't disremember that is my sister's age. When the war was declared, and freedom come, I was nursing and working at the white folks' home. They just got us niggers mixed up. I remember well when the people was drilling to free the slaves. That's why I know I'm older'n dat."

Memories of Slavery

The former slaves have not only retained memories of their earlier status, but have maintained a certain dignity and prestige for themselves by contrasting these memories with the pretensions to freedom of the younger generation. For these older ones it has been a part of the technique of survival to rationalize the social adjustments made. There are, at the same time, former slaves who, with a certain defiance, refer to slavery as an ill which they were fortunate and grateful to escape. This they do with vigor and eloquence, but also with a becoming caution. There is enough spirit in their recital of slave conditions, however, to set them apart from some of their brethren who, like many of their masters, find these memories glowing with increasing charm and romance as time separates them from the period.

The older Negro families are, indeed, divided rather sharply in their memories of slavery, and both groups have in turn passed them along in both practice and philosophy to their own offspring. Zack Ivey, for example, is one of the older heads and strong spirits of the community. He was more frank than is the custom of Negroes to be in contrasting his present condition with that of slavery. He complained: "I done had a harder time since I been free than when I was a slave. I never had such a hard time in my life as I'm having now." Then, with awareness of the implied treason of this remark, he added, compromising: "I'm saying this for myself. I ain't saying hit for nobody else. I wish I had stayed a slave." There was to him nothing offensive in his attachment to his master, particularly since his was a good master; besides, he drew distinction from the very power and wealth of his owner. "In slavery my master and mistress tuk care of me. I lived down in the quarters but I was always up at the house. Them quarters was 'ranged just like a garden. Here was a row and there was a row, and up there was the white folks' house. My mother had to see atta all the chillun in the quarters 'cause they kept so much fuss. I was small and light and done 'bout most as I pleased."

One does not have to look far to see the lively survivals of the early social attitudes in the present population which figure so largely in the memory of Zack Ivey. For a most significant feature of the culture of this group is the slow pace of its transformation. Life was regimented for Zack Ivey but not unpleasantly. The rations were especially memorable in the face of the dull monotony of their present daily fare. "In slavery days," he reminisced, "we et peas, onions, hog head, liver, cow's milk, butter, Irish potatoes, and everything what grows in gardens. That's why I'm here now. I'm just living on the strenk of that. Hit's the strenk of that done kept me alive." For Zack Ivey life was a simple, elemental process of love-making, child-breeding, frolics, and religion, very much as it is now in the community. "I had three chillun by my first wife and fifteen by my second wife. We had frolics. We had them in the white folks' yard. The white folks made you play and run and jump. Your feet an' things had ter be washed and you had ter be all clean and white ter set at table. We had guitars and blowing quills. We had the best kinda time. The only thing I didn't like they kept me in my shirt tail so long. I thought I was too big fer ter be in my shirt tail and ever' time they come round and tell me ter jump my shirt tail would fly up, and I'd say, 'You gotta put some pants on me.' I was keeping company wid my lady frien', going cross the creek, and I looked and there my shirt tail was a floating."

The difference in opinion as well as in memories on the question of slavery found frequent enough expression. So close was the group in the ordinary routine of life, and so well known the opinions, that they would frequently take the form of debate through the investigator.

Riny Biggers, a character of equal strength in the community, without being informed of the views of Zack Ivey, began her own reminiscences with a warning: "Don't you believe no nigger when he says he ruther be no slave. Things happen then too awful to talk about. If they catch you with a pencil in your hand it would be too bad. When de white folks' chillun would come through wid books from school by the quarters and dropped a piece of they school paper and if dey seed you pick hit up dey would clare you tryn' to learn to read and write, and over Sunday for a month you'd be put in a strait-jacket."

The immediate difference between these two types could be observed in the children of these old family heads. Riny Biggers made her own children learn their letters under the threat and free employment of a handy stick. When they had grown up and she was no longer capable of having children of her own, she adopted others and sent them to school in the same manner. Of Zack Ivey's eighteen children, five were dead; four had left the county for Montgomery; two remained with him; of the whereabouts of the

20

others he had no knowledge. None of them had had more than a few months of schooling, and the two who remained still lived with him, one of them an unmarried daughter with four children.

Riny Biggers, taking advantage of the extended privilege of her sex, was more aggressive about her freedom and made a fetish of education, although she herself was illiterate. The high value of literacy had been implanted in her in slavery as firmly as Zack Ivey's memory of the care-free days of frolics and food and courting. She was what one might call "race conscious." She told her children often the story of a figure who seemed to stand out in her memory as the heroic one of slavery. "Red Ann," as she was commonly known, knew the secret of letters when she was bought by Riny's mistress. It was a trade-off as unethical as selling a blind horse without confessing his defect. Red Ann's literacy in this case was her defect. Riny's mistress bought Red Ann from a speculator but she did not know that she could read. She was called "Red Ann" in contempt for nature's presumption to endow a slave with a swarthy Caucasian complexion and quite straight soft hair, sometimes referred to as Titian. When in the presence of her mistress, or any white person, for that matter, Ann carried a blank, uncomprehending stare. She would handle papers on which there was writing without showing the slightest curiosity. Once securely out of sight, she would read them and keep her intelligence to herself. Later she began to read letters coming to the house and, becoming still bolder, would show them to other slaves whom she took into her confidence. They watched as she read, then one day a slave, secretly jealous, whispered to her mistress Red Ann's secret. There was consternation confounded by unbelief. In a culture which denied the ability of Negroes to read, it was easier to believe as well as to wish that they could not. Suspicion grew and she was questioned. Red Ann persisted that she could not read. The mistress left notes around to trap her, but Red Ann was too clever. Finally, she wrote her mistress' name to a pass and disappeared.

This secret power was a lasting lesson for Riny, and she ground it into her own children from the day they were large enough to understand. For that reason she was accounted the equivalent of a radical in her society, and the variant fate of her children testified to the conflict between her own determination and the pressure of environment. Of Riny's first set there was one living and two dead. The living child, now in his fifties, eventually shook off the county, the state, and left the South forever. She knew only that he had a family in Detroit and children in school somewhere. Another son died at the age of ten. A daughter grew to womanhood, married, and died in childbirth. Of the second set, one daughter, Aggie, was living with her mother; a son, Arch, was killed in a fight with a white man; and still another, Jerry, had been away from home about fifteen years and had finally worked his way through a school in South Carolina. Two other children had died at early ages and there had been three miscarriages. With her now was the second of the adopted children which she had begun to rear. Her memories of slavery were fresh, no doubt from frequent rehearsing:

My master's people? Some of them masters would take they slaves and lock 'em in the house all day and you couldn't stick your head out of the door. We could lay on our porch and hear 'em hollering and working all night tel day. I seed 'em walk in sand tel they fell dead. Had been me I would been fightin' now. I come from the fightin' class, but I'm too old ter fight now. My master's brother's wife was so mean tel the Lord sent a peal of lightenin' and put her to death. She was too mean ter let you go ter the well and git a drink of water, and God come long and "squshed" her head open. One of the other masters was so mean he made his slaves crow. Whenever he got ready ter go ter Prattville he had him a chariot fixed up wid eight horses. Lak we settin' here done been two packs of hounds done passed chasing atta slaves and he had more slaves runned away.

"Salt-Water" Men

Another class of Negroes in relation to whom there is retained, in the memory of the community, an active social distinction is the "salt-water nigger." They were the freshly imported Negroes from Africa toward whom the Negro slaves felt a pronounced superiority. Cass Stewart, now over eighty-five years of age, could remember some of these. Said he: "I was wid de Africans. Dey couldn't understand what dey was saying deyselves. I seed dem salt-water niggers down my home near Selma. I knowed a man down dere working 25 acres, couldn't work wid half of 'em 'cause when you made one of 'em mad you made all of 'em mad."

The older slaves kept themselves aloof from the African, partly out of contempt and partly out of fear. In the community today there are contemptuous references to certain families as springing from "salt-water niggers." This situation provides an unexpected link with Africa which might indeed yield traces of other trans-planted culture traits.[12]

Old Farming Methods Surviving

The old people, despite differences of opinion on the matter of slavery, retained numerous traits in common as a part of their heritage from the institution. Most important among these was the method of farming. Sam Thomas, still feebly active, despite his nearly ninety years, and always able to raise some sort of crop, made an observation on the development of agriculture. The method they learned was for him the best method. He said: "The way they farmed here then was a hoss ter de plow and a hoss ter de hoe hand. *They works dat way round here now.* They had a leader and all lumped together in one hand master."

As a matter of fact, there has been practically no change in the farming methods except on a few advanced farms. The layout of the plantation is practically the same as it has always been. The perennial tenants go to the commissaries for food, clothing, and other essentials or get advances in small amounts of cash. The larger the plantation, the greater the prestige of the planter. From the importance of the planters the tenants draw their own social importance.

This man what we rent from got a big plantation, and he got it filled up, too. Lots of dem is renters and a lot of dem is jes workers by the day for him. He got a little commissary up dere at dat big barn where you

[12] One old resident, in quoting remembered expressions of these Africans, used terms strikingly similar to the African West Coast pidgin English, which was all the more unusual because West Coast pidgin is not common in the dialect of the Negroes in this part of the South.

can buy what you want. Dey puts it down on the book when you buy something. I jes tell de thing jes like it is. When you want a sack of flour or anything you go up dere and get it, but you don't have no money to buy it with. De people last year 'vanced around $8.00 and $9.00 to de plow. Long bout dis time last year we got a draw and no more. Course I scuffles round here and works a little extra to keep from being worried so much.

The man what owns dis place sold it and is living 'tween five and six miles of Montgomery. Mr. ——— stays near Montgomery. His men stays up yonder in the big house. He sold it to Mr. ———. Mr.——— was better than Mr———. Mr. ——— never did 'vance anything. Mr. ——— jes got tired of staying here and he sold to Mr. ———. These here people here is regular farmers. Dey get more land den anybody in Alabama. Got about 700 and some odd acres I guess. They got a lot of people on this place. I jes couldn't tell you how many farmers is on dis place. Dey is all back across in here and way back over yonder.

The acuteness of the struggle for a livelihood has issued from the effort to produce enough from the constantly weakening soil with the simple old tools of two generations ago. The reluctance to change has been bound up with the decreasing importance of the area itself as a cotton center, the increasing economic helplessness of the families, the high illiteracy, and the almost total absence of money. Even if these were different, there would remain to be overcome a group inertness and habituation to their status which was notable near the beginning of their new era of freedom, and about which the old people themselves remark in their stories of the past. For years after their emancipation they not only were unable to grasp the significance of their changed status, but automatically kept up the habits of earlier association in every detail and in spite of the assurance by their "white folks" that certain controls were no longer in operation.

Even atta we was free, the niggers wouldn't believe it. They kept going ter master and mistress atta passes to go off and they would say, "Steve, I don't give no more passes now, dem days is over; you is as free as me." The niggers couldn't believe hit atta they heard hit. I'm tellin' de truf. The niggers was still scared, too. You know the niggers and white folks b'longed ter de same church, and went ter de same church. The niggers would set behin' de 'titions. The preacher would tell 'em slavery was over and ter come on in the church, but they wouldn't.

Then the white folks got scared dat dem niggers might kill 'em. Dat de reason why niggers and white folks ain't goin' ter de same church now. 'Cause mattered not how the preacher would say tain't no mo' master and mistress now come on inside, some of them niggers wouldn't. They stood outside by them windows wid day heads stickin' in. Yes, honey, I 'members dis all.

Physical Survivals of the Past

Memories of the past are reinforced by numerous physical features—the old and sagging cabins and the decaying splendor of the big house, the rotting remains of the old plank road, and occasionally the untouched breastworks of the Civil War itself, which changed their political status. Will Daniels reckoned that the house in which he lived was ninety years old, and gave this explanation in support of his speculation:

There's an old man 'round here who used to wait on Dr. ——— and he's about ninety years old. The house was here when he was a boy. Old man Parker owned it in slavery times. The slave cabin was tore down when I moved here. The young Missus comes up here to see it sometimes now. She says she just likes to see the old place where she was raised. She showed us the print of the man's hand that built it. It's right there in the hall.

Stability

Year after year these families continue to live and move about within the county, but rarely leaving it. The tenant turnover is high. Their one outstanding means of asserting freedom is this mobility, although within an extremely narrow range. Planters can never tell which of their tenants will be with them the following year, but of one thing they can be fairly certain—that they will not leave the county, and in time, will rotate, of their own choice, back to the point of beginning. The past is thus kept ever alive, since it is never seriously broken. This restlessness is expressed in such statements as:

We moved here in 1925. Getting time to move now, ain't it? We been here too long now.

I just been here two months. . . . . I'll just be here 'til the last of the month and everything gets settlement.

25

We jest been moved out here from Montgomery this year, so my husband could get on his feet, but we expects ter move soon's cotton time's over.

When people ain't got no home they move back from one place to the other.

We moved here from Shorter, but 'fore we went ter Shorter we lived in La Place. We been farming all our lives 'cept two years when we was in town.

The statistical evidence from the 612 families gives more exactness to these comments. About 60 per cent of the 400 husbands, or male heads of the families, were born in Macon County. About

TABLE II

BIRTHPLACE OF THE MALE AND FEMALE HEADS OF 612 NEGRO FAMILIES IN MACON COUNTY

	Dead or Away	Border States	Some Other Southern State	Same State	Same Place or Neighborhood	Unknown	Total
Male heads of families......	152	1	15	270	7	8	453
Wives of female heads of families.................	33	0	11	354	7	2	407

34 per cent of these men were born elsewhere in the state of Alabama, and only about 5 per cent were born in other southern states. In the case of the 579 wives, or female heads of families, about the same proportions were born on the place or in the neighborhood. This seems to correspond roughly with the general immobility of the residents of the state. For the United States as a whole, 67.2 per cent of the population were born in the state in which they reside while for Alabama 87.5 per cent.

There were those who could point to the spot "where pappy was sot free, right over yonder." One old resident pointed his foot at the stove beside which his parent had died on the very plantation where he had served his master as a slave. The second generation was there, renting from the family of the former owner of his

26

father. Ann Weaver is living in the cabin given her by her white folks when they moved to Montgomery. "It's mine tel I die," she said with triumph. "She went down ter de courthouse and had it done, so dat effen she die fo' me they can't take it." One resident confided: "I've never been out of the state. Reason is, I wouldn't know what way to go."

The Tradition of Dependence

For those still living in the county there is, it would appear, one unfailing rule of life. If they would get along with least difficulty, they should get for themselves a protecting white family. "We have mighty good white folks friends, and ef you have white folks for your friends, dey can't do you no harm."

How this practical policy, so clearly a carry-over from the past, can extend to controlling advice on the most intimate matters is apparent in the domestic experience of Josh Walker, who sought the judgment of his white folks on the merits of his last wife.

This last wife I had, she was a blizzard, 'cause she was no count no way. Hers was her way and my way was my way, and she quit me and carried off all the money I had. I had done saved $80. She carried hit all off. That was six years ago. She was too old ter draw water and ter cook, but she had the devil in her. Hit tuk four men to carry her away. She went off. Said I'd be wid my chillen an' she gwine ter hers. *White folks tole me that I better let that hussy go and atta she left I jes shouted.*

The sense of dependence has crystallized into a sort of practical philosophy: "You know when you get where you can't behave yourself you better move. You got to be loyal, 'cause you know this is a white man's country." And again: "You can't do nothing with white folks agin you." Nor should it be supposed that all of this dependence upon the whites is based upon fear. There is a solid and sympathetic paternalism among some of the white planters toward their Negro dependents which is felt by them. Max Wheeler, for example, was a stolid, illiterate, but hard-working head of a large family who experienced the perennial difficulty of breaking even. Year after year he went to his white planter friend. Times were hard in 1931. Max explained sympathetically: "He

27

said he had so many folks on his place to feed, it was hard, but he wanted to try to give all of us a little feed." It worried Mandy Williams that she was "so sympathetic with white people." Sarah Owens, now sixty-eight, achieved her own freedom from the sense of dependence by claiming her white folks as her own. "Honey, them's my own good white folks. Done had me [in the family] since I been three weeks old and had my mother before me." Booker T. Washington, in a memorial address at Hampton Institute in 1893 on General Samuel Chapman Armstrong, was, no doubt, thinking of his neighbors back of Tuskegee when he asserted with vigor: "The greatest injury that slavery did my people was to deprive them of that sense of self-dependence, habits of economy, and executive power which are the glory and distinction of the Anglo-Saxon race."

The older members of the community who find ample satisfaction in the old culture are aware of some queer difference manifesting themselves in the attitude of younger members who have been away from the section. Caleb Humphries went to Montgomery to try to adjust a matter of compensation due on the death of one of his sons in France. He tells the story now of how he was sitting in the Red Cross Office in Montgomery when a white man, whom he promptly assumed to be the governor of Alabama, came in. "He was tall as a tree, and I said 'Good-morning, Master'—so uster slavery I still say hit. They [other Negroes] stopped me from hit 'cause dey say you don't hafta treat white folks like dat dese days."

The community is being affected at present by at least four factors: migration of a portion of the younger generation away to other states and to the North; return of a small number of younger members who have been sent away to school in Tuskegee and Montgomery; the gradually increasing literacy of the group, beginning with the children; and the introduction of certain programs of welfare from the outside. The interplay of these new influences with the old habits of the community may be observed in some measure against the background of the present structure and functioning of the Negro family in this area.

28

Father, mother, and their children are regarded by sociologists as constituting not only the elementary family but the fundamental social group. It is the universal pattern, and based on this primary structure, which, in our culture, places the father most commonly at the head of the group, principles are formulated regulating marriage, defining legitimacy, and determining what is respectable, even moral. The families of this area are, by this standard, considerably atypical. In the first place, the rôle of the mother is of much greater importance than in the more familiar American family group. This has some explanation in the slave origins of these families. Children usually remained with the mother; the father was incidental and could very easily be sold away. The rôle of the mother could be extended to that of "mammy" for the children of the white families.

The position of the Negro woman always gave her greater advantage in dealing with their white masters than the Negro men. Historically she has been the controlling influence over the children. Moreover, in the present economic arrangement, her earning power is only a fraction less than that of the male, and as a rule more sustained and dependable. She, thus, in large part escapes one of the most powerful factors influencing adversely the status of women generally in the American society.

A second factor marking a difference is the free grouping of relatives and adopted children in the households. Although the households kept themselves strictly separated (92 per cent of the families or households lived under separate roofs), there were 30 per cent of the families with one to six relatives living with them. The families with children were the ones most likely to add relatives to their numbers. Over half of the families had other relatives in the household.

In the third place, just about two-thirds of the families could be considered normal in the sense of having both parents living or living together with the children. To this circumstance is added another factor of the almost indiscriminate gathering under the same roof of half-brothers and half-sisters from various marriages, and of adopted children taken freely into the home. The makeup of households which sociologically may be regarded as families often constitutes a confusing picture. Mary Grigsby, of Hardaway, is head of one of the oldest families of the county. She gives an account of the present structure of her household. It contains some of her own children, her children's children, and half-brothers' and sisters' natural and legal children. It is, however, as stable as most of the others. As a matter of fact, it represents a sort of selection. Those members who find themselves too violently at variance with the codes by which the family is regulated move out and away, or are expelled.

My mamma she said I was born on ole man Chum Crack's place on Boyd's farm. After I married I left 'em, but I been here nigh on about forty years [in the neighborhood]. I been on this spot nigh about thirty years. My mamma died this year. She were about one hundred years old. This is my son and grandson. One of my sons he married and live over yonder, but this grandson lives with me.

Charlie [grandson] was born here. My daughter were in Birmingham, but she come on here. She went back for a while and stay with her husband, then she sent Charley back and give him to me.

Richard was born in Montgomery, and Dave, my son who is Richard's daddy, give him to me when he was three years old.

Sam Burkes is Charley's father. I don't know where he at. His home, though, in Birmingham. Mary Burkes, my daughter, and Charley was married, though, right down there.

Lena Parsons was Richard's mother. She and Dave wasn't married.

I was the mother of fifteen children in all. I got six livin'. Some come live, but didn't live no time, yet three got to be big chillen walkin' 'bout fo' dey dies. One boy got to be eighteen years old. He had that fever and from that spasms and spells and from the spells he fell in the fire and got burnt and never got over it. The other two just died with the fever.

Charlie [another son], he goin' on three years old when he died with the fever, too. With the others I go about five or six months and I lost 'em. I jest keep a losten em.

That the last one I saved right there [*pointing to another son*]. I had to work to save him. I had to go to the doctor. I got so weak I couldn't hold 'em.

Gregory wasn't the father of 'em all. He was the father of Janie and David [the oldest boy in Montgomery]. Robert Pitts is the father of the other four, Mary, Richard, Jessie, and Archie. I was married to Gregory by David Bracks. I wasn't never married to Pitts.

A further fact about this community is that in almost half of the families one or more of the members of the original family group were away in other parts of the county or state, or in northern states. Of the 612 families there were only 317 with no members away, or about half, and those include the families with no children at all. In 295 families there were from 1 to 10 members absent. One hundred and twelve families had 1 person away; 70 had 2 persons away, 40 had 3 persons away, and 61 had 4 or more persons away. Moreover, those absent members when they leave the state are often cut off completely from the parent stock.

In the case of the unlettered offspring, or even mates of the remaining family heads, the ties are sometimes carelessly allowed to break. It not infrequently happens, however, that children who leave push forward their education and become consciously separated by a vast cultural chasm. This had occurred in the case of the family in which the mother had remarried and given birth to three children by a second husband. Her two sons by a first marriage had left the county and begun their own education, which carried them through the State Normal School in Orangeburg, South Carolina. In her dreary two-room cabin, with one large bed as the only furniture, the fly-specked photographs of these two boys in collegiate cap and gown hung like strange, alien figures from the newspaper-covered walls. She did not know where they were or what they were doing. Nor had she seen them since they left. These photographs remained as almost mocking mementos of a separation as complete as death. Another family in similar circumstances had a son away who has become the head of a Negro educational institution, but who is likewise lost to them. Thus the community in throwing off its members escapes both the irritation of its disturbing miscreants and the elevating influence of its cultural misfits at the other extreme of the scale.

Size of Families

There were 1,344 children in these 612 families. Sixty-nine of these children were under one year of age and constituted 2.7 per cent of the 2,482 persons in all the families. This was higher than for the county as a whole. This age group constitutes 2.2 per cent of the entire population. Two hundred and twenty-nine of these children were under five years of age. This was 9 per cent of the entire group, or slightly less than the figure for the county as a whole, which was 10.0 per cent. Six hundred and thirty-two of the children were between the ages of five and fourteen and constituted 25.4 per cent of the 2,482 persons in these 612 families. This was

TABLE III

NUMBER OF FAMILIES WITH STATED NUMBERS OF CHILDREN

TOTAL NUMBER FAMILIES	CHILDREN											
	0	1	2	3	4	5	6	7	8	9	10	11
612.........	189	127	83	62	41	40	28	21	10	6	3	2

slightly higher than the figure for the county as a whole, which was 23.9 per cent in 1920. If we take into consideration all the families, there are, on an average, 2.2 children to a family. But 189 of these families had no children, and if the average number of children for these families with children is calculated, there are 3.1 children to a family. Table III shows the distribution of these families according to the number of children.

Types of Family Structure

The environment has produced not one but many family types which, however, have numbers of traits in common. It is not immediately apparent just what have been the predominant influences in shaping their differences. There are families which are fairly stable and adjusted to the environment and its social codes. They have a distinct background, certain family traditions, a consciousness of integration, and they are sensitive to certain patterns of respectability which represent the more reflective moral sentiments of the group. These families appear among both the educated and the uneducated classes of the population and in varying proportions among owners, tenants, and croppers.

The frequency in this community of the artificial or quasi-families seems to warrant their classification as a type. They have the semblance of a normal and natural family, and function as one, but the members of the group are drawn into it by various circumstances rather than being a product of the original union. There are, again, those families which, though not bound by the formal sanctions, are held together for years by the strength of affectional ties or the satisfactory character and mutual convenience of the arrangement. Multiple marriages are fairly common. Intransient family groups seem to be a product of the environment and are held together over periods by economic and other considerations of convenience. And just as these family forms are reflections of the environment, there have been developed physical adjustments with regard to both remarriage and the disposition of children. Equally important are the families whose organization and sentiments, though in accord with more advanced ideals of other communities, are in constant conflict with the dominant patterns of both the white and the Negro local community. Finally, there are those family groups which reflect definite disorganization as a result of the disintegration of traditional controls, and are yet unable or unwilling to adjust themselves to newer patterns of relations. All of these are affected in some degree by the social and cultural transition which the community is experiencing.

The numerical distribution of these types of families can be suggested in these figures: in the 612 households there were 404 married couples or couples living together in common-law association. There was no male head in 152, or 25 per cent of these families. The male parent was either away or dead. The wife or female head of the household was absent from 33 of the families. About two-thirds of the families were normal family groupings. In 231 of the 404 couples married or living together the man and woman were each married or in marital association for the first time. In 24

33

families the husband had been married more than once. In 74 families both man and woman had been married more than once. There were only 2 divorced persons who had not remarried. The community afforded no spinsters and extremely few bachelors.

Stable Old Families with Strong Affectional Ties and a Family Tradition

The Haygood family was rooted in slavery, but father and mother, both illiterate, were married and had lived together over fifty years, reared children, established a family tradition of a sort, accumulated a little property, and retained their affection for each other. Ellen Haygood spoke thus of her background and relations with her husband until his very recent death:

Yes, indeed, I may be old but I remember everything. I was born during slavery. Dem sho' was bad times. If the niggers hadn't been liberated by Abe Lincoln we'd still be the white folks' niggers. The way them folks used to beat us was shameful. My white folks want rich. They was just good livers and they want so bad. I ain't nebber forgotten my young mistress. She had the longest nose you ever seen, but she was sweet. Her name was S——. All the niggers on the place called her "Miss Sis" and when I sees her now I calls her "Miss Sis." She's done got powerful old but she still lives right on the old place over yonder near Honey Cup. Yes'm right here in Shorters. Folks would raise the fence and put your end on one side and your head on the other and beat and beat them niggers. I was the onliest little nigger on the place when freedom come. The Yankees come through and said slavery's done gone. Child, the niggers got to yelling and whooping all over the place. Some of 'em got kept in bondage as long as four years after freedom. The white folks jest wouldn't loose us. Abe Lincoln touched a pen for the sign of freedom but all the niggers didn't know. The Rebels didn't tell us until some good white folks let the cat out of the bag. My husband he was off in the war. That was Jim. He done told me so much I ain't nebber gonna forget. He got discharged right on Peach Street in Atlanta. Dere's his picture on the wall. I gits here in my bed some night and puts on the flashlight on the picture and says, "I'm still all alone Jim—still your Ellen." I know it ain't gonna be long now 'fore I goes to him. He sho' was a good husband. He used to cook and help me but we was married fifty-six years and I ain't missed cooking his vittels but once. He got mad then and hit me. . . . . Then he was sad and said, "Scraps (used

34

to call me Scraps), I hain't nebber gonna hit you no mo' long's I live," and he sho didn't. I loved that man.

The week 'fore he died he said, "Ellen, git my tax papers and all the pension papers. I'se gonna fix things so if I die you won't have no trouble. I'se an old disable soldier and I'se gonna take care of you." Well, we signed papers 'n' all. Then he paid Miss Jessie $1.00 to come here and write all our names in the Bible in ink. See, I couldn't write and Jim couldn't but he'd been carryin' all that in his head, and he knew if anything ever happen and it weren't wrote down, it be hard for me. He was blind, too. Got blind from cooking so much. All that smoke was too much for his eyes. Well, I come nigh going blind too. Jim paid $100 for my eyes to get better. A white lady come here and tended like she was gonna do a heap for us and said she'd send some glasses but she ain't done nothin.' After freedom I went to school 'till the one-legged man wrote me I couldn't go no more without no money an' we ain't had nothin' then. All we got we just cummulated. When my chilluns married I gave each one two sheets, three pillow cases, one half-dozen cups and saucers, and a piece of furniture. I treated 'em all the same. Just had to save to git all this, an' if anybody knows how to save and scrape, I do. I gits all the slop ready for the chilluns and it don't take much the way I fixes it. I done lost $700 in this Tuskegee bank when hit closed. I'se been saving that a long time and it sho' got me bad.

My husband died with the kidney trouble. He got drawed sores all on his legs. I got 'em now. Wait, I'm gonna show you. The children want me to go to Birmingham to the doctor. Dere's a doctor there who can look plumb through you and see everything. Spects my heart is like this cause everything I got is dead but me and three chillun. I done had to stop breeding for six years on account of bad misfortune. I got a milk leg and a risen breast. The doctor is scared to lance it.

Tain't easy for me to keep up with all my spenses. I miss Jim for that. He sho' could figure. Just two years ago next month he died. I make lines like this . . . . for dollars and circles for nickels. I send some of the money up North to the chilluns, but I done got careless and don't keep it up.

Families with Strong Maternal Dominance and with Specific Moral Codes

Frank Grice is forty-nine and his wife thirty-seven, and with their seven children, ranging in ages from eight to twenty years, they live in a five-room cottage which they are attempting to buy. All but one of the children are living at home. The house is old, has never been painted, has half of the windows missing, and is, in the words of Mrs. Grice, " 'bout to fall down." They are cotton farmers and for the past three years have tried to make a living from thirty acres of questionable cotton land which they rent. Last year they raised two bales of cotton, both of which went to the white man from whom they had purchased a mule with which to do their plowing. Besides the cotton, however, Frank Grice raised three loads of corn, two hundred bundles of fodder, fifteen gallons of syrup, and three banks of potatoes, and this provided the food for the family and their total income in kind for the year.

Jerry, next to the oldest boy, is the wanderer, and left home three years ago. They do not know where he is, and indeed have not heard from him since he left. But the family stands out as a distinct type in this neighborhood. Neither of the parents can read or write and none of the children has passed through the fourth grade in school. The parents wanted the children to be educated but even education was less important than "living decent." The mother is the stronger element of the family, and has pronounced notions about morality and respectability. All the children but one, Jerry the wanderer, live quietly in the community and in marked social isolation. The attitude of the family is unique and important for its revolt against commonplace practices in the community.

Yes, I's the mother of seven children and every last one of dem belongs to Frank Grice. I ain't stuck on dese stolen chillun; dat's why I married in my mother's house 'fore I broke my virtue. I just got 'omanish and nothin' would do me but to marry. Out of all of dem, I ain't got but one bad un. He ain't just say bad, but he wanders away. Been away now 'bout three year, and the last time I heard from him he was in Union Springs. No, he don't get into no trouble, 'cept last year he got into trouble for carryin' a gun. He didn't shoot nobody, but hits 'gainst d law to have one. He got out of it all right because we have mighty good white friends.

No, hit's been sometime now since I's been to church. In my condition I can't go. I'm lookin for the baby in September. I's so shame to go to church lookin like dis. You know yourself everybody would be lookin' at me with my stomach so big. Maybe if I could get me a loose dress I'd go. I 'speck this will be my last time to come around. Eliza

Rose, the midwife, tells me the time when my last child was born that I would have one more time to come, but she said, too, dey would be twins. I wish they would come twins, and den I knows I would be done for all time, 'cause I's just about tired of having chillun. Every time I look out de door I's like dis. I's so thankful for one thing: my oldest boy is such a good child.

Me and my family don't never git into no trouble. De peoples right up dere next to me stole two pigs last year. Dey can't git along wid nobody. No, I ain't have no fuss wid 'em, 'cause I ain't see no use. I just pray to the Lord and he takes care of everything.

Quasi-families: Female Heads of Assembled Families

The number of households with old women as heads and large numbers of children, although of irregular structure, is sufficiently important to be classed as a type requiring some explanation. The oldest generation is the least mobile; the children of these in the active ages move about freely and often find their own immediate offspring, while young, a burden, as they move between plantations. Marriages and remarriages bring increasing numbers of children who may be a burden to the new husband or a hindrance to the mother if she must become a wage-earner. The simplest expedient is to leave them with an older parent to rear. This is usually intended as a temporary measure, but it most often ends in the establishment of a permanent household as direct parental support dwindles down. The responsibility is accepted as a matter of course by the older woman and she thereafter employs her wits to keep the artificial family going. Charlotte Harris, in the subcommunity of Sambo, has such a family. When first visited she was in the field hoeing. On the way back to her cabin, Josephine, a small and grotesquely deformed girl-child of about twelve years of age, came reeling unsteadily down the path. She was groaning, moving her lips rapidly, and uttering unintelligible sounds. "She can't talk," explained the old woman. Then calling to the other children in the rear of the cabin, she commanded, "Come here, you chillun, and git de baby." Two of them, a few years older, appeared and led the child away. The old woman then began to talk as she cooled herself:

37

I don't know 'zackly how old I'm is. 'Bout fifty I guess. I 'member when slavery time was. The old marster uster have lunch up ter the big house every Sunday and call all his little niggers up to the house. No, they ain't been all one family. He had lots of niggers and he liked to show his friends how many little niggers he had. I wan't big enough to remember much.

At this time Josephine came back to the house and attempted to get upon the steps, but could not lift her foot high enough. The children helped her up the steps. She went into the house and came back with an armful of rags, then sat on the porch, staring, groaning, sucking her tongue, and hugging the rags.

I don't know 'zackly how old Josephine is. I think she 'bout nine years old. She old 'nough to 'menstrate. She kinder like a young lady. Looka here, got a little breast coming. You know she old. She is my granddaughter's child, who died the other day. Janie Lou and Ethel her chillun too, but I been had Josephine all her life. Dese other two just come since she dead. I ain't know 'zackly what she died with. Charlotte died in the hospital in Montgomery. Left five chillun. James and the other boy live over dere with his father. Dis one here is 'nother child, belong to my other grandchild. Charlotte named for me. The doctor said she had an abscess in her stomach.

Josephine ain't right bright. She ain't crazy, though. Been like dat all her life. She don't never git into no trouble. She burned her foot once but she ain't fall in the fire. She stepped on the hot coal. When I went to the burial last week she wouldn't go with me. I paid my brother Dan to stay here with the child 'cause I hates ter leave her here alone, but old people so contrary.

No, Josephine ain't foolish. Her mother said 'fore she was born that she stayed on the creek fishing too long. One day when she had been fishing, on her way back home somebody put a ground hog in the road. Somebody killed the ground hog and laid it on a sheet for her to pass, and it skeered her to death. Then when the baby was borned she started to walk but she ain't walk, just crawled like a turtle. Tried to talk; says "mama" sometimes. She always plays wid rags and sticks; gathers 'em up in a pile.

My husband been dead. I don't know how come he died. When he died he jest hollered. He was a good Christian, though. Said he had pains and all the misery was in his head. He went so naked I said he died with the pneumonia. He didn't wear no clothes atall. Yes, he had plenty of clothes, but too stingy to wear 'em. I don't care how hot it is, clothes made for the flesh. During cotton-picking time I talked to him but it ain't do no good. Had good clothes, den laid down and died and left 'em all here. After he died I called in the little boy and gie'd him a whole sack of clothes. I'd a worn 'em out to rags myself if I'd had dat many. Mine all full o' holes, but I does pretty well.

I gits the house and patch for nothing. John Henry Davis, my grand-daughter's husband over there, lets me stay here. I he'ps him some wid his farm and then I takes care o' the chillun. She gives me $2.00 a week, sometimes rations. Davis furnishes my food 'cause all of 'em been eating here since my granddaughter dies.

I plum' out of all the 'cieties now. Susie Williams was the president. I'll have to join some others 'cause my overcoat [coffin] cost too much. I was b'long to the Home Mission. Just throw my money away joining the Union Aid. I hate to lose all dat money. Got to work now to pay the $30 to the overseer. He buried my husband. I'll work till the Lord calls me, 'cause I ain't paid the overseer back yet. He wouldn't take my cow, 'cause he told me my cow was my living. He sure was good not to take my cow. The church give me $5.00. Mr. ———— said he would give me a chance. He wanted me to live on his place but I didn't 'cept the offer 'cause I mighta taken sick and had nobody to wait on me. I come over here to be near my granddaughter after my husband died; and then she died.

The Red Cross he'ped me once. Me an my brother Dan went over dere. The white folks was over der figuring and my brother looks like he wanted to talk imposin' talk. They was handing out letters to the folks, but they ain't had none for me. The white man got fretted so I pulled Dan's coat tail. Miss ———— told us not to blame her 'cause she only had letters for the people what give her they names.

I had one granddaughter to die with pellagacy. No, she ain't died here. She stayed here all last winter then went to her husband in Montgomery and then died.

Quasi-families: Male Heads of Transient Families with Shifting Family Members

Another and curious type of family is that in which the male head remains constant while various other types of relationship, including a succession of wives and their children by him, shift around him. The children and grandchildren and wives who fail to accommodate themselves to the pattern drift out and away, or are thrown off while others remain, constituting essentially a fami-

39

ly organization. An example of this type is the family of Grants. The husband, who in this case is the pivotal figure, is fifty-two and his present wife thirty-eight. Besides them there are three children: Lulu Harris, eighteen, the unmarried daughter of the mother and her two-year-old child; and two sons of James Grant, by other wives, twenty-two and fifteen years old, respectively. He owns a small two-room frame house. In point of organization there is no difference between such an adjusted type of family and a natural one. It is, perhaps, even more efficient when pointed toward productive ends—a circumstance which lends cohesion to the natural family. As a matter of fact, in spite of its transient nature, the family changes are, realistically viewed, little different from those which occur in course of the growth of children. What is conspicuously lacking is a family tradition, and this lack is not, incidentally, wholly confined to the transient family.

I'm about fifty-two years old, but I don't remember how long I've been living here in this county. It's been so far back. I just go by what the folks say. They say I was a little boy when I come here.

That's my grandchild, Lilly Mae's child. Will Jackson is the father. He don't live here. You know just about how it come here. Lilly is my wife's first husband's child. He somewhere. She got a divorce. I mean she didn't but her husband did.

Yes, I got a divorce in Union Springs for my wife. Mrs. Murray, the lady we was working for, got the divorce, and I ain't know how much it cost. This is my fourth wife. The first one died in Mississippi. I heered that she died and they fetched her back home in Mississippi. I ain't leave the second one; she got away from me. The third one, I ain't know where she is, and there is the fourth one right over there. I ain't got no divorce from none of them. I got two sons and a daughter done left home. One son left home around the war when the people got all stirred up. I don't know where he is. My other son and daughter, I don't know where they is neither.

Stable Non-legal Unions

Families cohere over a long period with all the semblance of stability, but without the legal sanctions. In the Johnson family are: Will Johnson, fifty-three; Mary Lucas, his common-law wife, thirty-five; Annie Lee, fifteen; Willie Lee, eight; Alice, five; Mamie, three; Thomas, two; and Salina, five months. Two other children died in infancy, and two of the father's children by a previous connection had been away in Montgomery about a year. The mother also has one girl from another unsanctioned alliance. Two of the children in the present household are able to work. The parents are unmarried, but this omission seems relatively unimportant. The arrangement is one of mutual convenience and desire, and has survived shocks sufficient to provoke permanent separation and divorce. Mary Lucas was muscular, large fisted, self-reliant, and not afraid to "hit the sun" in the field. Carelessness was added to poverty in their household and the children were unusually dirty and ragged. Will Johnson was vigorous but older. He had a heavy tangled beard, and one eye was missing. He would sit with his hand over his face and his evident self-consciousness suggested that the injury was not an old one. The mother spoke first:

He is the father of all dese chillun. No, we ain't married. I ain't never been married. I'm the mother of seven chillun. The other one ain't here. She is a girl. Ethel Harris is her name. She married now and lives over there in Hardaway somewhere. Dave Gregory is her father, and he is in Montgomery. I got two chillun dead. One died when it was a day old and the other one a few hours. Both of dem come too soon. Both of 'em was born alive with the eyes open. I knows they was alive 'cause they both cried. I fell out de wagon with the first one, and ain't nothin' wrong that I knows of wid the second one.

MAN: I been knowing her [Mary Lucas] a long time.

WOMAN: I was raised up under him. He lived 'bout half a mile from me. My mother knowed his mother 'fore she dies. They been well acquainted.

MAN: Yes, I's been married once, and my wife, her name was Mary Hunter 'fore we married and then she named Mary Johnson, live now in Montgomery. Had two chillun and they with her in Montgomery. I don't know how long they been gone. I thought of marryin' Mary once. Just as soon as I git able I goin' to get married. May be a good while and it may not.

WOMAN: I likes him all right.

MAN: I likes her better than any other woman in a way [*speaking very hesitatingly*]. She understands the way we gits along. We done talked this thing over. . . . .

The last time I went to the doctor it was fer my eye. I went to

Dr. ——— and he charged me $24. It been 'bout three years ago. Dat woman over dere hit me in it.

WOMAN: Dat what he say. I have to say like he say, and he said like it was. He hit me the fust lick. If he hadn't hit me I wouldn't a hit him. I hit him wid a stick. I didn't mean to hit him in the eye. Tried to git around it. Didn't mean to hit him in the face, let 'lone his eye.

Non-agricultural Families

Some of the male heads of families are able to let their wives stay at home. The arrangement is easier where the man is engaged in work other than farming. Albert O'Neal is a laborer in a log mill, earning seven dollars a week. He has held this job for seven years, and he makes a point of keeping his wife at home. They have been married eight years and seem happy, although the wife has recently developed a keen interest in education, and confessed that if she were not married she would be going to school somewhere. Her husband is a hard-working man who seems to live for the happiness and comfort of his young wife. But she is bored with the life of the community. Said she:

I love my husband but it seems like he has such a hard time keeping up his family. I married in 1923. I was going ter school and my father had died and I had ter take care of myself. My mother just died last year. She had pellagacy. I stayed with my godmother in Milstead. I never did stay with my mother. She left and went ter Louisiana and never did return. She left papa. She never could git along. I met my husband in Milstead and we married in Godmother's house. We done been going tergether when we married 'bout three years. I uster like the farm all right tel they wasn't gittin' nothin' for cotton.

We would be living in town but my husband can't git nothin' ter do up there. I gits tired out here sometimes. I wish I was in town. I'm tired of picnics and suppers and ball games. That's 'bout all we hafta do. My husband goes ter work wid sunrise ever' morning and works tel dark. I git up 'fo day and cooks his breakfast. He don't come back home ter dinner 'cause hits so far. Hits 'bout seven miles from here. He comes home 'bout dark, half dead. Then we eat supper and 'round a hour he's sleep.

Stable Legal Unions

Domestic relations are rarely ever continually peaceful in the households, but the real test of the union is the ability to sustain

42

the shocks of marital strife without following the easier path to separation. The Keys have been married twenty-seven years and have never separated. Their two sons and a daughter-in-law live with them in the household. Cotton farmers all, they raised not only three bales (1,270 lb.) of cotton which they sold for cash at eight cents a pound, but also 200 bushels of peas and 27 gallons of syrup. Together they raised chickens, had seven hogs, and, what is most important, have been buying their home for the past six years.

We been married twenty-seven years and ain't never parted. We fight and scratch and I stay right here. He has never fought me. I get mad, throw chairs, and stay home, 'cause if I ever left I would never come back. . . . . We done lost much money in lodges, and it's been so long I can't remember. My husband was a member of the American Workmen and I use to be a member of the Sons and Daughters of Job. The man what organized it called hisself the Grand Debit.

I's had two miscarriages. I toted some wood under my arm and mashed its head.

Disorganized Legal Unions

The influence of exposure to the city of one parent, while the other remains at home is marked in another type. In a more general sense, there is revealed a family organization in contact both with the culture of this isolated section and with certain externals of the culture of the city. In the family of Robinsons the organization remained stable as long as the husband remained in the county. Then he got a job as a section hand on the railroad and eventually got passes to town. Mr. and Mrs. Robinson have been married about eighteen years and have eight children, including the twins, Isaac and Isaiah. There have been four stillbirths. The mother comments on her family:

Mary stays here wid us. She jest started here Friday. She and her sister's husband can't get along, and she and her sister neither. Bama ain't no good. She named after me. She sick all the time wid her eyes, and I jest keeps her home. I don't rent. They jest let me stay in here; as long as they got work fer me ter do I work.

The children done all stopped school 'cause they had ter help take care of theyselves. I couldn't support 'em by myself. I is a day laborer and makes 50 cents a day. Mariah works by the day and makes 50 cents a day to help. Lizzie [the oldest girl] ain't here. She is in Detroit. She runned away and married and went there. She sent us some money but hit was stole out the letter. I got the letter but didn't seed no money. I sho' didn't like hit fer her ter git married.

We owes this man, and he gives us two $5.00 a week for working, and he takes half of it and we have ter live off the rest. I didn't have nobody ter help me and I had ter go down there ter git stuff 'nuf ter live off at the end of the fall. My husband left us a year this July. Say after they laid him off the railroad he couldn't find no job ter do and he wasn't going ter work on no farm. He worked on the railroad with the Phillips gang, and when they cut him off he jest went 'bout his business. I aint' heard of him, but the last concern I heard of him he was in Montgomery, and I knowed that 'bout all the far he could get. I ain't going ter look fer dat man. He might have some rotten woman there who might jump on me. I'm jest going ter stay here and do the best I can. We was married in 1914, the fifteenth of July. He was an awful gambler and sold ever' thing he could git his hands on. He even sold my clothes and the cows we had. I stayed wid him 'cause I cared for him. I uster worry over him, but I don't think 'bout him now. Better leave this marrying business alone, Honey, 'cause these men will git you a house full of chillun den up and leave you.

The mother and all the children were barefooted; and far into the day the beds in the two-room cabin were unmade, the bedding sticky and black with dirt, piled in the center of a corn-shuck mattress.

Stable Families with Advanced Standards

There is the type of family which in organization and sentiment is out of harmony with its local environment. It takes its pattern and social codes from other and more advanced areas. While the family lives in the community, the members take but small part in its life. They are, however, not isolated even though contacts with the outside world are limited and rare. They are usually owners of both their homes and their farms, and are not dependent upon the prevailing economic system for their support or their ideals. Their homes are conspicuously out of place as Negro homes and are readily mistaken by the stranger for the dwellings of one of the white planters. There is usually a reason for their remaining in the locality, and some extraordinary circumstance out of the line of normal development responsible for their independence.

The Hennings were born in Macon County and have lived in their present home for nineteen years. The father is fifty, the mother fifty-two, and there are three children—twenty-seven, twenty-five, and seventeen, respectively. Neither parent has been married before, and all of their children are with them at home. The five-room house is a frame cottage, well built. They own a small automobile and a piano, and subscribe to a daily and a weekly paper. The father is a machinist in the L. and N. Shops in Birmingham and comes home every two months for a week-end. All the children have been sent away to school: two to the Alabama State College in Montgomery and one to Fort Valley in Georgia. The living-room of the house is furnished in conventional style with duofold, bookcases (containing some two hundred or more volumes), and a phonograph. On their farm they raised during the year sixty bushels of corn, six and one-half bales of cotton, and a considerable quantity of peas, potatoes, and peanuts. They kept a budget and had exact figures on income and expenditures.

The circumstances enabling this family to maintain a cultural level above that of the majority in this community are as follows: A grandfather, who had been an adventurous migrant, found his way to Oklahoma and before his death purchased some land on which oil was later found. At his death he willed a sum of money to each of his two sons and to his grandchildren. In the family to which the head of the present Henning family belonged there were six children, each of whom received $600. This was used to make one-half payment on the farm on which they now live. After a period he went to Birmingham for work and from his savings, while his children were still young, completed the payment on the house and farm.

Sixty-one of the 612 families (about 10 per cent) owned or are buying their homes. Four hundred and forty-three families rented as tenants or croppers, and 108 lived in cabins on plantations. Again, the majority of these families live in either two- or three-room cabins; there are 259 families (42 per cent) in two-room and 176 (28 per cent) in three-room cabins, and 59 families live in one-room cabins. In two of these one-room cabins there were seven and eight persons, but in most of them only one or two persons resided.

Chapter II

THE FAMILY

COURTSHIP AND MARRIAGE

BEFORE a child reaches the age of twelve there are duties demanding, with the same insistence felt by his parents, his presence in the field. The routine of cotton cultivation has lent itself with a fatal pliancy to a division of labor capable of extension with each stage of growth from childhood to maturity. Where there are children there is always work to be done to earn the bare living they require. Where there are no children it is less possible to perform all the tasks required to earn enough to survive. Herein lies a first disorganizing factor in the family organization of the community. Immediate as well as remote survival imposes relentless demand for children's labor and the exactions of an economic system of ever increasing severity impose a forced growth upon the children from the moment of birth. Every aspect of the life urges to the earliest possible attainment of adulthood. Where there is early maturity we have come to expect early marriages, especially for women. There is, as a rule, among Negro women generally a greater tendency to early marriage than among white families, and this tendency is accentuated in cities. In southern cities it is much more pronounced than in southern rural areas, but in this special group studied the tendency is considerably less than in other southern rural areas.

The trend in this community runs in an exactly opposite direction from that of the population in general. For the general population not only are there earlier marriages in the country, but, on the whole, more marriages. Ogburn and Groves explain this by observing that women are the ones most markedly affected by

47

urban trends. They become dissatisfied with their rural economic and social status in a monotonous environment, and move to the city where there is more life and greater economic opportunity. This independence in time results in surplus of women at the marriageable ages in the cities. The men are more rooted in the soil.

There is a population unbalance in the rural Negro group studied but the heavier migration has been on the part of the men. The women are the stable element. There is ample support of the statistical differences observed in the large number of women heads of families, their importance to the agriculture of this area, their approximation to economic equality with the men, and their present dominant rôle in the family.

Other factors play an even more important part in accentuating this difference. The organization of the Negro families in this area to make it the most efficient economic unit tends to discourage early marriage of either men or women. When a young person marries the original family unit is seriously disturbed. The economic returns from the period of nurturing unproductive children come only when the children, male or female, reach an age which enables them to contribute to the support and earnings of the family group. Custom and practice recognize this situation. Young people are simply not expected to marry early, and, apart from the insecurity of such a venture, when such marriages occur they encounter a pronounced disapproval. When such early marriages occur the couple is expected to live in and become a part of the household of the parents of the boy or girl.

The situation of economic independence of women in cities is reversed in this community, and is reflected rather strikingly in the economic independence on the part of the Negro women in the country. Their earning power is not very much less than that of men, and for those who do not plan independent work there is greater security in their own family organization where many hands contribute to the raising of cotton and of food than there is for them alone with a young and inexperienced husband. It is practically impossible for two young persons alone to attend all the details of cotton cultivation on a scale sufficient for adequate support of themselves. Likewise, it is extremely unlikely that any young man will be able to accumulate sufficiently to "get on his feet" before marrying.

The condition most favorable to early marriage of a girl is that in which the girl is being sought by a widower considerably her senior, who has had years of experience with the system and who, at the same time, has already some other persons in the household; or a condition in which a young girl is sought by a younger man who is working as a plantation hand with no personal responsibilities at all. In this latter case the addition of a wife, young or old, is welcome as an additional farm hand. The experience of one of these girl-brides will make this situation more real. "I married 'fore I was fourteen years old. I run off and got married; no preacher ain't married me. The man, Mr.————, that my husband worked for, married us. He didn't tell me to go back home, 'cause he knowed I was a good hand and then he could have me there too."

The postponement of marriage in the section which has been noted does not preclude courtship, but accentuates it, and gives rise to other social adjustments based upon this obvious economic necessity. The active passions of youth and late adolescence are present but without the usual formal social restraints. Social behavior rooted in this situation, even when its consequences are understood, is lightly censured or excused entirely. Conditions are favorable to a great amount of sex experimentation. It cannot always be determined whether this experimentation is a phase of courtship, or love-making without the immediate intention of marriage, or recreation and diversion. Whether or not sexual intercourse is accepted as a part of courtship it is certain no one is surprised when it occurs. When pregnancy follows, pressure is not strong enough to compel the father either to marry the mother or to support the child. The girl does not lose status, perceptibly, nor are her chances for marrying seriously threatened. An incidental compensation for this lack of a censuring public opinion is the freedom for children thus born from warping social condemnation. There is, in a sense, no such thing as illegitimacy in this community.

The community tends to act upon the patterns of its own social heritage. This is true of sex relations as well as of economic relations. The tradition of the plantation in relation to morals, sex relations, and marriage never has conformed to that of the world outside. Unique moral codes may develop from isolation. It has happened elsewhere. Even in America there have developed patterns of sex relations among white communities not very different. In rustic villages of Bavaria, Austria, Norway, and Switzerland the presence of illegitimate children is not a handicap to women who wish to marry, but the conditions there have been different.

In the families of this study the customary courtship period is observed, but in conformity with a tradition older than the county itself, when pregnancy follows this relationship it is not socially imperative that marriage follows. A woman may have several beaux but only one with whom she is intimate. This was more than once mentioned in the course of this study, as an approximate virtue. The character of the present concern about premarital relations is to some extent apparent in the comment of one of the women:

The first man I ever courted got me in "family way." I uster live on P——'s place 'fore I married. My baby was ten months old when me and my husband married. I was trying to wait 'til he got on his feet and got something 'fore we married, but he never did get nothin'. . . . . He knowed it was his child, 'cause he looked jest like his daddy, and after he was born we went on together jest like we was at first. I never did fool around [have sex relations] with nobody else but him, though I had other beaux and he knowed it. Then after a while me and him jest got married.

Another woman, now the mother of five children and married to a man from one of the older families in the section, remarked casually and frankly: "Our first child was born before we was married. Then he wanted to marry me, so I married him."

Younger people may court, but their affairs are not often of long duration or binding. Church meetings, church suppers, festivals and frolics, and the Saturday trip to town are the occasions on which they usually meet. At the church suppers and other more public affairs the younger men and the younger women group separately. The men entertain themselves loudly with jokes and stories, frequently ribald, and with various actions to attract the attention of the girls or to provoke laughter. The young girls when together, whether experienced or not, affect shyness but are rarely, if ever, unaware of the boys. In the course of the evening a boy may take one of the girls aside for more intimate conversation which may then lead to a less decorous intimacy.

The courtship of older couples is from the beginning a more serious adventure. When one of the older men is courting, either a young woman or one nearer to his age, a change is noted in his personal behavior. At public affairs he leaves off the familiar overalls and "dresses up." The act conspicuously alters his personality. He escorts the young woman to parties and buys ice-cream or pigs' feet or chicken or chitterlings for her. The relationship is thus noted by their friends. Where courting has gone on publicly and the sanctions thus recorded, marriage tends most often to follow the legal and approved form, whether the divorce has been legal or not.

In so general a condition of uncertainty and indifference about the legality of marriage or divorce the question is not often raised, but it is nevertheless true that for the particular ones—that is, those who have begun taking over the pattern of the new culture— the fact of legality is worth mentioning, with at least the expectation of approval.

Jealousy and the violent expressions of this passion are manifested by both men and women during the courtship period, by legally married couples and by companions in a common-law relationship. Because Ben Mason began courting Alice Harris' daughter another woman shot him five times. But Ben Mason had not himself the best reputation. A few years earlier he had accidentally killed one girl while shooting at another who had spurned his attentions. The gossip of the community for the greater part of a month centered around the murder of a young woman at one of the frolics, by a man who came in a blind rage of jealousy to kill his wife because she was "running 'round with other men." The story comes most vividly from the mother of the murdered girl:

My little gal got killed just one week ago today. She was a good chile. Never give no trouble. Yes, she was married and had a baby two years old. She and me went to one of those suppers the other night. I was sitting on the bed in one room and all of a sudden Jake Johnson run in and said, "Willa's done been killed." I run out there and there she was all heaped on the bed—limp. The house was so full, but I just screamed and run to her. I picked her up in my arms and her brains was all shot out in her hair. When I put her down I was covered with blood and I couldn't do nothing but scream. Some nigger come in there to kill his wife 'cause she was going running 'round with other men, but he missed her and put a steel bullet in my baby. This is the dress she got killed in. And I'm going to show you her wedding dress, too. The society I belongs to paid $40 for the burial. I didn't lose nothing that way. That was such a good chile; she was a good wife. Her husband said he'd get that nigger yet, but they found him. The sheriff's got him now at Tuskegee. I sure hopes they punish him good 'cause he's caused me so much pain.

In one family the wife displayed a face grotesquely twisted. Her teeth protruded through a vicious slash in her upper lip. She said:

My husband did it—jest jealous-hearted. He hit me right up there with a fence post and it wasn't bout nothing. . . . . . Lots of times we'd get to scrapping off of nothing. I used to could do as much wid him as he could wid me, tell he got me down, then I'd stop him. Folks used to say, "Carrie, you must be mighty bad." But I tell 'em no I ain't bad, and if they'd look at the starting of it they would see it was his fault. We hardly ever have any falling out now though. He said he didn't believe I was doing all them things he 'cused me of, but he would git in behind me for fear.

Older and more experienced men have decided that jealousy does not pay. It is a disturbing force capable of sapping the spirit of every activity.

HUSBAND: My wife and me, us been married, this coming Saturday, nigh forty years. I slapped her once since I been married. Any friends we know she meets 'em, kiss 'em, and we go right along. I ain't going to let nothing disturb me but the Lord. When you jealous you don't live long.

WIFE: You be jealous and you may be up at the church but you can't rest. The meeting won't do you a bit of good; you may be thinking about that man riding with some woman.

Sex, as such, appears to be a thing apart from marriage. A distinction is very well drawn by one unmarried middle-aged woman with several children who said: "What I wants now is a husband not a man. I wants somebody to help me take keer of these chillun." The legal relationship had little to do with her romantic life. Jealousy is manifested not so much when infidelity to the institution has been discovered as where there is evidence of a transfer of affection, whether it involves sexual intercourse or not. A woman came back from her parents' and found her husband with women in her own home. He became angry at her intrusion and began swearing. When she responded he struck her with a stick. She went home and considered herself permanently separated. The objection was not primarily to the irregularity of her husband's association with women, but to the fact that he beat her.

Tom Bright was my husband, but he fight me so I just couldn't live with him. He treat me so bad. I didn't do nothing a-tall. I uster cook his breakfast and he'd come home with a big stick and beat me. Said I didn't have breakfast done. He drank but he wa'n't drunk when he beat me. One time I went away to mamma's and come back I found some women in my house. When I come in he got mad and went to cussin', so I packed up and went back home.

The comment of a woman of twenty-five who had been married twice suggests an attitude from the other side of the picture. The husband was jealous but trifling. The woman seemed to feel that he had no right to be jealous unless he was also useful.

The first man [husband] wasn't no good—just trifling. I soon got rid of him. First we kept separating and then going back. Then I met Major and my first old man started right away to getting jealous. So I left him, but I did right. I went down there to Montgomery and got my divorce. It cost me $32.50, but it was worth it, seein' it 'liminated all his 'tachment to me.

Ceremonial recognition is more often given to weddings than to any other event in the life of the family. Even though this seldom occurs now, there are sufficient traces of an old custom to allow it to be revived when it is especially desired to give formal public sanction to marriage. On these occasions the nuptials are celebrated with wine and cake and festivities, by the friends and relatives of the couple. Occasionally small tokens are exchanged. There has been a practice, tracing back several generations to slavery, of making this an occasion of festivity. Slaves, although not always encouraged to marry, and deprived of the civil sanction of a ceremony, when there was mutual desire, provided it was within the limits of the master's circumstances, were allotted a cabin, given small tokens by the master and mistress, and a ceremony, conducted by a Negro preacher and patterned after the custom of the whites. It is spoken of now by some of the older members of the community, and little change is noted in the forms of the ceremony. Speaking of slavery, one said:

The folks married then jest like they do now. They did jump over a broomstick [a custom now abandoned] but the preacher had a Bible and married them. Sometimes the sheriff married them. If you and this sister come engaged you would ask Mr. ——— for her and he would say, "Do you love this nigger?" and he would go and ask if she loved you. Then, whatever place you stayed on your master would have to buy whichever one would come there.

The Ideal Wife

Young men when they marry want someone whose labor can help them "get on their feet." Middle-aged men want younger women who can combine this labor with some of the feminine graces. Old men want companionship. A good woman, it is conceded, can be of moral assistance to a man.

I always tell my old lady that every man ought to have a good woman to 'courage and help him. My old lady and me always says the young married folks gets along better. She and me, we don't have no difficulties, but Lordy, you ought to a see that chile I married first! She was a pretty little thing, but she up and died and never had no chilluns.

A man of thirty-five, still unmarried, stipulated three conditions which a woman should meet before he would be willing to marry. She must be able to work, she must be nice looking, and she must be willing to acknowledge him as the head of the house.

The most desirable mates for girls in those families ambitious to

54

maintain a stable unit are men who can assure further stability. Unfortunately for romantic love, the economic arrangement under which they live does not develop many eligibles for daughters of such families, and family authority is exerted, sometimes to the point of physical force, to keep the girls from marrying at all, because it would seriously disturb the economic balance of the original family unit. Elopements have been a means of escaping these complications.

Me and my husband was courtin' a long time, and we jest 'cided to git married. Hit was on a Wednesday night and me and my brother went down ter my cousin's to carry a turkey hen, and I seed a light of a car and we got in the car and drove home. We stayed home 'bout half a hour, and I had done got my clothes and carried them over ter my girl friend's house, then to my grandma's home. I set up till all went to bed. So I pretended I was going to set on the front porch, and I got my coat and started running. He was up the road. I got scared after I got out of the house 'cause I knowed papa would know my clothes wasn't home, and if I went back he'd kill me. We got married, and I didn't have time to drink no wine and cake, and we went over to his mother's house. We heard the horn coming and runned in the house, and sho' nuff it was papa, and he axed my husband's mother, "Is my little Gracey here?" He had a shot gun and he was so mad my husband's mother told him I wasn't there, and he left. Reason I didn't ask papa, I knowed he wouldn't give me away. Mamma done said it was all right with her, but papa always said no, 'cause he wouldn't give my two oldest sisters away.

The conflict here is between the basic requirement of the family group for the added value of the services of its grown children, the prospect of transferring this service to another family, and the imperatives of romantic love.

Hodman Speeks was a widower about fifty-eight years old, and reputed to have saved some money over the years. He owned his home and was now ready to marry again, and felt that he could afford to select a wife without being bound by the usual economic considerations. He was not particular about the women of his community. He had seen too much of them. They not only were a disappointment, but failed also to respect sufficiently his own valuation of the advantages which he, as a husband, could bring. But if a young and attractive woman came in from the outside he would attire himself in his old Prince Albert coat, a cane, and a high collar, and begin a round of visits in the neighborhood.

I'm looking for a good woman right now [he confided to a visitor to the neighborhood]. You know a man gits filled with betterment after he gits a good wife. Now, I tells you, I'm this kind of a man. I feels that 'tain't a man's place to slave a woman to death. I'm going to take care of a wife. When my other wife got taken sick I had a doctor to her in less than fifteen minutes. I owns this home, but 'tain't fit for a woman. I got some money and I'd build a new house. I know something 'bout telephones, too. I'd see that they git a telephone put in here. My wife could have her own little patch and we'd be right happy together—she'n me. 'Tain't meant for a man to be all alone in the world—reckon he gits too reckless with hisself.

Neither the young women of the country nor the old ones, however, were much impressed with the widower. As he passed the house of one of his neighbors a woman remarked, "Here comes that old man Speeks. He ain't got good sense. He got more land than he knows what to do with, but he's so mean and foolish nobody goes near him."

The Ideal Husband

When a very young woman marries it is usually for security. A more mature young woman marries to insure herself the exclusive attention and earning power of a man who is already or likely to be the father of her children. The middle-aged woman offers herself or accepts a husband on approximately equal terms of working value. An old woman, when she marries at all, seeks companionship and that shadowy security afforded by a man of her own age. Unlike the men, an old woman does not often marry a person younger than herself. A mother of a young girl set this ideal before her daughter: "I wants my daughter to marry a good man, so she won't haveter work in the field and be diggin' here and dere, like me." Millie Williams had been married once, but was separated from her husband, who left the section and went to Pittsburgh to live. She was carefully considering remarriage, and thus described her ideal:

Rubin is so good to me. He buys me groceries; sometimes $1.50 and sometimes $1.75 worth, every two weeks. You know he is jest a young man, only twenty-five years old, and a preacher, too. He is sure good to me. He works at the Veneer plant and gits $1.25 a day, and he sure sees after me. We going to git married pretty soon.

Although the young women frequently marry older men, they are sometimes brutally contemptuous of them once their earning power is affected. "That old man, if he could do something I could tell you how much we made. But he don't do no work. He's jest a lazy nigger." Another said: "Aw, my old man won't do. He ain't no count now nohow. He's so old he can't do nothing. Can't even see." This particular husband was about fifty and his wife thirty-seven.

Color consciousness plays a part in the selection of mates. On several occasions women remarked that they wanted a husband, but he "must be good and dark," meaning by "good" in this case "completely" and by dark "black." There are few mulatto women in the community, and mulatto men have a reputation for being "run-roun' men" and poor providers for dark women.

A man who has been unsuccessful in holding other wives is not regarded favorably as a prospect. "No, indeed, I don't want him. He done had two wives and couldn't keep 'em. Ain't nobody goin' to live wid dat man." Men who do women's work are similarly unpopular. "You know when a man's used to washing and cooking for hisself, jest like a woman, he's hard to git 'long wid." Physical strength, dogged industry, and a good disposition were the chief virtues hoped for in a husband. They took precedence over all considerations of possession of money, social position, education, physical attractiveness, or that kind of ambition which sought to abandon the familiar round of life.

THE CHILDREN

In a system which requires the labor of the entire family to earn a living, children of a certain age are regarded as an economic asset. They come fast, and there is little conscious birth control. The coming of children is "the Lord's will." The number of miscarriages and stillbirths is extraordinarily high and the infant mortality great. There is pride in large families. "Good breeders" are regarded with admiration. One woman quoted a doctor as explaining that she was "sickly" because she "needed to breed." For men the size of the family is a test of virility and for women fecundity has tremendous weight in their valuation as mates. This was a conscious boast: "Course my wife she done been laid up with dead chillun until she marry me. She ain't never lost no chillun by me, but that other man she had made her chillun all die." Interest in children and in large families, and the high fecundity rate, may indeed carry over from the period of slavery when social status among Negro slave women was in an important measure based upon their breeding power. Again it may reflect adjustment to a high mortality-rate which demands a correspondingly high birthrate to insure a balanced survival in the population. Assertion that a woman cannot have children by a man constitutes a slur. Some of the most cheerful women were those with large families. The contented comment of one very large and comfortably sprawling mother of thirteen children offers a good illustration of a sentiment not uncommon: "Lordy, I'm jest building up dis world wid babies, and can't help it. Well, dey says it's healthy to have chillun, so I jest goes on."

Mary Harris, another mother of a large family, had been married to Jim only six years, but they had fifteen children. Jim's wife had been barren but Mary was not, and, although unmarried herself, she gave Jim ten children before his wife died. Then they married and she presented him with five more, and may yet present others.

Children, in the average family group, once a part of the family are accepted good-naturedly and as a matter of course. There were indications of conflicting types of interest in children. The uncontrolled fecundity, the almost universal set for large families, and the acceptance of parents, mothers particularly, of the responsibility for supporting any number which they happened to have, point to a fundamental interest in children, whatever the motivation. This interest as expressed, however, was almost without exception in "children." There was little indication of individualization of attention, or recognition of separate personalities, and very imperfect expression of those sentiments of strong emotional attachment to separate child personalities which are noted in the more advanced families. The affectional relationship was manifest, but not emotionally stressed. Parents as a rule clung to their children as long as they could provide them subsistence. The harsh and frequent incidence of hard times created so many occasions for failure in this respect, particularly if one of the chief breadwinners withdrew, that passing over children for adoption was fairly common and the community had attempted to meet this need by making adoption a simple and natural procedure.

Frequently there was confusion on the matter of names and ages of children. Numbers of mothers could not remember the names of all the children, unless they were looking at them. This may have been due to the habit of ignoring names of children, and supplying simple "pet names" for identification. Ages require a reflection and counting which is not always done accurately in communities of higher literacy. On a visit to the home of a family in which there were fifteen children the question of the ages of the children came up. The mother, squat, dark, and glistening with perspiration, sat on her porch, making her breast available alternately to an infant in arms and one about a year old. When asked about the names and ages of her children her first response was one of exasperation that she should be expected to remember a mass of details of this character. She shouted to one of the children, "Go in the house and git the Bible, 'cause God knows I don't remember how old them chilluns is." After a moment she said, "All dese you see here ain't mine, but most of 'em is." Actually, there were several adopted children in the group who were so completely incorporated into the family as to be considered her own. She had to separate, in her thinking, those whom she had "birthed" and those whom she had acquired by other means. The names and ages of seven were read from the Bible and she assented, and thought these were all. Then the name of Robert was mentioned, and she explained that she had forgotten to account for

59

him. Later three other names were mentioned by the children which had not been listed in the Bible. "All dem mine too," she said. "Jest been having chillun all my life."

On another occasion when a large family was being visited, the father was trying unsuccessfully to name his children as his wife returned from the field. She scolded him for his ignorance and began naming them herself. When she failed it became a hilarious joke, and the husband ran into the yard rocking and roaring with laughter.

The families cited in this connection are exceptional in the sense of having a large number of children still alive. The fecundity rate is very high, but the number of children who survive even the first period of infancy is comparatively small.

I got so many chillun dead I don't know how long they been dead, 'bout six of 'em. The first boy was a grown man, twenty years old. He died with consumption, but I ain't had no consumption. The other girl I don't know how come she died. There was one that I "overlaid."[1] I went to sleep and the child was nursing, and I give so much milk that she smothered. The other boy was four years old. We had a mule and Mensifield [the husband] wanted to come to the master's home. Louis [the son] was right smart so he jumped at the mule data way. I was in condition [pregnant] at that time. Said to him, "Mensy, don't you spose dat mule kick you in de side?" It raised a knot on Louis' head. He tuck to his bed; had a hot fever, and died.

Jest one child I had had fits. She had two spasms, and I jest giver her a little pepper and salt and she ain't had no more. She grown now and got a cowpen full of chillun herself.

The actual number of cases in which children were given away to other relatives or friends and the fact that adopted children taken into these families with such small distinction between them and the natural offspring suggest that the ties between parents and children, especially where the families are large, are as much influenced by the opinion current in the community as by the interests of the family as a separate unit. Parents hesitated to give away their children to non-relatives for adoption, although this

[1] Accidentally smothered to death in a crowded bed.

happened numbers of times, but very frequently turned them over to another relative, usually the grandparents of the children.

In the economy of the family the relationship of members of the family to one another is not so strongly stressed as in families of the conventional type. Once out of immediate contact, the affectional basis of the relationship was perceptibly weakened. Interest frequently dwindled away and the child most often became a recognized and permanent part of the family of the grandparents. The fathers showed much less concern than the mothers when these physical ties were broken. This is the general situation pattern which fosters so considerable an amount of child adoption. The frequency of separations of families with children and the large number of children born outside of formal family relations normally throw a considerable burden of responsibility upon grandparents, and this responsibility, in turn, is accepted as a matter of course. Actually there was a marked sense of social obligation to children, expressed more by grandparents than by parents with numbers of children.

Sadie Thompson not only had a family of her own, now practically grown, but had undertaken the rearing of some of the grandchildren and other adopted ones. She had enterprise and initiative and both virtues were required to keep up her household. There was in her solicitude for the children a feeling rarely expressed, whether experienced or not, by families regarding their own immediate offspring. And with this feeling there was mixed some appreciation of the economic value of the children themselves.

I got these little motherless children here and got nothing to give them to eat. I never had a mouthful to give them yesterday and last night Mr. Walker just give them boys a dollar and I couldn't buy nothing but a little meal and a spoonful of lard. These children got a father but he don't give them nothing. These my dead daughter's children. Sometimes I look at them and tears get in my eyes. We made fourteen bales of cotton last year, and didn't get a penny for it. The little children was barefooted and didn't have a thing. If they hadn't had a little pig and I made some syrup I don't know what the little things woulda done. Every time they go to the white man they say they can't let you have nothing. Something is wrong somewhere but they ain't letting the nigger know where it is. I hate to go so far and not get nothing. "I don't reckon we will die," said one of my sons. But you will die 'cause every one of you all look sick in the eyes and it's cause you ain't had enough food. This is a starving land. . . . . This is the worst place I ever run on in my life. If you could jest get out of it all you put in it you could live happy. This is good rich land, and you could make money if we was treated right. The mules ain't even got nothing to eat, and we have to pull up the little corn and feed it to them. I look at my children sometimes and I'm sorry I ever born a child in the world. I believe in living like people. My children is smart 'cause I taught them to work. Us never do hire no day hands. We all help one 'nother get through with the chopping. They busy all the time. How they hold up I can't see.

Economic considerations almost without exception constitute the nexus which binds parents and children, and in the constant economic stress of the section it is what would be expected. "All my children is big enough to work, but three, and I got ten here. I got two children by my first wife and got 'bout two or three more 'sides that. I don't know where they is."

It was, however, impossible to escape the observation that once separation came it was complete and final. Once children leave home they rarely return. There was, besides, the frequency of paternal desertion, the uncertainty of support for the children loaned to friends or relatives, the frequent confusion and indifference about their names and ages, and the failure to remember the dead. Children who had died were seldom referred to in terms which suggested emotional ties. They were merely lost children. It was as if the rôle of fate and numbers was blended with a dour philosophy which accepted these crises as inevitable incidents of the struggle for survival. Moreover, it was apparent that hopelessly crippled or deformed children, like the hopelessly decrepit old, were not objects of pathos or sentiment. They were tolerated with some fortitude despite the general economic strain as a phase of the mutualism of their community relations. A woman was asked if she had any crippled or deformed children. She responded promptly: "No, I ain't got no cripple chillun. If I had I 'spect I would uv kilt 'em." This was probably an extreme expression, under a situ-

62

ation of economic stress, of a very real sentiment. Actually there were few such children in the community. It would indeed be difficult for them to survive in a situation which made survival difficult even for normal children in infancy. Another woman was explaining the presence of a female relative in the home: "This lady who stays here is my husband's cousin. She gonna have a baby soon. She got two more, but she gie'd dem away. She ain't married; the child's father he 'round here somewheres." In this instance the responsibility of children would obviously be a burden to the woman. The family to which she had given her children regarded them freely and easily as their own, but their own children were regarded primarily as potential helpers in the severe struggle for existence. The comments about their children, and almost always about the adult ones, were followed by some such consideration: "She's a good chile. . . . . She bring me something to eat when she can." Or: "I can't let dat boy marry. He all I got to help me."

Separations and divorce frequently divide the children or leave all of them with one parent. The natural handicaps, for illiterate people, of communication contribute to a stretching-out of filial ties, often to the vanishing-point. "My girl, Fannie Mae, is with her father in Pittsburgh. She been gone 'bout ten years. I ain't heard 'bout her since Christmas 'fore last. I speck she still dere."

There are, on the other hand, examples of strong and more obvious attachment between parents and children above the age of dependence, who remain at home, and this is especially true of widowed mothers and their sons. One of the most extraordinary instances of parental devotion, however, was observed in the case of one family, incidentally one of the few farm-owners in the area, whose son had been prostrate and deformed from infantile paralysis for more than ten years. The father had made himself a character in the town, stalking about like one in a daze, and asking the white doctors with annoying persistence and regularity if the doctors outside (medical science) had discovered anything yet to cure his boy.

Pregnancy

Pregnancy is treated both in fact and in the verbal allusions to it occasionally with a moderate gesture of concealment, but just as frequently with practical matter-of-factness. A woman is "close to the bed," or "cripple," or in plain terms " 'bout to have a baby," or "stomach stickin' out." The situation of most of the women permits little opportunity in the period of pregnancy to experience exhilaration and consciousness of the psychic values of such functioning.

I's cripple and ain't able to lift nothing. When I says cripple dat means what you see, dat I's going to have a baby. I jest been spitting and heaving all over this house. Dis heat make it worse. Girls what ain't married don't never ought to get deyselves no rainbow. First thing she be so sick and heaving and all de man is gonna say is "You'll be better soon," and go 'long 'bout sumpin else. . . . . My mother is staying here till my cripple is better. That what I done to git this here baby sho' ain't worth all this sufferin' and sickness.

The economic consideration is evident even in the incidence of this temporary handicap. When John Edwards was asked why all of his six children were born in July, he said people teased him about this, but, whether intended or not, "It's lucky for me, 'cause she [his wife] can hoe up till 'bout time and then she's ready to pick when fall comes."

Adoption

Adoption of children is a fairly common practice. Several factors appear to be responsible. Children after a certain age are, as indicated earlier, an economic asset. Childless couples, for whatever reason, have not the social standing in the community of families with children. The breaking-up of families, through desertion or migration, results in the turning-over of children to relatives or friends, and since little distinction in treatment enters, they soon are indistinguishable from the natural children, and assist them by dividing the load of heavy families. Moreover, adoption is related to illegitimacy, and frequently the children in families which are referred to as adopted are really the illegitimate offspring of one's own daughter or neighbor's daughter. The child of an un-married daughter becomes another addition to the children of the parents of the girl with all the obligations. Discipline is in the hands of the original parents and the young mother's relationship to her son is in most respects the same as her relationship to her younger brother. These children call her by her first name and refer to their natural grandparents as "mama" and "papa." It has happened that men have adopted into their legitimate families extra-legal children by other women, and with no apparent distinction that would make them unfavorably conspicuous among the other children. Again, children orphaned by any circumstances are spontaneously taken into childless families.

This girl, we find here when us come down here. She be's both orphan by mother and father, and nobody to look atta her. So we jest tuk her as one of the family, and don't sho' no difference. We don't tell no difference. This little boy is my sister's boy. I can't 'dopt him long as she live, 'cause I don't want no dissatisfaction. But he won't stay with her. She carry him home and have to bring him back.

One way of getting rid of children of low mentality who are likely to become an economic burden is to give them to childless couples.

His wife left him [the adopted son]. He's my boy. He thinks I'm his mother. She give him to me when he was a baby, and I ain't never told him no better. He's not right bright, but he's got sense nuff to treat you right, and he is so much help. His mother wasn't right bright either. I kept him in school till he was twenty, but he never did finish the first grade. The teacher said I was doing my duty, but he jest couldn't learn. Course, he can write and read, too. When he is away, he writes to me, and he can't read his own letters. He's jest sort of frenzy.

The ease with which the adoptions are made is interesting. There are few families, indeed, however poor, that would not attempt to rear a child left with them. Adoption, in a sense, takes the place of social agencies and orphans' homes.

No, I ain't got no husband; he ain't dead, I don't guess. I ain't seen him in eight years. He left me here wid these chillun, so I try to take keer of them. The girl is my niece. Her mother and father both dead.

Me and my wife been married thirty-two years. We ain't got no chillun of our own. My wife 'dopted this little boy. He eleven years old. His mamma gie'd him ter my wife soon atta he was born. His mamma 'round here in Shorter somewhere. We don't know nothing 'bout his daddy. His mamma ain't never been married as we knows of.

Children and School

This much is recognized—that when educating children is considered, the economic advantage of having them disappears. Almost unvaryingly, too, an interest in education goes along with landownership.

We moved here in 1905. My father started buying this place. Getting time to move now, ain't it? I own 110 acres here. The rest of them chillun didn't want to stay on the farm. They just got tired and moved different places. My father just worked this place up from the muscle. Nobody didn't help him. He was a old slavery-time fellow, and lived to get about seventy-two years old. It's about 166 acres in the whole place. I got four tenants. My brother was off when my father died but he was here when my mother died. He's got I don't know how many chillun. He's most too smart for me. *I ain't got but one and she cost me 'bout as much as his whole crowd, I reckon.* She goes to Tuskegee. It costs a lot of money to educate children. She fell down in one study, and she is going to summer school to catch up in algebra. I have to pay her tuition and buy books and carry her to and from school every day. It costs something, I tell you.

Children Born out of Wedlock

The sexual unions resulting in the birth of children without the legal sanctions are of several types, and cannot properly be grouped together under the single classification of "illegitimate." Children of common-law relationships are not illegitimate, from the point of view of the community or of their stability, for many of these unions are as stable as legally sanctioned unions. They hold together for twenty and thirty years, in some cases, and lack only the sense of guilt. Again, there are competent, self-sufficient women who not only desire children but need them as later aids in the struggle for survival when their strength begins to wane, but who want neither the restriction of formal marriage nor the con-

66

stant association with a husband. They get their children not so much through weakness as through their own deliberate selection of a father. Sexual unions for pleasure frequently result in children. There is a term for children born under the two latter circumstances. They are called "stolen children." "Stolen children," observed one mother, "is the best." A woman with children and who has been married though later separated from her husband may add other children to her family, without the benefit of the formal sanctions. These are "children by the way." The youthful sex experimentation, which is in part related to the late marriages, often results in children. These are normally taken into the home of the girl's parents and treated without distinction as additions to the original family. Finally, there are the children who result from the deliberate philandering of young men who "make foolments" on young girls. They are universally condemned. These children, as circumstance directs, may be placed with the parents of the mother or father of the child, an uncle, sister, or grandmother. They are accepted easily into the families on the simple basis of life and eventually are indistinguishable from any of the other children. Even if there were severe condemnation for true "illegitimates," confusion as to origin would tend both to mitigate some of the offenses and to obscure them all from specific condemnation.

The sense of guilt may be noted in some of the more advanced families but within the community as a whole social censure is not severe, nor is there any notable loss of status because of "illegitimacy." It does not appear to be regarded as severely as, for example, the use of certain artificial forms of birth control, or "being closed out," which means having all of one's crops, stock, and tools taken over for debt.

The church recognizes illegitimacy as a "sin of the mother," and if the mother is brought into church meeting with other evidences of "sin," like card-playing or frolicking, she may be "put out of church"; but readmission is possible with a solemn promise not to do it again. Actually, there is less stress placed by the churches upon illegitimacy as a "social sin" than upon card-playing and playing ball.

The danger, from the point of view of health, is the promiscuity of relations and the passing-on of venereal infection. Some men in this section of the county have numerous children scattered about, as a result of their tireless love-making with single girls, married women with children of their own, and with widows.

The sense of shame and lowered status follows illegitimacy when the family has, for one reason or another, become compact and self-conscious; when there has been exposure to recognized standards of a higher level, as a result of children returning from boarding-school, or when the family has acquired some education. Under such circumstances families are more careful about the opinions of outsiders, and frequently force the father of the child to marry the daughter. Ownership of property tends to restrict illegitimate relations because of the economic complexities introduced, and the effect of loose domestic relations upon credit and leadership in relationships beyond the immediate community is a restraining factor.

An attempt was made to measure the extent of illegitimacy. One hundred and twenty-two women in 114 families had had 181 illegitimate children. The illegitimate children were present in all but 3 of these 114 families. It is necessary, however, to make clear, as far as possible, the condition under which illegitimacy was found in these families. In the case of 24 couples now married the wife had a child before marriage. In 14 of these 24 cases the father of these children was the present husband, and in 10 cases the woman had had the child by another man before marriage. In 2 cases the women, who had subsequently married the father of their illegitimate children, had had 4 children each. There were also 3 widowed women who had had illegitimate children since the death of their husbands. In 13 families the mother was living alone with her illegitimate children. Two of these mothers had 4 children, 2 had 3 children, and 4 had 2 children each.

One unmarried mother of thirty-three years of age had 6 children of whom 4 were living. The oldest of those living was a girl of twenty-one and the youngest a girl of ten. The father of all of them was a man legally married, with a considerable family of his own. The oldest daughter was unmarried and had 2 children. Neither of the fathers of the children had offered any support and the women have not asked for it. The mother is a one-half-share cropper, and with the children she manages her farm about as successfully as the average family with a male head. There were 8 women, separated from their husbands, who had illegitimate children. In one case the separated woman was living with her mother. Illegitimate children were also found in the case of 10 common-law couples. In 8 of these cases the children were by the men with whom the wives were living, and in some cases there were 5 or 6 illegitimate children in the family. In 31 of the families a daughter had 1 or more illegitimate children, and in 1 family 2 daughters had an illegitimate child each. Illegitimate children were also found in 9 families in which the daughter, who was the mother of the children, was dead or away. In some cases the illegitimate children in the home had been adopted. This was found to be the case in 9 families. In 6 of the families the illegitimate child belonged to relatives, as, for example, a cousin, or a sister of the mother, or a nephew's child outside of marriage. In 2 families a son's illegitimate child had been taken into the home, and in one case the father's illegitimate child had been taken in. In 5 of the families the illegitimate child belonged to a granddaughter or to a great granddaughter.

How the Children Come

I got so many chillun I don't know where they all is. I got four living and one dead that Mr. ——— is the father of. I been married once, but me and him separated. They tell me he lives some place there near Tuskegee. I ain't get no divorce. Don't know whether he left me or no; we jest 'cided to depart, and it's been a good while ago. C—— B—— was the father of two of my children. I ain't know nothing else 'bout the father of any of the rest of them, aside from them that he [pointing to Mr. ———] been the father of. I can't 'member nothing 'bout them. I got frost-bitten one time and I can't 'member so well.

The daughter emulated the mother. When asked about her daughter's child, she said:

How can I know who is the father of Corinne's baby? We done had her over there in school, and she come back and brought the baby. Whoever he is, he don't do nothing for the baby.

These is Carrie's chillun. She ain't married. She was jest sixteen when the oldest child was born. Jimmie Hall is Leonard's daddy, and Ernest Watts is Leroy's.

No, sir, they ain't all got the same father! Them three is, but these two darkest ones ain't. I ain't seen the daddy of the first ones since year 'fore last. He married and don't give no help. I love him but I don't want to marry him. We started going together when I was a girl and jest kept it up. I ain't seen these others' daddy since before this last one was born. They tell me he over the creek, but I don't know and I ain't worrying myself none about him. He ain't like Hall. I like Hall and we jest kept on going together till bad luck happened. If my mind keep on like it is, I'm going to marry a man and trust him to take care of the children.

I wasn't married to the boy's father. We was engaged to marry but he done some shooting and had to leave and he never did come back till my boy was a big boy, so I jest didn't care 'bout marrying him then. I been married to somebody else now 'bout twelve years.

On one plantation a group of Negro women were living openly with white men. Their children were mulattoes. One of the women interviewed stated that the white man for whom she had been housekeeper recently died and just left her with the house. Her job had been ringing the bell for the other Negroes to go to work, and she had been greatly disliked by the other Negro women on the plantation. In still another situation the woman and a mulatto daughter cooked for a group of white men. Said she: "They come here three times a day to eat. They provide my clothing, food, and this house." Neighbors said they were the men's "women."

Twenty-four couples among the 612 families were living together without legal sanction, in a first association. The time which these couples had been together varied from one to more than thirty years.

The frequency of children born out of wedlock and the fact that no actual disgrace attaches to irregular birth occasionally work out to the advantage of the child. Adoption has been given increased importance. There is a demand for children to adopt, and an increased social status for families which adopt children.

Adoption in turn is commonly a convenience for children without the protection of a family organization of their own. A motherly old woman said: "These chillun here, they mother in Plaza. They father somewhere 'bout near here. They all got the same mother but different fathers. The two oldest ones was born 'fore they mother married. I tuk them all soon atta they was born."

Older families, and especially old and widowed women, look upon adoption as more of a privilege than a burden: "Lord, I almost like to not be able to raise me that child; he was so sickly at first." The sentiment is sometimes carried to the point of surrounding the child with an importance which many children in normal families lack.

SEPARATION AND DIVORCE

The actual number of divorces is small. In the 612 families there were but 2 heads of families who could be classified as regularly divorced and not married again. There were other heads of families who had been regularly divorced but who had remarried. Taking account of the 8 individuals single and living alone, and the 105 who were widowed, less than half, or 231 of the 612 families, were those in which the husband and wife were married for the first time. Among the group of 105 widowed heads of families some of the mates were dead and others had gone away without declaring their intention to separate permanently. Voluntary separation in the community really amounted to divorce, for many of the parties involved remarried without regard for the legal status of their first marriage.

Divorce is one of the legal formalities introduced from the outside in regard to the meaning and purpose of which the community is profoundly confused. Some of the families thought that going from one county to another gave them the legal right to remarry. It was believed that crossing the "line" (Mason and Dixon) meant divorce. One such remarried woman exclaimed: "My husband done cross de line; don't hear nothing. He may be living or dead. Ain't dat divorce?" The simplest interpretation is that the act of separation is divorce.

TABLE IV
Marital Status

Single—living alone	8
Unknown	4
Married—times unknown	1
Both married once	231
Husband married once, wife more than once	24
Husband married more than once, wife once	75
Both married more than once	74
Married but separated	52
Widowed	105
Divorced	2
Unmarried couples living together	24
Unmarried mother with children, living without father	12
	612

"They say when you separate from your husband you already 'vorced." The term "giving a strip," in common use, refers to the act of a man or woman writing or having written on a piece of paper the statement that he or she is divorced, and this stands as final.

I been married three times. My other husband's 'bout Wetumpka somewhere. We jest couldn't git along, so he revorced me, and me and the second one fought like cats and dogs. One night he fought me so I had to call for help. He left that night and the next day he got the wagon and moved, and he *asked me for a revorce; so I give him a strip. Marion Wood write it. If I had time I'd ramble round here and find that strip they sent me from Wetumpka.*

There were other individuals who believed that the act of re-marriage of their spouse, even though no divorce was secured, conferred upon them the freedom to marry again. "You see, my other husband, when we separated, got married again first, so that divorced us." A man and woman, aged forty-eight and forty-six, respectively, had been married eighteen years. It was the second marriage for both although neither had secured a divorce. Of her first husband the wife said: "My husband didn't leave me, but he got into a little trouble about some cotton situation and went away. He wanted me to go too, but I didn't want to leave my mother. He was gone a long time before I married again." The husband explained: "My wife just went away, and she's over in Cecil. I didn't have to get a divorce, because she been gone a long time."

A man who had been drafted during the World War was positive that he had been exempted by the government from any further marital responsibility: "I's an ex-soldier. They told me when I went to the army and come back that the government had done 'vorced me, and I didn't have to git naire 'vorce." The arrangement of convenience is pushed at times with an almost brutal severity. Old Amos Boyd said: "My wife she stay over in La Place. She over there for her health. She come home 'bout once a week, so I'm thinking 'bout 'vorcing her. Now a good time to 'vorce her." When Minnie Toles was sick her husband left and went to Cecil. When he came back she told him she didn't need him, and he was thereby divorced.

It would seem, again, that divorce is needed only in those cases in which there was objection of one party to the separation. "Me and him jest come here to live and she [his wife] ain't claim him, so I don't speck he need a 'vorce." The uncertainty about the meaning of divorce contributes to the uncertainty about security in marriage. One man was troubled because his wife had been gone for more than a week on a visit to her mother, and he was not sure whether or not she "had up and divorced" him. Another sent his wife away on a visit in order that he might not be embarrassed by her presence when he "made out a slip" for her divorce, which he intended to do before she got back.

There is indication that the mores are in process of change in the fact of the now serious and frequent discussion of the meaning and purpose of legal divorce. This discussion took place between a husband and wife and a visiting neighbor:

NEIGHBOR: My husband don't help me none with the child. He jest throwed me away and I was sick. I wasn't down in bed. He done married again. He didn't had to git no divorce 'cause I didn't want him no more.

WIFE: You know good and well he didn't git no divorce, 'cause you'd a knowed something 'bout it.

HUSBAND: He could a had a divorce and you not know nothing 'bout it. I had a divorce six months before my wife knowed anything 'bout it. You git a divorce through and by money. They git a pencil and figure it out for you 'thout the wife knowing nothing 'bout it.

NEIGHBOR: He jest a "run-about" man anyhow.

One reason for the small number of divorces and the curious beliefs regarding this formality has been suggested as the cultural one of introduction from without of a new device for the regulation of marital relations. Another is the actual cost of this legal procedure. Divorce, after all, is a personal matter and the introduction of a lawyer not only beclouds the issue but brings a demand for cash which few of them have. The attitude of the courts toward this omission is not severe. Rather, the disposition seems to be to ignore it as a serious offense. So long as the practice affects no one but the Negroes, and they accept it as a part of their lives, there is no necessity for insisting upon a standard which, it is assumed, they have not attained. From the point of view of the Negroes, so long as no one is seriously inconvenienced by the permanency of the separation or the fact of remarriage, it is considered an unnecessary expenditure of money to get a divorce through the courts. There is always more frequent demand for the permanent separation than there is money.

There are instances of use of the external pattern of divorce but without complete understanding of its real meaning, as, for example, when a man goes to town and "buys" a divorce for a woman he hopes to marry, even though this woman's husband may still be living in the community.

74

WIFE: This husband I got now bought me my divorce.

HUSBAND: I paid thirty or thirty-five dollars for it. It's different with different people. It depends on how long they been separated and what they separated for, and the lawyer too.

The influence of new ideas was evident in the family of Quarles. Both had been married before, but they had been living together about five years. The wife now thinks she should have a divorce from her first husband, and her present husband plans to go to town sometime and "buy" her one.

Causes of Separation and Divorce

Separation, like marriage, is regarded very largely as a personal matter. Desertions are frequent and almost casual, growing out of various kinds of disharmony. The woman deserts almost as frequently as the man. There are at first temporary separations following minor dissatisfactions. At any point, however, the separation may be made permanent by the remarriage of one of the parties, or some change in circumstances which places either out of reach. Couples separate six and eight times, each time returning because of the greater convenience of the existing arrangement, only to discover that the old basis of dissatisfaction had not been removed. It is more "respectable" to separate, and even to experiment further with another mate, than to tolerate certain conditions with one's legal mate.

The position of women in the community increases the rate of separation at the same time that it decreases the social consequences of this separation. A deserted woman is not entirely helpless, and occasionally her economic burden is lightened by the withdrawal of the man. The large number of women heads of families may be accounted for in part by the desertion of the men, in part by death, and in part by the withdrawal of the woman, with her children, to set up an establishment working as a tenant farmer or renter on some other plantation.

An underlying provocation to separation is the lack of functional balance, with respect both to the business of earning a living and to temperamental differences. The hard and drab life of most of the families places a severe test upon this arrangement, and the weaknesses of the social restraints of the community encourage change. Separations which may be classed as desertions are, perhaps, the most numerous group and include among the underlying motives general dissatisfaction with the association, trifling or lazy husbands or wives, and such sentiments of resignation as "he jest liked some other woman better."

I divorced my first wife and I'm separated from the other one, but she ain't divorced. We didn't fuss or nothing, we just decided to quit intelligent.

Me and my wife went to Georgia, and me and her couldn't agree and she stayed in Georgia. I don't know what come of her.

My wife talking 'bout quitting me 'cause I ain't got no money. Good time to quit now when I ain't got nothing.

My ole lady jest walked off; say she goin' be her own boss.

My wife jest left. She didn't ask for no 'vorce—just told me to quit writin' to her in her name 'cause she was married. Dey didn't git no 'vorce. After she married I didn't have no 'vorce. I didn't know she'd quit me till her father told me.

An old man, calm and deliberate as he smoked his pipe, recounted this series of disturbances in his domestic life:

In all I been married four times. The first wife, somebody poisoned her with Paris green. An old woman poisoned her 'cause she couldn't whip her. She lived nine months and died on the Jordan place near Downs. The second wife, Mary Ann, I quit her. She over there in Bullock County. The third wife caught fire and died. The next one been gone since March, 1929. I didn't quit her; I was gwine ter quit but she didn't gimme time; she quit me. She wouldn't listen to me. If I say "don't go" then it's best for her not to go.

In a situation in which separation is so lightly regarded there is little occasion to make specific the causes.

Me and my fust wife separated. Don't know where she is—me and her jest parted.

My husband lives in Bullock. Don't know why he leave me. Jest picked up and left. He don't give me nothing. I don't know whether we separated or no. He jest lives over there and I lives over here. He got three of the children over there with him.

Of the specific causes of separation, cruelty is perhaps the most frequently mentioned. Here, again, the women are not always at a disadvantage, for they know how to fight back. Where this resistance is effective there follows a mutually respectful truce, or a separation based upon incompatibility.

Tom Kerns was my husband, but he fight so I jest couldn't live with him. He treat me so bad.

I have been married two years. We went to the courthouse in Tuskegee. I have been back home to mother's more than ten times since we been married. Sometimes I stays two days and sometimes two weeks. My husband don't go away and leave me. He jest likes to fight and do's lots of things then I go home. My mother tells me to go back home.

I been married but my husband been too mean. Dis man ain't like him.

He was jest too mean. He was too old, too.

Me and my husband been parted three years. He was mean and lazy.

A second specific cause of separation and divorce is mismating with respect to ages. Although there is apparently complete freedom of selection, other factors of importance enter and are soon

	No.	Per Cent
Husbands over 40 married to women 5 years younger....	63	26.5
Husbands over 40 married to women 10 years younger...	42	17.6
Husbands over 40 married to women 15 years younger...	53	22.3
Husbands over 40 married to women 20 years younger...	17	7.1
Husbands over 40 married to women of same age bracket	53	22.3

manifest in family discord. The tendency is emphatically in the direction of a wide disparity in the ages as between men and women. Of 238 male heads of families, forty years old and over, only 53, or 22.3 per cent, had wives within the same age bracket. This story of youth married to old age, as told by the husband, sheds light on some of the indefinable dissatisfactions at the bottom of many of these separations:

She was just too young for me. She was only eighteen when I married her and I was about forty-five. I lived with her several years, though. She was a little woman, didn't weigh but ninety pounds. She fust went off and stayed a week, then she come back and we stayed in bed till 'bout noon, then I got up and went to the field and she went visiting. I didn't know whether she was gonna stay or not. She come back and asked me for the key so she could take a nap and I give it to her. I guess she took a nap. I know she stayed up there a long time, then she come back and give me the key and told me goodbye. I just kept my head turned till I knowed she was out of sight. Look like to me if I'd a turned and seed her going way from me I'd jest hollered so loud. Look like it would a killed me when she fust left. Yes, I did like her, but I'm gitting along all right without her now. Course I could a got a divorce without paying all that money. I could a paid a man to say he done something, but I wouldn't do it. I wouldn't slander her 'cause she'd been a good wife to me when we was together, so I jest said if I had to give anybody money, I'd jest give it to her.

Family interference has been noted among the causes of separation. The pull of family, on both sides, is frequently strong enough to exercise an important influence over relations.

Me and my husband was gitting long fine when we went to live with his people. Den when I be in family way his people didn't treat me right. I tole him we oughta move. There was so many chillun in that house. There was twelve in all—my three and then some of the rest of the chillun done married and brought their chillun back home. We all uster work on the farm together, and when I would go in the garden to get some onions his mother tell me to stay out of the garden. I couldn't get nothing outa the garden after I done help to plant it. I kept on like that till one day my husband packed up my things and sent me back home to my people. I ain't blaming him for what he did, 'cause he was home with his peoples and he done what they say. You know he be's a child at home jest like the rest of the chillun.

A course of regular and unemotional breeding has been given as a cause of separation, and is explained in the observation about men "getting you with a house full of babies and leaving." Before the limit is reached, however, the woman may leave.

78

Incompatibility, based upon color difference, has figured in the list of separations. "She was light-complected and nothing suited her. We jest couldn't 'gree on nothing much, and so we quit." In this instance there was another factor. The present wife chided the man about not telling all of the truth. "How come you don't tell why you separated? He caught her with a white man. I believe in telling the truth."

Women have become disgusted finally with men who "run 'roun too much," and have left them. "I been married twice. Both my wives left me. They jest said I run 'bout after the women. But they 'cuse me wrong."

Separation seems to place little strain upon the relations of the various parties concerned in these affairs. Alice Jackson's common-law husband and her first husband, from whom she had not secured a divorce, worked on a job together. Her legal husband was contentedly settled with another woman and her children. "This my third husband. We ain't married. He was the chillun's pappy. Den I married a man and couldn't get along, so I come back to live wid him. He works with my real husband." The sister of another woman's husband continues to live in the family although her brother has been displaced entirely by another and more congenial mate.

What happens when there has been exposure to new standards is clear cut and unmistakable. Jacob Wagner is a widower with one married and three unmarried daughters, twenty, eighteen, sixteen, and fifteen years old, respectively. His wife had been dead about six months and the responsibility for their care was upon him. Although he had only gone as far as the fourth grade in school, he had been a member of the First Baptist Church School Board, and work on the railroad had carried him frequently out of the city. He knew the significance of separation and divorce and had taught it to his daughters. When he mentioned the possibility of marrying again because he needed a wife "to help me with the girls," the daughters were indignant that he could think of marrying again so soon after the mother's death. Discussing the question of the oldest daughter's marriage, he made it clear that it

79

met every requirement. "If he [her husband] had never obtained a divorce he could never have married my daughter. Anybody marries my daughter's got to plumb the line."

WHAT IS RESPECTABLE?

The families of the community do not act upon a single standard of propriety or of morals. Ideals and life-conceptions vary strikingly, not only with respect to content, but with respect to definition and emphasis. There is, moreover, an extraordinary overlapping and fusing of traits and heritages in a community which holds its members with varying degrees of cohesion. Notions of respectability rest upon the social customs which have grown up with the group, upon an adaptation of the early social patterns to which they were exposed, and upon the newer patterns which are being slowly introduced.

It is possible to trace roughly some of these standards by reference to degrees of isolation. Geographical remoteness from the centers of sophistication and cultural change is important but not the only determining factor in isolation. The old traditions persist virtually unchanged in some families, whether they live near the highway or far in the back country. The present picture, however, is one of confusion, arising from the conflict of different ideals and ways of life. A family will reflect one set of moral ideas regarding marriage and another regarding divorce, or one regarding legitimacy and another regarding extra-marital sex relations. Generally speaking, home-ownership and education tend to mark these differences in standards.

It is important to point out first what seems to be a conformity to the conventions of the group itself without reference to outside standards and ideals. One family with two unmarried daughters, both of whom had several children, had very positive notions about what was respectable and what was not. The father stressed the responsibility of his family to the children of his daughters, discounting the value of marriage as such. He was satisfied to keep out of contact with the law. In personal relations his attitude was that of the frontier, relying upon his ability to effect a personal settlement of differences which ordinarily are handled in the courts.

Ain't none of my daughters got married but dey is my chillun, and I take care of all of dem. The fathers of dey chillun don't come here less dey come right. I tell 'em all to stay way from my house. I don't git into no trouble with nobody. I am dis old and never been to jail, never been handcuffed or had a fight. My brothers git into trouble, but I ain't never had a fight. I keep my gun near 'cause if anyone tries to bother me, gonna shoot 'em shore. Gonna shoot 'em shore.

It is not regarded as the proper thing to demand or even to ask the father of an unmarried woman's child to support the child. "No, these babies don't git no help from dey daddies. Help, nothing! I wouldn't let them beg them to do it for nothing in the world. I wouldn't bother them for a pocket handkerchief. They don't git no help atall from dey daddies' side." Another woman with children "by the way" explained: "Sherman Biggers is the daddy of two of dem. Sherman gives Bertha a dress now and den, but he don't give her no money. I don't worry him for it 'cause I don't see him have it."

On the other hand, there is the suggestion of approval if the responsibility of the father is assumed without prompting. "This here baby is my daughter's baby. She is jest fifteen years old herself. The father paid the doctor bills and give it clothes."

Community gossip exercises restraint, but in certain cases in which the question of "illegitimacy" was an issue, the direction of this control was away from marriage. The mother of a young girl who had a child by the son of a neighbor refused to let her daughter marry the boy, in spite of mutual desires, because the mother of the boy had made uncomplimentary remarks about the girl. "My oldest daughter ain't married and she has a baby seven days old. The baby's father, why he's up the road there 'bout two miles from here. His mamma jest talked 'bout her so I wouldn't let her marry him. She tried to 'scandalize' her name." It would be a mistake to assume from the practices current that there is indifference to standards. Indeed, there is a rather rigid conformity to those standards of the group which are distilled from personal experience rather than from the abstractions of moral philosophy.

There are limits to the sexual freedom tolerated, and when these limits are reached violators are treated with unmistakable group disapproval. The community, for example, has its gay Lotharios, who exploit existing conventions to their advantage. A young man, illiterate but loose and boastful, was discussing marriage. He said if he married and could not get along, "then I quits and marries again. I got six more [wives] coming." Someone remarked that his father had been married to the same woman forty years, and he replied: "De Bible say go 'round and see about the ofren [orphan] chillun." This last was intended as a ribald paraphrase of the Bible to give swagger to his sexual promiscuity. Community disapproval was certain and severe on the man who violated local usages by refusing to assume any responsibility. "He's a yaller boy who ain't done nothing but go 'round and fool all these girls. That was the second time he done make foolments on her, too, 'cause she lost the other one." The community also has its "fast women," but they are not the familiar "prostitute" type. Rather, they are women who flaunt, with their sex, the dominant economic concern and interest of the group. They are the ones who maliciously, and to no useful end, steal other women's men and through the men the earnings to which another woman has made an important contribution. One woman in commenting about such a character said: "She go 'round braggin' she don't spend no money. She got 'em workin' for her. You be workin' and she goin' 'round dressed up like 'Miss Ann' while you go naked." The usual connotation of "fastness" in women had less relationship to sex morals than to age of sexual maturity. "I was a fast little thing; up and married at thirteen. (That man jest kept goin' and comin' back, till finally he jest didn't come back at all.)" There are women who give their favors freely, but seldom on a purely commercial basis.

On the other hand, there is a strong current of approval of alliances, whether legal or not, which offer the highest chances of survival in the environment. A mother who had never been married said: "I ain't want no husband myself, and I don't care if Alder

82

[her daughter] marries or no. Willis [father of Alder's child] is a smart man. Alder's father asked me to marry him, but I tole him I don' want no husband."

A common-sense view of marriage in this setting classifies it as a serious hazard. There is no more steady, hard-working woman in the community than Della Promise. She knows how to keep herself and her house clean, belongs to church and to several societies, manages her children with notable success, and in other respects is regular and reliable. She has never been married, and has no apologies to make about it. Seriously and with conviction she said: "Everybody don't git married, and if I can't git the one I want I don't want to git married. I never seen but one boy I thought I could marry, and me and him had ways too much alike, and I knowed we couldn't git along, so I jest has my chillun and raises 'em myself." Married life imposes certain obligations which are, in the feeling of this element of the community, more binding than necessary or practicable. It gives license to mistreatment; it imposes the risk of unprofitable husbands; and it places an impossible tax upon freedom in the form of a divorce. For example: "Men jest git you a house full of chillun and leave you." Or again: "I been married but my husband been too mean. He beated me too much. Dis man I'm livin' wid now ain't like him. He's nice. I like him. I been thinkin' 'bout marrying, but I don't want to marry now."

It is, in a very practical sense, less respectable to be beaten by one's husband than to be living with a man peacefully and happily, though not married to him. The lack of legal obligation acts as a restraint upon mistreatment, for the services of the woman are of very real importance to the man. As Artie Joe McDaniel, who has been living with Robert Jackson for several years, said with some pride in her independence: "He's nice all right, but I ain't thinking 'bout marrying. Soon as you marry a man he starts mistreating you, and I'm not going to be mistreated no more." Experience dictates numerous expressions of caution on the part of the older women.

If you ain't married don't you eber go git yourself no *rainbow*. First thing you know you'll be sick of it.

Ain't nobody got nothing to give me but God, and if I don't trust him I'm lost.

Men ain't nothin' but overalls.

Better git a good holt 'fore you git into this marryin' business, 'cause there'll be some tight times if you don't.

Gambling is condemned. This is no doubt a result of the influence of the church with its prohibition of indulgence in certain forms of worldliness. Any form of life-activity which does not involve obvious and direct manual labor may be said to be under suspicion and disapproval. A possible exception is the religious ministry, and most of the preachers who reside in the community are also farmers.

Likewise, the influence of the prohibition of the church is seen, somewhat unfortunately, in the ban on baseball, but with profound wisdom in the disapproval of the secular "frolics." "I don't go to them frolics. People git drunk and comes back and tries to show everybody who dey is." Frolics are not respectable. One woman, expressing her disapproval of them, based this disapproval on the fact that "they don't show the right respect for women." She explained the meaning of "respect" by saying that they had "splashed a woman's brains out last Saturday night." The following account by the mother of a boy who had killed a woman at another of these affairs both characterizes the "frolics" and helps to define the proper sphere of women.

My son John was a good boy. They tell me that the woman what he killed was dancing on the floor that night. She hadn't been long settin' down. It was jest awful. John didn't give up till yesterday, and when he did give up they got the boy what lent him the pistol too. See how kin folks git one 'nother in trouble? I guess, though, they can't do nothing but make him pay for loaning John that pistol. He wasn't after that chile he killed. He jest couldn't rest, I reckon, till he give hisself up. If John hadn't had that pistol he wouldn't a shot it, and if that woman had stayed at home she wouldn't a got killed. I don't believe in women goin' to these suppers. They ought to stay at home where they belong.

Quite apart from the question of sex, respectability has other concerns in this level of the culture of the group. One of the most frequent assertions in evidence of respectability is the fact that no one of the family has been in jail. The Boyd family is one of the oldest in the community. There are 26 children in the family, of whom 11 are still living—5 girls and 6 boys—all born since slavery. Said one of these: "Papa rents from the man what set him free. We have never been nowhere else but right here. Papa died right over there; all of us live on this plantation. None of us ever been in prison or in suits or nothing. We are always in hopes of getting something." An old man who had several grown sons in the neighborhood gave this formula of success: "I works hard to keep out of lawsuits and trouble. Nobody don't bother me, and I don't bother nobody."

A practice which has the disapproval of the group is begging. The sentiment is well expressed by one of the older members of the community in her comment when she heard that a neighbor had asked a stranger for some money for food and snuff. She was caustic in her criticism: "I don't 'cept charity from nobody. I don't tote a bucket 'round under my dress beggin'. Work is honorable and good. I believe in it. 'Tain't livin' right to go beggin'." Work is a virtue even though there are lazy members in the group. Women are justified in leaving husbands who are lazy and trifling. More than this, the values attached to work transcend those attached to legitimacy. "Me and my husband been parted three years. We couldn't git along. He was so mean. He ain't helped me none. He was jest so lazy, he didn't wanna work. He ain't none of my child's father. The daddy is dead. I never was married to my child's daddy." The community standing of this woman and her own self-respect were such that she felt completely free to censure the behavior of the young school-teacher who came from the outside. "She was pretty good, but last year she wasn't nothing but a little courtin' girl. The big boys wouldn't go to school. She was so young they didn't want her to teach them."

Begging is, however, different from mutual assistance between neighbors. This is probably the root of that same mutualism which is reflected in the case of newly arrived southern immigrants to the North. They are at first most reticent about applying to the public agencies for relief, despite their poverty. There is a common disposition to help one another with food and shelter. When they become more sophisticated they discover in these agencies a mysterious means of getting something for nothing, which holds dangers both to working habits and to self-respect.

The families in the community, clinging to their own standards of respectability, found it difficult at first to adjust themselves to the policies of the Red Cross, although these services are now widely used. One of the families, although poor, was outraged and humiliated by the organization's method of determining the need for assistance. Said the wife:

My husband went to the Red Cross to get the money they owed him, 'cause his son died in the army. The Red Cross ain't never give us nothing. When my husband gone down there they was so pikus and close, and ain't give us nothing. There was an old man down there wid a lot of chilluns, and they ain't give him nothing neither. They jest lecture and act indifferent. They make you feel so shame over the way you have to git it, you don't want it.

When Fannie Ford, who had worked all her life and lived hard, reached the point of being unable to purchase either food or clothing, she still maintained her pride. "Folks say, 'Sister Fannie, you go on down to the Red Cross.' I said, 'Jesus don't send me there,' but they ain't done nothing anyhow. No, I don't ask 'em. I don't like to be a charitable person. I jest went 'long and made out somehow." Thus, an enlightened piece of human engineering which provides a device for necessary relief may arouse a conflict of ideals of respectability no less significant than in the clash of two cultures.

Clearly enough, a transition from the imperatives of one cultural level to that of another is taking place, and this change is being manifested in other ways more advantageous to the group. There is a reaching-out for the new standards, although these standards are not as yet always adequately conceived. Definitions of the situation are frequently mixed and confused. Illegitimacy, for example, though regarded by some families as something not entirely to be countenanced, is considered by others a lesser social evil and affront to decency than desertion following a forced marriage. Mary Blyden was conscious of a certain personal superiority over her neighbors. She attributes this advancement, of which she is pardonably proud, to the fact that she likes to associate with "cultured people."

I don't get into no trouble 'cause I love to be with cultural people. They always trying to have something. Them others they always trying to git something for nothing. The Bible say "seek and ye shall find," and they got more time to seek then we have, 'cause while we out there in the field they 'round seeking. This is my daughter's child [illegitimate] here. His father's name Asbestos Key. He Maggie Key's son. He ain't do nothing for the child. You know these young people has a peculiar way of doing things now. They go from house to house dropping chillun just like an old house cat. I don't believe in forcing 'em to marry, though. I had a cousin once and her father forced the man to marry her and after the marriage was all over he walked out one door and she the other, and they ain't seed one another since. This 'suading and coaxing and begging 'em to marry jest ain't get you no place. It's my child so I take it as my 'sponsibility.

A shade removed from this attitude is that represented by a family in which the mother showed no sensitiveness about her daughter's illegitimate children, but the daughter, on the other hand, withdrew in embarrassment when the subject came up. The younger generation is slowly picking up new notions although they cannot always escape the current of the old life to make the shift to the new.

The female head of another family, with four children in school, felt warranted in setting her own notions to the conventions of the community. She said with pride: "I don't believe much in these stolen children. Me, I married in my mother's house before I broke my virtue."

Freedom from the economic compulsions of the life of the community carries with it almost invaryingly a corresponding freedom from many of the social customs. The family of Cox's have lived in the community over eighteen years, own eighty acres of land for which they paid twenty-two dollars an acre, and have sent their children to school. One daughter, who teaches a four-month-term school in Russell County, has attended a summer session at Alabama State College. When the mother was asked about the marital status of her children, she said none of her girls was married, and added emphatically, "Neither of them has had any children either." The remark, as well as the emphasis, was offered without prompting and reflected a new consciousness to the changing mores. The father in this family raised cotton but also did public work and hauling. By this means, and aided by his sons, he accumulated enough cash for a part payment of one thousand dollars on his house and farm. The family wore very good clothing but adhered to the custom of going barefoot. The family organization follows roughly the essential pattern of the community with respect to the family economic unit, but this has been modified in such a manner as to avoid the ordinary stresses of the system. The sons live in the household but cultivate plots which they rent from their father, paying him back in cotton.

Thomas Germany has lived in the county twenty-seven years. He owns his farm of one hundred and twenty-nine acres for which he paid twenty-eight hundred dollars in 1904. He can "read a little," although his wife is illiterate, but all of the five grandchildren whom they are rearing are in school. They made a point of stressing that they had never "been in trouble." The mother still uses the community midwife instead of a doctor, although she has now lost respect for this practice. She is convinced that she lost her last baby through the ignorance and carelessness of the midwife, but the pressure of the group impels her to continue using a midwife rather than get talked about. Although the house is in poor repair it is inclosed with a fence—something very unusual in the section. There are blinds at the windows and a lightning rod on the roof. They have planted a fruit orchard. These were indices to the family. It happened that the wife had been married before, and she was asked where she secured her divorce. The answer was a retort with considerable feeling: "Where else do you suppose I got the divorce if not at the courthouse?" The family had few friends in the community and wanted but few. They get along now by "tending to their own business." One of the grandchildren is illegitimate and the family is miserably conscious of the sin of the daughter.

Edgar Hill is one of the few mulatto men observed to be married to a woman of perceptibly darker complexion. They have a pleasant home life, and although they are not home-owners they have well-defined notions about marriage and family relations. There was an expression of indignation when the question was asked if the woman was the mother of all the children in the family. "She is my wife; who else would be the mother?" Similarly, the man raised his eyebrows in shocked surprise when asked if they had ever been separated and shouted "No." To still another question regarding sleeping with the windows open (a practice extremely uncommon in the community) he answered, "Yes, we sleep with the windows open and doors too."

A further indication of the changing mores appears in the experience of Sherman Riggs who has thirteen children—eleven by his wife and two by a woman neighbor. He regards himself as an upright man, trying to do what is best. He was an officer in the church and is in good standing in the societies. Conflict in his mind arose over the question of marrying the woman by whom he had had several children, to satisfy new notions about legitimacy and respectability.

I get lonesome lots of times but a man is crazy to see something won't do and then walk in it. I done tried it [referring to his period of common-law association with his woman neighbor]. I mean by that just like you have a pencil, if you saw it wouldn't write you wouldn't bother with it. A new broom sweeps clean, and when I marries I wants to marry for pleasure. The fellow pecking the rock can see more than the fellow not pecking the rock. I like Minty all right, but now a fellow's got to use common sense. *The world is so critical now a fellow is scared to do anything.* I left off most of my frolics when I was young. But common sense got to come in. You tak' a cow and tie it out before a lot of grass—the cow will bite first one bunch of grass then another, trying to see which one he likes the best; so that the way with a man.

Despite the unevenness of life, the amount of sexual freedom, the frequency of separation and realignment of families, the number of children born out of formal wedlock and the customary provisions for them, codes and conventions consistent with the essential routine of their lives do arise which represent a form of organization adapted to the total environment. Where social processes such as these proceed largely unconsciously, the surviving folk ways may reasonably be presumed to have a foundation in the fundamental needs of community and human nature. The marriage relation under slavery, despite its lack of the sanctions by the dominant society, had some seriousness of purpose for the slaves and was forced to accommodate itself to the convenience of the institution of slavery with respect to continuity, fertility, selection of mates, change of mates, the quasi-eugenic demands of the institution with respect to breeding, and similar circumstances.

It is scarcely conceivable that the isolation of this group at any point could be so complete as to prevent the introduction of a different body of sentiments and practices in accord with a more advanced conception of life and of social relations. The total situation, thus, would be expected to represent different stages of cultural evolution, from the almost complete acceptance of the original sanctions of the group under slave tradition to the fullest acceptance of the new codes introduced, whether thoroughly comprehended or not. Disorganization is most acute where these sanctions are in conflict and the individuals are firmly rooted in neither of the patterns of life-organization.

SHELTER AND FOOD

". . . . Somewheres to sleep and sumpin' t'eat."

The cabin of the Jenifers can be reached by a ragged and winding path half obscured by a field of growing cotton. The path, although beaten down and fresh with use, does not trace a direct course, but meanders almost furtively through the field, down the side of a gulley, then over and around a tongue of thick-set trees and brush, all without apparent reason. If you ask a neighbor how to get to the Jenifers' house, he will first point to a wide arc of a road over which a team of horses could travel, and which skirts respectfully the proprietorial boundaries of the cotton fields.

(Tramping through the cotton is something akin to vandalism.) When and if he is surer of you, he will point to the path under your eye and suggest that you follow it "a little piece over the way."

The home of the Jenifers is set in the midst of a new stretch of cotton beyond the trees, and once there, no other dwelling is visible. Around the dwelling is a cleared space packed hard and yellow. On the left, and beginning a few feet from the house, is an inclosed area about the size of a bedroom. It is the family garden, and into it has been crowded a patch of cabbage, greens, and onions which the family has attempted to shield from marauding animals and the younger children by a fence randomly constructed of sticks, tin advertising signs, tar paper, and stray bits of canvas. The house itself is constructed of upright boards about a foot wide with thin strips down the seams to keep out the weather. It is set rather precariously about a foot from the ground upon four up-rights of rocks placed one upon the other and held plumb by the weight of the house alone. On first sight it gives the appearance of two single-room cabins set close together and joined by a roof. The passageway, however, has a rough flooring like the two inclosed rooms, and this passageway is called the "dog-run." The soft wood of the floor has been worn into smooth and grimy ruts, testifying to the habits of the family.

The dog-run is an important part of the house. It is the sitting-out place, and in summer, especially, it is the meeting place for the family. They rest, eat, doze, and gossip there. Two benches fashioned after a simple pattern are planted against the wall. On the end of one of these is a battered wooden water pail covered over with a damp cloth. A pair of overalls and a man's hat, both frayed and dusted white with earth, hang from a nail support. A tub and washing stick, a pair of men's heavy shoes, a rusty water-dipper, and pieces of firewood also find a place in this areaway. From the front of the house there is a sweep which permits a view of the family well at the rear with its box-shaped covering, its sagging and insecure sides, its top open and exposed to sundry deposits.

Doorways lead off the dog-run into the two rooms. In one of these rooms, where Father and Mother Jenifer sleep, there is a large bed with a double mattress, one of shucks, the other of feathers, and they are covered over with a quilt patched laboriously from an indeterminate variety of cloth scraps into an intricate pattern of squares. They call it, modestly, a "crazy quilt." The bed is the outstanding piece of furniture. Besides this article there is a wooden box spread over with a newspaper, a rocking chair, and a small table on which stands a kerosene lamp with a broken chimney. Some pride of home has gone into the effort to select newspapers with colored pictures for the wall covering and to keep it reasonably fresh. There are no glass windows. For light and air a board window is pushed open. But this can be done comfortably only in spring and summer, and at other times the family contents itself with light from the open fireplace, where, incidentally, the cooking is also done. On any day when the window and door are closed, sharp slices of light, from the sides of the house and from the roof, spatter the room with shadows. When it rains or the winds blow cold, these interstices bring a great deal of inescapable discomfort.

The second room is little different from the first. It has its bed under which most of the miscellaneous possessions of the family are stored, a larder consisting of a couple of shelves in one corner of the room, and underneath this a pile of seed cotton. There is an accumulation of soiled and worn clothing and bed coverings in and near an open box.

This is the home of the Jenifers, father, mother, two sons, a daughter and her infant. The other belongings of the family, to be precise, are one plow (now in serious disrepair), two hoes, two frying-pans, an iron pot, several tin plates, four pounds of salt pork and a bag of corn meal, church clothes, an insurance policy, a Bible, two almanacs, and a bottle of "Black Draught" medicine.

The family is not a fictitious one but is taken directly from the largest group in the physical classification of homes. Over half of the 612 families live in the one- and two-room cabins, and 175, or 28 per cent, live in three-room cabins. One hundred and sixty-two of these cabins, or 25 per cent, had been standing over thirty years;

OVER HALF OF THE 612 FAMILIES LIVE IN
ONE- AND TWO-ROOM CABINS

NEIGHBORS

74 per cent of them had been built more than sixteen years before. Few of the houses have glass windows, only blinds, and there were some with no window spaces at all. Many of those families who had windows in their cabins slept with both windows and doors tightly closed in summer and winter, professing variously to be afraid of prowlers, mosquitoes, night air, thieves, and ghosts. Five hundred and thirteen of the 612 families, however, had small gardens. Seeds for these gardens had been distributed by the Red Cross during the year, and proved to be a most valuable contribution to this group.

With the exception of a few homes owned by Negro farmers, the dwellings available for the tenants present a dreary monotony of weatherworn cabins. The physical pattern varies but slightly, and there are not enough houses of better model and construction about to incite interest in anything different. It is a standard of housing so widespread and so far inferior to the towns as to make extremely difficult any comparable measurement. For greater convenience and exactness of measurement, the physical features of the housing of this area have been projected on a simple scale. This, at least, has the advantage of objective description over the more indeterminate classification of good, fair, and bad. This scale takes into account the materials of the structure, age, condition of roof, windows and floors, porch and steps, space, modern conveniences for the farm home, kind and condition of heating, lighting and sanitation; and gives a reasonably balanced valuation for each item in a total of 100 points.

Six hundred and eight dwellings were measured. A frame house, for example, which had been recently painted, was five to ten years old, with sound roof, floors, windows, screens, running water, an inside toilet or septic tank, a bath tub, electric light or perhaps kerosene lamps, and a stove for cooking, may receive a score of between 75 and 90. Exceptional dwellings may reach the full 100 score by the possession of quite reasonably attainable modern conveniences. A lack of any of these items, as in the matter of defective flooring, broken or missing windows, leaking roof, would register in lower scores.

93

Of these 608 homes in Macon County, the largest number, 185, or 30.4 per cent, rated between 30 and 40. The modal house was thus about a third of what would be expected for minimum efficiency. The mean score was 35, or slightly over the mode. The lowest score was 12 and the highest 60.

Ownership of occupational implements and of cultural artifacts may be taken roughly as an indication of rural efficiency and, perhaps, of the extent to which new material traits are being acquired. In order, thus, to relate the ownership of these articles to

TABLE V

Scores on Physical Housing in 608 Families in Macon County, Alabama, June–July, 1931

Scores	Homes	Stores	Homes
0– 4	0	45–49	55
5– 9	0	50–54	23
10–14	1	55–59	6
15–19	2	60–64	2
20–24	16	65–69	0
25–29	72	70–74	0
30–34	185		
35–39	138	Total	608
40–44	108		

the home, additional values were given to the total of 25, and these combined with individual housing scores. In 608 families there were 392, or 64.4 per cent of the families with neither agricultural implements nor cultural instruments of any sort. In 736 families in Gibson County, Tennessee, an area of mixed farming, 116, or 15 per cent, of the families fall in this classification. The central scores were least affected by the addition of these values while the higher physical housing scores and those just below the median were considerably improved.

The low average of these scores not only corresponds closely with direct observation, but stands out conspicuously as low scores when compared with another rural Negro county of a different type of background. The area used for comparison is Gibson County, Tennessee, which is not a plantation area but one predominantly of small farms. It is one of the poorer sections of Tennessee, and has no tradition of the plantation since it has always been an area of small farmers. The Negro population is only 30 per cent

CHART I

SCORES ON PHYSICAL HOUSING IN 608 MACON COUNTY HOMES AS COMPARED WITH
SCORES ON PHYSICAL HOUSING IN 736 GIBSON COUNTY HOMES

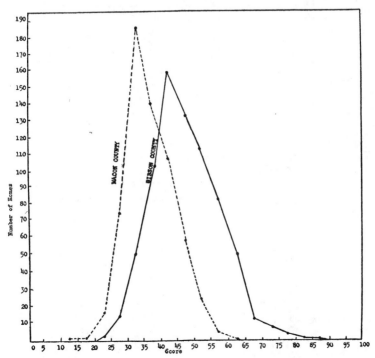

of the total, as compared with 82.3 per cent in Macon County, and 31 per cent of the Negro population own their homes as compared with 10 per cent in Macon County. The difference, as measured by the same scale, is most striking. The median in Gibson County is 46.6 as compared with 36.01 in Macon County. The lowest score in Gibson County was 23 and the highest 91. Homes

TABLE VI

Total Scores of Physical Housing, Cultural Instruments, and Occupational Implements in 608 Families in Macon County, Alabama, June–July, 1931

Scores	Homes	Scores	Homes
0– 4	0	50–54	64
5– 9	0	55–59	21
10–14	1	60–64	17
15–19	1	65–69	10
20–24	9	70–74	3
25–29	46	75–79	1
30–34	106	80–84	2
35–39	118	85–89	2
40–44	112	90–94	1
45–49	94	95–99	0

TABLE VII

Scores on Physical Housing in Macon County, Alabama, as Compared with Scores on Physical Housing in Gibson County, Tennessee

Scores	Macon County Homes	Gibson County Homes
0– 4	0	0
5– 9	0	0
10–14	1	0
15–19	2	0
20–24	16	2
25–29	72	13
30–34	185	50
35–39	138	101
40–44	108	159
45–49	55	134
50–54	23	114
55–59	5	85
60–64	2	48
65–69	0	14
70–74	0	9
75–79	0	3
80–84	0	2
85–89	0	1
90–94	0	1

CABINS IN THE COTTON

of owners in both states had consistently higher rating than those of tenants.

It is possible to give more specific description of these houses in relation to ratings. Dwelling 165 has a score of 35, which approximates the median score of the dwellings. It is a two-room, unpainted board structure with a lean-to kitchen, and has been standing over ten years. The roof leaks, the floors are weak, and the steps are broken. Well-paned windows let in light and air. Kerosene lamps are used for lighting, and a stove and fireplace for cooking and heating. There is a well within fifty feet of the house but no means outside or within are available for sewage disposal or bathing. With respect to cultural and occupational implements, there are no books, musical instruments; neither hoes, plows, rakes, nor other occupational tools.

Dwelling 87 has a score of 35. It has two sleeping-rooms, a lean-to kitchen, a projecting porch, and is some thirty years old. Its occupants had whitewashed it ten years ago. Dim vestiges of this coating now remain. The roof leaks, the porch is tumbling down, and the broken and paneless windows lend an air of desertion to the place. There are, however, good steps and substantial floors. Six people live here but without a source of water supply on the place. They go to the neighbor's well for water. Projecting itself behind a clump of bushes, about twelve yards from the house, is an open privy in advanced disrepair. There is no provision for bathing. Kerosene lamps are used for lighting and the fireplace for cooking.

The Townsends live in a house which is given a score of 59. This is one of the better homes. It is a one-story frame structure of five rooms. Each room is ventilated and lighted by one glass window and all of the windows are intact. The house, however, has never been painted since its erection fifteen years ago. Roof, floors, steps, and porches are substantial. The family has a fireplace and stove, kerosene lamps; uses well water, and has an open privy. There are no special facilities for bathing and no modern conveniences other than an automobile.

The Jones family scores 56. Five months before the family had moved to their present quarters to "better conditions." The age of the house was approximately fifteen years, but it had not been painted since erection. Floors, roof, steps, and porches were in good condition. Windows and doors were screened. There was an open privy but no bath. Kerosene lamps were used but there was no water on the place.

The best dwelling in the group was an owned home. It was a brick-and-frame structure, recently built and painted with roof, floor, porches in good repair, and all openings screened. There was an open privy in the yard but no running water. The family had an automobile but no other modern conveniences.

The lowest scores of 12 and 18 merely illustrate the egregious extremes in physical housing possible under the prevailing conditions of life in the county. No house in Gibson County approached the lowest group of buildings in Macon County. The score of 12 was given on a perilously dilapidated one-room log cabin known to be over thirty years old. It was without windows, the roof was buckled and crumbling, the chimney had caved in and constituted a constant menace to the occupant. There was no water near the place and no toilet, no floor, no provision for bathing, no lighting. It was occupied by an old woman and her adopted child.

The attitude of tenants toward these dwellings varies interestingly. For some, their quarters are "all right for common folks like us." They neither know nor want anything different. There are others who are satisfied to live where they are although they are aware of the inadequacy of their shelter. Some voice complaints with vehemence; some whisper them out of fear of incurring the displeasure of the landlords; and some accept their discomfort with the good-natured tolerance which they exhibit toward other facts of a hopeless situation.

When one tenant housewife was asked about her house, she remarked with resigned disgust: " 'Scuse me, but dis ain't no house. We stayed here outdoors all last year, waiting for Mr. ———— to come fix us a place to live, but he ain't come yit. When it rains we hafter git up alongside the wall and when the rain's over we hafter put all the stuff outside to dry."

Another woman commented: "My house is so rotten you kin jest take up the boards in your hand and cromple 'em up. Everything done swunk about it."

These observations were by no means exaggerations. The extremely cheap construction of the dwellings and their age made it inevitable that they should soon become uninhabitable except for persons adjusted to a primitive type of dwellings. The extravagance of their disrepair prompts some of those who must nevertheless live in them to equally extravagant though harmless statements of disgust. At one home the mother was asked if her house leaked. She seemed to be overwhelmed by the naïveté of the question and controlled herself before answering, because she had just experienced a rain. "Do it leak in here?" she repeated with complete amazement, and then answered, "No, it don't leak in here, it jest rains in here and leak outdoors; dis ain't no house; it jest a piece a house. I got a great mind to take a hammer and knock it down." Other complaints, where there was the spirit to complain, followed the same type:

He [the landlord] come here five years ago and say he going to fix this old house up. All he's give us since then is a few planks to fix the porch. Its nothin' doin'. We jest living outdoors.

This house so open I get plenty of fresh air. I raised up seven girls and two boys right here. . . . . . I'm jest staying round here fighting and praying. I'd be glad if I could git me a comfortable home but folks won't let you have nothing less you mortgage it and when you git it all fixed up they come in and take it. So I jest leaves it like it is.

This house is mighty cold in the winter time. I'm old and my blood is thin. I got seven quilts and I put all them on the bed and I almost freeze. The wind jest shoots through the cracks and gets the bedticks cold and I can't get warm for nothing.

My health was good 'fore I come here. I had't took no medicine from a doctor in fifteen years 'fore I come here to this house; it was jest so cold in here I got a cold and took the flu and had to have the doctor that same winter I come here. I said it was this old cold house 'cause I come out of a sealed house; this old cold tin give it to me.

99

As to toilet facilities, 310 used open privies near by the house, 296 had no sewage disposal. Two hundred and fifty-eight used open wells for their water supply, 243 used well-pumps, 32 used springs, and 81 families had no water on the place at all.

Such dwellings and surroundings constitute a dreary setting for families and their children. One reaction to this is the constant wandering-about in search of something better, with respect to both housing and labor terms. The crowding-together of families in these small rooms destroys all privacy, dulls the desire for neatness and cleanliness, and renders virtually impossible the development of any sense of beauty. It is a cheerless condition of life with but few avenues of escape even for those who keep alive a flickering desire for something better.

Diet

The chief foods are listed, as a simple indication of food habits. These items of food in winter are salt meat, corn or flour bread, and syrup or sorghum. Few vegetables are eaten. There is a common belief that "greens are feverish." Milk is sometimes used, but few have cows. Sweet potatoes are used when available. The meals vary little, even during the day. "I don't eat no supper 'cause I git tired of the same thing all the time." Breakfast consists commonly of corn bread and syrup. A heavy meal with meat is eaten for supper. The fortunate ones are those who have been able to put away potatoes for the winter and who have a "shoat" to kill at Christmas. A large number of families—sometimes for reasons of taste, sometimes for lack of money—did not eat vegetables in either winter or summer. Occasionally a chicken is killed for Sundays. It was difficult to get accounting of the items of food even of the day before. A list was made of the foods of the current day. Gardens were drying up and food was scarce, but such accounts as the following were among the most common:

We get a 24-pound sack of flour and that will last us two weeks. These boys won't eat nothing but flour bread, if I don't make 'em, so I buy a peck of meal once in a while and make them eat some corn bread. Then I buy ten or fifteen cents' worth of beans or cabbage sometimes and once in a while a can of "ramatoes." I eat oatmeal regularly. The boys don't like it, but I like it and when I can't get milk, I just put sugar and water on it and eat it.

An old couple at the dinner meal sat on the front porch eating beans out of a rusty pan with their bread crumbled up in a bucket top. The bread was of corn meal and had been cooked several days. It was cold, as were the beans which they were eating. The wife was drinking milk along with her portion. They were slowly eating with their fingers. "We buy 'bout a peck of meal and it costs 40 cents a peck. I buys a dime's worth of sugar 'bout once a week." Other food habits were such as the following:

We country people have to eat rough food. They won't even let us have fertilizer. We ought to have oatmeal, grits, and things like that to eat but we can't get it.

The baby have to eat what we have and that ain't much. I got one old rooster. I wanted to kill him but I ain't got no grease to cook him wid.

No, I don't eats chicken. I like 'em all right but I has to put 'em up in a coop for two weeks 'fore I can get 'em clean enough. I can't eat 'em right out de yard.

If the rations give out 'fore Saturday we just don't eat nothing 'till Saturday evening. Mostly we use is white meat and bread and white lard. I ain't got no taste for it 'cause I was raised on plenty vegetables. Sometimes we have peas. If it don't rain these people ain't going to have nothing to eat.

I know how much groceries us buy every two week, but I ain't never stopped to figure it up. We always buys one bushel of meal, two pounds of flour, and five pounds of meat. Sometimes rice and sugar and like dat.

In the hunting season they may shoot a squirrel, and in the summer they fish. The families of larger means raise their own meat and vegetables and can fruits.

We always had plenty meat, we kill our own meat, we'll have good meat this year. I reckon I'll be able to put me up some berries if I can get some rubbers and tops—first time I ever bought tops. . . . . You know we don't suffer in the meat line but our bread's out.

My husband makes a plenty something to eat all the time. . . . . We got fifteen cows here and I could run a dairy if I wanted to. We use about three gallons of milk a day. We are crazy about milk. I really don't like corn bread 'cause it will give you the pellagacy. I just can't enjoy corn bread somehow or other. Don't leave fresh meat out 'cause I love it. With five of us here we can drink all the milk we get.

On the Saturday trips to town they may be seen sitting around chatting and munching peanuts, bananas, and frankfurters and drinking soda pop. These are a part of the excitement of the journey but contribute little to the dietary deficiencies everywhere so manifest. The Red Cross has provided yeast for many of the families, and this has been salutary where its purpose has been understood sufficiently to insure consistent use. The people die, and with good reason.

Chapter III

ECONOMIC LIFE OF THE COMMUNITY

THE DIVISION OF LABOR

THE life of the area is agricultural, the staple and inevitable crop is cotton, and the occupation of practically every member of the community old enough to work is farming. The whole of life is bound up with the slow and tedious decadence of the plantation system which, in Phillips' significant observation, formed the industrial and social frame of government in the Black Belt counties, while slavery provided merely the code of laws for the perpetuation of the system.[1]

Without the structure of slavery and the resources of new lands, it could not survive in health. Its greatest success carried with it the fatal corollary of industrial stratification, the crushing-out of yeomanry, a disastrous competition, and an unbalance of production which lead in the end to dependence. The attempts at adjustment of the system to new demands of agriculture have presented the curious anomaly of these original values of the plantation in conflict with powerful imperatives of the new agriculture. Modifications of the system into the share system with its tenant farmers and croppers lacks both the material and the social support of the past, and while it tends to serve more the end of decentralization, peasant proprietorship, and independent farming, it serves less its own and most unique advantages. The shell of the past hangs on in the agricultural economy of the community under study. It is present in the high proportion of Negro tenantry, the almost exclusive concentration upon cotton, the crude unskilled

[1] Ulrich B. Phillips, "The Decadence of the Plantation," *Annals of the American Academy of Political and Social Science*, January, 1910.

labor in need of land and skilled supervision, the credit system and advances, the tradition of dependence upon planters on the part of the Negro tenants, and the tradition of dependence upon capital on the part of the planters. It is in itself a transitional phase of agriculture as the modes of life of the Negroes are a transitional phase of the culture. The waste of the soil, the overproduction of cotton, the constant involvement of the credit system, have brought on an inevitable stagnation, both for planters and for the Negroes whose lives are linked with its ever declining fortunes.

TABLE VIII

STATUS OF WHITE AND COLORED FARMERS IN 1925

TENURE	COLOR	
	White	Negro
Full owners..................	248	277
Part owners..................	26	61
Managers....................	5	2
Total tenants.............	294	2,258
a) Cash tenants.........	135	541
b) Croppers............	54	655
c) Other tenants........	105	1,142
Total....................	573	2,578

Any analysis of the present economic status of the Negroes in this area must take into account the detailed division of the population into the customary and essential classes of cotton culture. In 1925 there were 573 white and 2,578 colored farmers in Macon County. Two hundred and forty-eight, or 43 per cent, of the white farmers were full owners, while 277, or a little more than 10 per cent, of the colored farmers owned their farms. Table IX gives the status of both white and colored farmers in 1925.

Nine-tenths of the Negro farmers are tenants. The census has distinguished three types of tenants: cash tenants, croppers, and other tenants. In our group of 612 families it has been possible to make finer distinctions in tenure found among the Negro farmers.

Sixty-four of the 612 families (slightly over 10 per cent), or about the same proportion as found for the county as a whole, were owners of their farms. Landownership is, indeed, not so easily acquired. It means a break with the system and such meager security as it holds. One farmer explained:

I got 186 acres of land. I pays instalments to the Macon County Bank. I pay from $65 to $45 in taxes. Jest 'nough to kill folks. We rents out about 25 acres. Last year I made three bales of cotton. We didn't do so much farming. I came out behind last year. . . . . When my father died he left 460 acres and hit was a crowd of us chillun, and my brother—the oldest—and my mother, they lak to run through wid ever'thing.

I been trying long back ter done paid this land off. . . . . My whole debt is $900 and some off now. Ever' year hit increases. They give you sich a little discount. . . . . I had a drove of cows and the bank tuk them too. . . . . I got nineteen chillun. Eight of them is dead; seven of them was misfortunes.

TABLE IX

DISTRIBUTION OF 612 NEGRO FAMILIES IN MACON
COUNTY ACCORDING TO TENURE

Owners.............	64	Laborers:	
Managers...........	2	Farm.............	70
Tenants:		Other............	18
Cash.............	177	With relatives, etc.,...	22
Cotton...........	132	Miscellaneous........	21
Croppers...........	99	Unknown...........	7
		Total...........	612

The Owners

Present owners, for the most part, secured their lands a number of years ago, when it was both cheaper and more fertile. Recently there has been a season of bad crops. Their earnings are small, but they keep themselves in food by cultivating patches, or raising corn, peas, and potatoes in addition to their cotton. Ownership has been consistently declining over several decades.

Few outstanding Negro farm-owners were encountered among the families studied. Such as were recorded were persons of very moderate personal accomplishments who were finding ownership almost as onerous as tenantry. A fair average is suggested in a family consisting of man and wife and five children, two of whom were away, from whose experience a citation will be made. Their home is a frame structure of five rooms. While the frame building is badly in need of repair, it is evident there is some degree of stability and ambition to achieve the status of a property-owner. The family has lived in it for twenty-four years. It is inclosed by a fence. The green window blinds and the lightning rods on the roof can be seen from the road. Just in front of the house is a large fruit orchard with pears, plums, peaches, and apples growing, and in between are planted green vegetables. At the rear of the house is a small cabin which might have been occupied by the former owner's servants. Said this farmer:

In 1902 I moved to C——'s farm just across the way. I came here from S——'s place in Parell, Macon County. I had $500 when I first came, with which I paid my rent and started to farm on 129 acres of land. Times were good then and I made 40 bales of cotton the first year and 36 the next. Paid Mr. —— 6 bales the first year and 7 the next, and sold the rest for 12 and 13 cents a pound. I then saved up enough money to buy this place and paid $2,280 cash money for all this land, 129 acres. I planted the fruit trees myself. I wish very much my children would a stayed here. They didn't know what hard times was. I don't know how much it's valued for—you know when you say a big amount then you hafter pay lots of taxes—so I just don't say. When I first came here I only paid $12 taxes, now they done gone up to $34. I wish me and my wife didn't have to worry about expenses, for pretty soon we will be too old to work. Since I saved all the money in 1902 I ain't been able to raise that much cotton since, not even half that much. For the last few years I only been able to raise one or two bales.

A detailed account of his earnings for the year, from all sources, is as follows: In 1930 he raised 2 bales of cotton (900 lb.) and sold them for 9 cents a pound, which brought him $81. In addition, he raised 2 banks of potatoes, 200 loads of corn, 32 bushels of ground peas, and 22 gallons of sorghum. All of this he used for his own family and stock. There are three small houses on his farm; two are rented and one is vacant. From one tenant he received $18 for rent of a house and farm. From another he received 200 pounds of

CHILD OF A SUCCESSFUL FARMER

A NEGRO-OWNER'S HOME

lint cotton, valued at $12. The fruit from the orchard is consumed by the family. He raises a few hogs, chickens, and cows. The family eats the chickens and hogs, and he sells eggs for cash.

Another owner gave this account of himself:

Nigh as I come to it, we been here about 17 years. Times are harder than den they ever been. Little corn, cotton, and cane standing in the field, but it's been now since 1927 that we had a decent crop. If it wasn't for the boll weevil, it was the drought, and if it wasn't the drought it was the flood. Got plenty stuff planted now in my garden, but it just drying up because we need the rain. Yes, times harder with me than it is with dem what ain't got nothing, 'cause it is just as hard to figure how to keep what I had. I hafter keep doing and looking, too. When we bought this home, near twenty years ago, times were much better. Cost us $20 an acre and the whole thing cost us $1,200. We paid half of it in cash. Bought this land from Mr. ———. During them times we raised as high as $100 for our cow.

His income for 1930 was as follows: 3 bales of cotton (1,500 lb.) for which he received $140, 2 banks of potatoes, and a quantity of corn which he kept for his family. He sold chickens, eggs, and hogs for extra money.

Below are given significant fragments from the experience of other owners:

a) I farms fer myself. I made 7 bales of cotton last year. There's 'bout 500 ter 550 pounds ter a bale. I raises peas 'sides cotton and corn, and saves some of them fer hogs and some ter eat. I owns 80 acres myself, and hit's all paid for. I rents 5 acres and a patch ter that lady's husband. I hafter hire day laborers sometimes. I hired 4 laborers ter help me chop cotton, and paid them 50 cents a day. Sometimes I hafter get 5 and 6 ter help me pick. I paid 50 cents a hundred last year.

I made 7 bales. One ain't sold. There was 525 pounds in each bale. I got 9 cents a pound for the 6 bales I sold. I had my fertilizer and helpers ter pay outa that. I still got that bale of cotton left. I made part of this money ter buy this land 'fore I come here. I don't know how much my house worth, but I'd sell the horse and mules cheap, 'cause they ain't no good.

b) I been owning this place about thirty years, and I been farming all my days, but I just come over here 'bout six years ago. I ain't go very far in school. Just been right 'round here to these little local schools. Didn't get to go away to no high school. I never did carry the term out, 'cause I had to work. I reckon I been 'round here in this community about fifty-two years. Been sick and ain't able to do much work, but I buys all I kin. I paid $3.50 an acre for 75¼ acres of land. I ain't satisfied with the house, but I ain't in no shape to do no better. It's just a shame, an old hull, but I don't seem to be able to make enough to do nothing.

The difficulty, as one of these owners explained it, of holding on to what they have, is a very real one, and this fact is given support, not only in the small number of owners, but in the number of former owners who have lost their farms.

This place was to be mine but the man done closed me out. I had an automobile and when he closed us out he told me to nail up the car out there, let it stay there till he come back. When he come he tuk my mules, cows, and ever'thing. I made a mortgage on the place and he come and take all my things. Take all my stock. I borrowed money from him. The first time I got $20 and then for four or five months I got $20 each month. Then I drawed $10 a month for ten months. Said I done paid all back now, when he come back the last time, but he had been here before and tuk all my corn and cotton. I done let him have a carload of corn, 'bout 250 bushels, 6 bales of cotton, 600 pounds and over each. Me and my boy give him another carload of corn. He got so he tuk every-thing I made for a while. Yes, he tuk two mules, a wagon, two cows, two calves; taken my plows and that ended it with me, cause he had done tuk the second time 5 bales of cotton, weighed 500 pounds each, and then he had come again and tuk one bale, 500 pounds. Come back three years. That was all I made and he tuk that. Said he satisfied when he got all that. He come here last year and closed out John and ———. He done let us had some of the stock, and the mule he let us have was the same mule returned back.

Twelve of the sixty-four owners rented land in addition to their farms. In a few cases these farms which they owned were too small to support a family. One of these families will be sufficient to il-lustrate the pressure of circumstances which forces such an exten-sion of the small ownership status into tenantry. The husband and wife live in an attractive, well-kept house, which they own. They own two acres of land and rent three more acres at two dollars per acre for farm land. The man lost his arm while working in a cotton gin about thirty years ago. He received no compensation, in spite of the fact that there was a lawsuit. He estimated his last year's

"I ASK LANDLORD TO 'VANCE ME ER PAIR OF OVERALLS,
AN' HE SAY HE NEED OVERALLS HISSELF"

earnings at twenty-five dollars above his rent. Neither of them has been to school, but the husband can read and write, and takes a paper daily. The wife was divorced from her first husband, but this is the husband's first marriage. They have two daughters living in Macon County. One of them lives near and owns her home. One daughter and one son live in Birmingham; one son in Ensly, Alabama, and one son in Chicago.

In other cases the owners rented land and had tenants or laborers working for them. In the case of four of the owners they were either buying their farms or there was a mortgage on them.

Tenants

The first distinction which should be made clear in regard to the tenants is that between those who have made arrangements for cash payments and those who have contracted to pay a stipulated amount of cotton. There were 177 tenant heads of families who had arranged to make cash payments, and 132 who paid rental in a stipulated quantity of cotton. Usually these tenants paid forty or fifty dollars for one-horse farms. The tenants seem to have no definite idea concerning the actual number of acres in a one-horse farm, but from the best available sources it seemed that a one-horse farm was from fifteen to twenty acres in extent. Tenants who pay their rental usually give a bale and a half for a one-horse farm. Here, again, the arrangement varies according to custom, or the terms of the landlord. The tenant may pay rent in cash, or in cotton and other produce; he may or may not receive advances from the landlord in the form of cash or rations. A renter may subrent. Again, he may apply for a government loan or borrow from the bank.

a) We pay 400 pounds of lint cotton. We made nearly 6 bales last year and he sold it hisself, but we still owe 'bout $50. We ain't got no advance, but we borrows from the bank. I think we pay 10 cents on the dollar. We sold cotton for 9 cents last year. We could a got 10 but just kept holding it. Old man J—— [landlord] won't do a thing. He come by here five years ago and said he was going to fix this house up. All he's give us since then is a few planks to fix the porch. It's rotting down. We're just living outdoors. We rents out our ox for $12 a year, and the folks feed him.

b) I ain't got no children and me and my husband works a one-horse farm and we got 'bout thirty acres. Last year we made 6 bales of cotton and rented the thirty acres for $60; fifteen acres we used for cotton, the rest for corn. We kept the corn and didn't sell none hardly. At ten cents a pound the six bales would bring $300. We has $10 advanced for four months. We turned it all over, and they took out the $40 advanced, $30 for fertilizer, and $60 rent. We got through and then they say we come out $72.43 in the hole.

c) Tenant received no advance, but paid 400 pounds of cotton as rent. He raised 2 bales of cotton [around 800 lb.], sold the other, and received 10 cents a pound [$40]. He also grew 3 bushels of potatoes, 16 rows of sugar cane, and 4 loads of corn.

d) Tenant received no advances. He raised 2½ bales of cotton and paid 1 bale for rent. He cleared $25 on the sale of 1½ bales. He also raised 12½ bushels of corn, 1 bank of potatoes, and 6 gallons of syrup.

In more prosperous times when there is a reasonable assurance of returns, the landowners made advances both to tenants and to share-croppers. It is a most frequent complaint of the tenants now that they cannot get advances. One said: "I ask Mr. ———— to 'vance me jest nuff for a pair of overalls. He tell me he needs overalls hisself." In other cases advances to tenants have merely been reduced.

Last year I drawed $10 to the plow [meaning $10 a month for from four to six months for each 20 acres cultivated] but I ain't getting but $7 this year. I rents the whole place [400 acres] and then subrents it, and pays 4 bales of cotton for rent. But I don't never make nothing offen it. Didn't clear nothing last year. I paid out $200 last year. Interest steps on me time I pay my rent [for money borrowed from the bank] and interest cost 15 cents on the dollar. I haven't made nothing since 1927. I clears $210 then and ain't cleared nothing since. I got 21 cents for cotton that year.

Another explained:

They don't give nothing now. Use to 'low us $10 provisions a month, but dey done cut us way down. The white folks say some of these banks done fell in; dere ain't no money to be got. That's all. Said this is the suppression time.

Another type of tenant pays a good rental in cash and receives advances.

We farms 60 acres and pays $150 for rent. That's $75 to the plow. They 'vances us $15 a month for five months. I come out jest $175 in the hole.

We run a two-horse farm. We was due to pay $150 rent last year, but I don't know what us is paying this year. We cut down on the land we was using. We made 22 bales of cotton last year, and it was selling at 8, 9, and 10 cents when we turned it in to the man. We didn't git nothing back. You see, the man had been carrying us for two years. I took 'sponsibility for the whole patch and let some of it out to three other parties, and stood for them. Besides the cotton the men took 13 loads of corn, but I saved about 200 bushels for myself to live on, and I sold some peanuts and corn.

The normal earnings of a man and wife, if both work as tenants on a one-horse cotton farm, would probably average $260 a year in cash value. However, they pay about half of their cotton in rent, use the corn for their stock, and eat the potatoes, peas, and sorghum which they grow along with the cotton. As a result very little cash is handled. They manage to live on the advances, or by borrowing for food and clothing and permitting their crop to be taken in satisfaction of the debt. It becomes very largely a paper loss or gain. In the case of loss the tenant may move away, leaving his debt. In the latter case he may be conscious of having earned more than he got, or of paying for some other Negro tenant's default.

We got right 'round sixty acres and one-half of it is in cotton. We working on halves. We got a two-horse farm. My daughter got one and I got one. I farmed with Mr. P—— last year. We had thirty acres over there and made 5 bales of cotton and paid $100 for rent. We gits $2 a month in cash and $10 in rations. We came out $200 in the hole last year. *I don't have to pay that off 'cause I let that went when I come here* [he had to give up farm tools, etc.]. I been farming all my life 'cept two years when we went to Virginia. . . . . I worked in the coke field out there. That was the year the war was.

One daughter lived at home. Four boys were away living in cities in Alabama. One grown daughter lived in the county and worked with them. One grown son was dead—"got knocked in the head" seven little children had died between the ages of two and four.

Share-Croppers

There is another type of farmer, the share-cropper, who, without tools or any form of capital, farms on the condition that he give the landlord one-half of the crop. There were ninety-eight families working on this arrangement besides one woman who gave a fourth of the crop for the rental of her small farm. The arrangement varies with the landlord and the condition of the tenant. When the tenant is furnished tools and work animals in addition to the land, he may get only a third of the cotton raised. Most commonly, however, it is halves, and he may find it necessary to rent a mule for his plowing.

The share-croppers frequently are subtenants for small white and Negro tenant farmers, or for their relatives. It is at least a means of beginning, and a good share-cropper can, with good fortune, place himself in position to undertake the responsibilities of a full tenant later.

I works a one-horse farm on halves. I get 'bout $12 a month in rations. Last year [1930] I worked for the Tallahassee Mill Company, and made $9.75 a week. My wife was working by the day for 50 cents a day. We been married 'bout four years now. I moved here from Tallahassee 'cause I was lacking for sense. The white folks liked me down there and everything, and I moved. I called myself liking ter farm best.

Farm Laborers

Seventy heads of families were farm laborers who worked on other people's farms for a stipulated wage. Eleven of these farm laborers had small patches of their own which they were permitted to cultivate rent free. The wage usually paid these laborers was 50–65 cents a day, the women receiving more often 40 cents. The following statement of a farm laborer indicates the conditions under which this class works.

We jest work by the day and pay $1.50 a month for this house. It's jest a piece of house. I gits 50 cents a day and my husband and the boy gits 65 cents each. We have to feed ourselves and pay rent out of that. My husband is pretty scheming, but sometimes he can't git nothing to do. I don't know how much time we lose, but he works most of the time.

Course the boy stops and goes to school in the winter sometimes, but if he can git work to do, he works too.

The husband lives with his wife and her sixteen-year-old illegitimate boy. The boy was caught with whiskey on him and stayed in jail a month before his aunt could bail him out. He is only in the third grade in school, and his mother gives this as the reason for his retardation. He had to work out the $105 bail which his aunt paid.

Among these families there were also laborers who were working on railroads, logging, and on county roads. There were eighteen of these laborers, including seven whose wives managed a small farm or a patch as a means of contributing to the family support. The wife of one of these laborers related the following history:

My husband and me married eight years. He works at the Hardaway log mill and makes $7.00 a week. He been working there four years now . . . . We don't have to pay no rent. The man he works for pays for hit. I don't do nothing but stay home. . . . . My husband was in debt when we left Milstead but he ain't much in debt now. He don't owe but 'bout a dollar or two. He don't lack this man he's working for 'cause he don't pay him but $1.10 a day. The man's name is Mr. S—— and he is mean to work for. He got 14 or 15 working for him down there at the log mill 'sides my husband. If we git hard up and want some money, he don't help us. He don't do nothing but run you away from there. . . . . My husband goes ter work wid sunrise every morning and works till dark. I git up fo' day and cooks his breakfast. He don't come back home ter dinner cause hit's so far. Hit's 'bout seven miles from here."

Casuals

Probably the lowest class of farm laborers was made up of the four farm hands who did not receive a stipulated monetary wage, but were to get what was known as a "hand's share." This, seemingly, just amounts to enough to keep them living. One old woman who lives by herself in a one-room shack and works for a hand's share told the following story:

I works for a hand's share in the crop with the folks cross dere. My husband *been* dead. I ain't never had but one child and dat's de son what's right down dere. . . . . I been up north in Birmingham with my sister . . . . but I come back here, 'cause dese chillun kept worrying me to come on here to live wid them. It's mighty tight on me to have to go working in dese fields half starved, and I ain't had a bit of money to buy a piece of cloth as big as my hand since I been back. I washed fer white people in Birmingham, and dey was good to me. I am jest gitting long by the hardest. I works for dese people for a hand's share in the crop. Dey gives me a load of corn and a load of potatoes. I gits some of all the other stuff what's made, and when selling cotton dey give you a little money out of the seed. I don't see no money on time. Dey gives me a little something to eat 'cause I works wid dem and dey gives me a little groceries. I never was in this fix before in my life. I had good money when I come from Birmingham. I had two fives and five single dollahs. I sho' gonna git what I works for dis year.

Eight women who were heads of families were employed in domestic service, and one of these women had a small patch which she cultivated. There were twenty-two persons, some of them very old, in other cases dependent relatives and in a few cases children, who were living on their parents' or relatives' farms, without being required to pay any rent. Two very old couples were living in this manner on white men's places, where they were permitted to sustain themselves on small plots of ground without having to pay rent. One old couple, now too old for much work, had been given a place by a white landlord. The man said, rather wearily:

I jest got a little patch, 'bout an acre. The people plows it for me, and I works it. I could work more [land] but I jest ain't able to plow it. He lets me have what I make. I don't raise no cotton, jest corn. You see I got hogs and I have to feed 'em and we have to have bread. When the corn gives out I works 'bout by the day, and git meal that way.

I used to be doing well; I used to rent a great big farm and rent it out. I had lots of stock. Oh, they died. I had to git rid of some. I had plows, hands, and everything. Oh, they ruint me, jest making one bale when they coulda made five, and me standing fer it. It jest broke me.

The old man is eighty-four years old and has been married twice. His wife is seventy-two years old. A white landowner allows them to live in the house and work the patch free. This white man and his wife often bring food to the old couple.

Among these 612 families there were 7 from whom it was impossible to learn the conditions on which they farmed. In one case, for example, a woman knew that last year she had farmed on halves but did not know what the arrangements would be for the present year. In two other cases the white landlord had been sick and there had been no opportunity to make arrangements. There were also persons in this group of families drawn from many different occupations. There were two pensioners, a midwife, a mechanic, a preacher, a teacher—who lived in the "teacherage"—a chauffeur, two managers or overseers of a large plantation, and a bootlegger whose wife was a cash tenant.

TABLE X

OCCUPATIONS OF WOMEN IN 612 FAMILIES
IN MACON COUNTY

Occupation	No.	Occupation	No.
Unknown	9	Business	1
Dead or away	35	Domestic service	20
None	9	Housewife and mother	31
Professional (nurse, teacher, etc.)	2	Farmer-housekeeper	470
Midwife	3	Farmer-laborer	32
		Total	612

Women Workers

Nearly all of the women in these families assist on the farm. Only 31 of the 579 women who were heads of families devoted themselves exclusively to the work of housewife and mother. Thirty-two of them worked as day laborers on the farms. Four hundred and seventy of them, or 81.1 per cent, combined the duties of farming and housekeeping. In some cases the wife's farming activities are confined to cultivating gardens. These gardens are necessary to supplement the efforts of these farmers in making a living. The type of garden a farmer has determines the kind of food he eats and the extent, very often, of his dependence on the landlord. Five hundred and thirteen of these 612 families had a garden.

Not only does the wife engage in work on the farm, but the children and other members of the household also work. In 252 families, or 41.1 per cent of the total, there were two persons working; and in 67 families, or 10 per cent, there were four persons at work. In 89 families, or 14.5 per cent, there were from five to nine persons at work.

TABLE XI

DISTRIBUTION OF 612 FAMILIES IN MACON COUNTY
ACCORDING TO NUMBERS WORKING

	No.		No.
Unknown	3	Six	17
None	4	Seven	17
One	94	Eight	10
Two	252	Nine	1
Three	103		
Four	67	Total	612
Five	44		

Child Workers

In many cases the arrangement between the landlord and the tenant or cropper includes the work of the children on the farm. In about 20 per cent of the 612 families all of the children were employed. But noticeable differences appear for the three types of families classified according to the education of the mother. Of the 64 families with children in which the wife was illiterate, 47, or about 74 per cent, of them had children employed. Of the 140 families with children and in which the wife had a fourth-grade education or less, 101, or about 72 per cent, had children employed. The significant difference appears in the next type of families, in which the wife had a fifth-grade education or more. Of these 169 families 103, or about 61 per cent, had children employed. A better basis of comparison of the employment of children in these three types of families is obtained by calculating the actual percentage of children in these three types of families who are at work. Ninety-three, or 56.3 per cent, of the 165 children in the first type of families were at work. In the second type of families, 230, or

51.1 per cent, of the 450 children were at work. In the third and highest type of families there were 235, or 41.8 per cent, of the 562 children employed.

There is great mobility among the tenants and share-croppers especially. In the group of 612 families there were 340, or 55.5 per cent, that had changed residence during the last five years. Many of these 340 families had moved several times during the five years.

TABLE XII

NUMBER OF FAMILIES WITH SPECIFIED NUMBER OF CHILDREN EMPLOYED

Education of Mother	Un-known	None	One	Two	Three	Four	Five	Six	Seven	Eight	Nine	Total
Dead or away	1	21	3	4	3	0	1	0	0	0	0	33
Unknown....	1	24	13	9	1	3	1	0	0	0	0	52
Illiterate.....	1	66	24	12	4	0	3	3	0	0	0	113
Four years or less.......	1	88	35	30	17	8	8	2	0	0	0	189
Five years or more......	1	122	40	29	13	8	8	3	0	1	0	225
Total....	5	321	115	84	38	19	21	8	0	1	0	612

They give various reasons for moving, such as "jest got tired of livin' down there," or they heard the soil was better in the present location, or in one case they wanted to move from the place because they say so many of the family die. One tenant gave rather specific reasons for moving. He said:

I moved here 'cause I jest didn't like Jim ——— and got tired of it. We made 10 bales last year but look like we poorer than ever. We didn't get but $12 'vancement for five months from that cotton; course we owed him some from the year before. I don't know 'zactly how much it was he [former landlord] got for the cotton; but he tole me he got ten, seven, eight, nine cents for some of it. He was a fellow who wouldn't let you know his business and course you couldn't do a thing but take his word for it. He got all new people this year. All of them is pretty much from new communities. About six or seven families moved out, and I believe about twice that many moved in. He had to go over to Warriorstand to get the people 'cause nobody in this part would move in; so he got some new folks that didn't know him.

His first wife and her first husband are dead. They had one child to die from "thrash" at the age of nine months. His two children by his first wife live with his mother in Birmingham. They have one child by the second marriage.

Ownership of Work Animals and Farm Implements

The total number of work animals owned by the 612 families was 237. These were distributed as shown in Table XIV.

In the absence of motor-driven machinery there can be no cotton without these work animals for plowing, at least. Thus it comes to be that a farmer's mule is as essential to his ability to sustain

TABLE XIII

Work Animals Owned

	One	Two	Three	Four	Five	Six	Seven	Total
Horses.....	38	3	1	2	0	0	0	44
Mules.....	119	54	4	5	0	1	1	184
Oxen......	6	3	0	0	0	0	0	9
Total....	163	60	5	7	0	1	1	237

himself and his family as land. But ownership of animals carries with it the obligation to feed them through the long period between seasons, and food, throughout the year, is difficult for the farmer to secure for his family. "My husband was groaning all night in his sleep. Say, 'Lord, that po' mule ain't had nothing to eat and I ain't got nothing to feed him.' He up this morning early, say he going to find something to do to get something to eat for dat mule."

For those who cannot own a mule or horse, it is possible to rent one. The cost varies from $15 to $25. Some landlords furnish work animals and make an adjustment on the crop. Between the Negro farmers there is a practice of exchanging services. The owner of an animal will plow for a person who does not own one, and in turn get his services in hoeing. The farm machinery and tools owned by these families were almost without exception the simple imple-

MAN AND MULE

"DIS OLE MULE LAK' ME—HE AIN'T MUCH GOOD NO MORE"

ments the type of which has been in service in the area for fifty or sixty years. As simple as these were, there were 299 families, or nearly half of them, who owned no farming implements at all. Table XV lists such as could be found. This table gives all of the tools actually owned by families. It is usually assumed that every farmer has a hoe and most of them a plow. This is not the case

TABLE XIV

FARM IMPLEMENTS OWNED

	One	Two	Three	Four	Five	Six	Seven	Eight	Nine	Ten	Eleven	Twelve	Total
Cotton planters....	21	....	1	....	....	....	....	....	....	....	....	....	22
Cultivators........	11	4	....	....	....	....	....	....	....	....	....	....	15
Fertilizers.........	6	....	....	....	....	....	....	....	....	....	....	....	6
Hoes.............	36	49	26	16	8	3	2	1	....	1	....	....	142
Mowing machines..	4	....	....	....	....	....	....	....	....	....	....	....	4
Pitchforks.........	4	1	....	....	....	....	....	....	....	....	....	....	5
Rakes............	9	7	1	....	....	....	....	....	....	1	....	....	18
Scrapes...........	1	....	2	....	....	....	....	....	....	....	....	....	3
Scudderstocks.....	9	2	1	....	....	....	....	....	....	....	....	....	12
Shovels...........	4	1	1	....	....	....	....	....	....	....	....	....	6
Singletrees........	2	....	....	....	....	....	....	....	....	....	....	....	2
Slanter...........	1	....	....	....	....	....	....	....	....	....	....	....	1
Stalk-cutters......	5	....	1	....	....	....	....	....	....	....	....	....	6
Sweeps...........	54	55	4	4	3	1	....	....	1	1	....	....	123
Turnplows........	114	102	19	24	6	4	2	....	....	....	1	1	273
Wagons...........	28	....	....	....	....	....	....	....	....	....	....	....	28
Total.........	309	221	56	44	17	8	4	1	1	3	1	1	666

with these tenants. It is expected that these tools will be provided with the land. The heavier farm implements are owned almost exclusively by the independent Negro farmers.

THE PRESSURE OF THE SYSTEM

When an owner or a tenant has borrowed cash or rations from the landlord or the bank and his crop fails, he risks losing a portion or all of his collateral, whether in crop, stock, tools, or anything usable. When everything is taken, he refers to himself as being "closed out." This is about as serious a misfortune as can occur to one who lives by the soil, and closing out a Negro tenant is not always a pleasant proceeding for the white landlord who has had dealings with these tenants. Sometimes they extend the credit. Sometimes they are forced by pressure against themselves to bear down upon the Negroes. Sometimes it is an impersonal procedure in which they are not aware of the suffering inflicted. When there is absentee ownership the blow descends swiftly and impersonally. But the bitterest complaints are against the cold process which relieves these tenants and small owners of their possessions because it can be done without fear of successful protest.

I made 5 bales of cotton and was due to pay 1½ bales for rent but they took it all. We all 'vanced from this same woman and they had taken her place and taken what the folks on this place that she had 'vanced made too. They took the place, debt and all. She had 'vanced us [his family] $75. Not a bit [in answer to a question as to whether they gave him anything back when they sold his cotton]. They jest took it all and went ahead. They took all the cotton and corn too and they took the mules, plows, and everything else. I made 'bout a hundred bushels of corn. I was buying one of the mules and renting the other from Mrs. S——, but they took both of them.

Unjust Settlements

It is, of course, impossible to determine the extent of exploitation of these Negro farmers, so long as the books are kept by the landlord, the sale price of cotton known only by him, and the cost and interest on rations advanced in his hands. In the case of many new tenants, however, who could have no standing indebtedness, their "suspicions" of being paid short were warranted. Said one tenant, "White folks take it when they git ready and you looking right at them."

We had 60 acres last year and paid $200 for rent and made 13 bales of cotton and turned hit all over. [This should have netted $400 at 10 cents.] The thing about hit, we ain't had no settlement. All we got last year was $51 in trade, they claimed. I ain't nothing like satisfied. I was settin' there at dinner looking at the house and the condition. I was settin' under that tree there last night studyin' 'bout the same thing. Me and my wife ain't had a string of nothing ter wear in two years.

'AIN'T MAKE NOTHIN', DON' SPECK NOTHIN' TIL' I DIE"

"DIS OLE FENCE NEED FIXIN' TOO"

Singleton Thompson's family, which included two married sons and their families, was renting from a woman planter. She sold them two mules, a wagon, and two plows, which were to be paid for in instalments. The first year they raised 10 bales of cotton, some corn, and hay for the mules. When the time for settlement came the woman took the 10 bales of cotton and presented a bill for $623.25, which they could not pay. She then took the mules and wagon, the hay, and 37 bushels of corn. The Thompsons moved and tried it again on another plantation.

The Adams family rented 37 acres and agreed to pay $100 rental. They raised, by exact count, 4 bales of cotton, 100 bushels of corn, 23 gallons of syrup, 300 pounds of pork, 25 bushels of peas. They had received $50 in allowances, and had been buying a mule for two years, the total cost of which was $115. The owner of the land took all the cotton and corn, and in addition the mule and their wagon, and informed them that they still owed $53. They asked for a "bill that said how for each thing." The owner refused to send this but instead became angry and informed them that they were $308.98 in the hole. The tenant said, "When you working on a white man's place you have to do what he says, or treat, trade, or travel. He jest closed out and got all we had."

Undoubtedly, the appearance of success, together with an uncertain appreciation of his proper social status, may provide annoyances which take on serious nature and in the end deprive the too successful Negro of his holdings. The story of one such experience is given in some detail because of its picturing of a combination of several elusive though not uncommon factors.

We all in the same condition here. This man call themselves giving us $6.00 to the plow but we hardly ever git it. . . . . My people made 43 bales of cotton last year and they didn't git a biscuit for Christmas morning. It ain't been a month this year what we ain't been hungry. I bought a little place and owed $500 more on it, and had two more years to finish paying for it. It cost me $1,350. . . . . They give me six months in jail for cutting two cords of wood closer to the line than I oughta been.

A man come down there where I was cutting and said, "Well, L——, what you doing, cutting wood?" and I told him yes, that I had to do fust one thing then another to help out. Then he told me to come walk down the swamp and show him where I been cutting, and I carried him down there and then he said, "You closer to the line then you ought to be, ain't you?" I told him that I bought that place and if I was close to the line I didn't know it, and if I was off I didn't know it. He said that B—— A—— [colored] said that I was cutting on somebody else's place. I asked him why didn't A—— come and tell me instead of going all the way to Tuskegee to tell somebody I was cutting 15 yards closer on the other man's place. I had two cords of wood cut. He said, "I tell you what to do; you take this wood and sell it and take the money to the bank on Saturday to Tuskegee."

I went on home, and in jest about a hour the man come up to my house, and I was shucking corn, and he said, "What did I tell you when I was here a while ago?" I told him what he said and told him that's what I was going to do. He said, "Would you mind walking out to the road with me?" I went out there with him and the sheriff was there and said, "Hello, old boy, still working hard? Get up in the car, I want to talk to you a while. L——, old boy, I been knowing you all my life, nearly, but did you know I got a warrant in my pocket for you?" I said, "What for?" and he said for cutting timber closer to the line without a permit. This other white man was standing there, and I said, I thought we had straightened that out as that man had told me to sell it to the Macon County Bank. The sheriff asked me why he was having me arrested if he told me that and he said, "Well, the land didn't b'long to him." Well, I said, "I haven't had any dinner yet and will you go by home with me?" He said he would go and wait for me to eat. When I got ready I asked my wife to give me 15 cents to get me some tobacco, but he told me not to bother with that cause he would buy me some.

He carried me on to Tuskegee and I saw that they was gonna lock me up, and I told them it wasn't no need for them to lock me up that I could make bond for cutting that little wood. He said, "Tell you the truth, people said we couldn't put you in jail, so you can sign up bond tomorrow." Well, the next morning I told them I was ready to sign up that bond and he said "I'm 'fraid they done run you bond up so high you can't make bond. It's $2,000." I said, "Man, I ain't killed nobody, how could you do that?" I could stand $1,000 but they kept me on in jail, calling themselves getting more than one case 'gainst me. I stayed in jail two months and they put my brother E—— in jail and J—— F——. Mr. W—— pulled my people out here by fooling them. He made them move off my place over here, and told me he was going to get me out of it. When the little case came up it was put off till May and then June and then July. They come in one day and said, "E——, did you know we was fixing to send you up to the penitentiary?" We went up to the courthouse and called the case against E—— R——, L—— R——, and J—— F——, and the judge said, "We going to give all you boys six months in jail." I got up and said, "Look here, Judge, will you 'low me to speak this one word?" He granted it. "Before you send me off, I want to ask you not to send E—— and J—— off 'cause they ain't guilty of nothing. Just give me ninety days of hard labor." They let E—— and J—— off. I went off and now I'm back to that tale-telling man what said he was going to help me.

When I got back, he said, "E——, you are looking mighty well. I didn't want you to go to the penitentiary." I said, "That's right, I'm back all right, and I come to see after my people, and get all straight and settle up with you and see about the cotton they made last year." Then he begins to start talking 'bout another crop and told me he had pooled all the cotton and couldn't sell it right then, but for me to go ahead and start another crop and he would pay my people. I was big-enough fool to believe he would be a man of his word, and I started another crop. I told him if he would settle with them for 10 cents a pound we would be satisfied, but he said he just couldn't get to it right now. He said that he believed we could make money this year, and we would settle this fall. . . . .

If you move to a place and find out you at the wrong place the best thing to do is to move, ain't it? These people been making enough cotton here to be double millionaries. There is one man over yonder who made 25 bales last year, and you know what he got out of that cotton? One ten-dollar suit; that is all he got after working all the year and making the white man 25 bales of cotton, and when they give you a suit they think you have made a lot.

The matter of government loans has offered opportunities for profit, in which some of the Negro farmers have failed to share, although they understood these loans to have been made in part on the basis of their tenantry and application.

I don't believe the white folks are doing right by these farms. We have no water, the place is in a bad condition, and we was supposed to get a federal loan. He had all the men come up to his house and sign for it, and said he would waive the rent 'cause he couldn't get it 'less he waived the rent. He signed for all the tenants and got $1,600, but he kept the money and made us pay the rent and all the loans we owed him, too. On top of that, he issued groceries for just 5 months last year and after that he give some $6.00 and some $7.00, and some $10. This year he just give some of them a few groceries and he's still holding to that money.

Few of these families handle any cash money. They get their food and a few clothes from the commissary or store, where advances are made. Two hundred and thirty-seven of the tenants and croppers received no advances. There were 67 tenants receiving advances in cash only; 39 were receiving advances in provisions only; and 21 were receiving advances in cash and provisions. These advances are mainly for food, but sometimes the farmer manages to get a few necessary clothes for his family. These are usually secured at the time they make settlement, or when settlements are not made they turn in their cotton in the fall.

An attempt was made to draw together the varied arrangements with landlords on which the tenants work, to estimate the yearly money earnings and the amount of cash handled. A very large number of these heads of families did not know how much they had earned and how much they had netted above current expenses for food and clothing, usually in the form of advances.

Twenty-six per cent of all the heads of families went into debt, four of these for more than $500; 61.7 per cent emerged without gain or loss—"broke even"; and 9.4 per cent registered profits. Fifty-six per cent of all the families had a gross annual income of less than $100. This, however, does not include varying amounts of food raised in their gardens and consumed by the families. This served principally for the summer and early fall and consisted of corn, potatoes, peas, and sorghum.

A measure of refinement is brought to the figures on income by sources of income. The largest group, 237, is that of tenants receiving no advances. Seventy per cent of these were receiving less than $100 per year in money. Fifteen, however, had gross incomes of more than $500. Fifty-seven per cent of those who rented homes received less than $100 and of the home-owners 69 per cent earned less than $100. At this period at least, home-ownership is no guaranty of greater earnings. The actual cash handled by the majority of families is between $70 and $90, normally in the form of advances, or loans out of which comes payment for a portion of the food; for clothing; for health; for education of the children; for church, lodge, and insurance dues; and for some amusement.

Branson and Dickey found in two Chatham County townships in North Carolina that black renters and croppers held property valued at about $305 per family, and the white renters and croppers $415 per family. The average property owned and cash per family handled during the year for each economic class was as shown in Table XVI.

TABLE XV*

AVERAGE PROPERTY OWNED AND CASH PER FAMILY HANDLED
DURING THE YEAR FOR EACH ECONOMIC CLASS

Economic Classes	Property Owned	Owned per Family	Total Cash Income	Cash per Family
135 white owners.............	$624,642	$4,627	$ 84,553	$626
41 black owners..............	93,856	2,407	21,708	597
38 white renters.............	19,999	526	9,525	251
18 white croppers............	3,279	426	1,993	153
66 black renters.............	27,016	400	19,053	289
36 black croppers............	4,113	123	2,777	197
329 farmers.............	$772,905	$2,349	$139,609	$424

* R. C. Branson, "Farm Tenancy in the Cotton Belt: How Farm Tenants Live," *Journal of Social Forces,* March, 1922.

That this is a more prosperous area with greater likelihood of Negroes acquiring ownership of property is evident in the fact that a fourth instead of a tenth of the Negro farmers are owners and they own three-fourths of all the Negro property.

David R. Coker, of Hartsville, South Carolina, estimated the average cash income on the cotton farms of the South at $600. This includes owners and tenants, whites and Negroes. Moreover, this is all gross income. The net is impossible to secure because of the lack of bookkeeping records of the various expenditures, and cost-accounting of any sort for general farm work. That the net is small, however, is evident in the extreme smallness of the gross.

The Dreary Cycle of Life

The weight of generations of habit holds the Negro tenant to his rut. Change is difficult, even in the face of the increasing struggle for survival under the old modes. One intelligent old farmer had sensed an important element of the natural conservation of these tenants. He said:

Farming is like gambling. If I get out I ought to get back and work a smaller farm next year. But you take an old farmer and if he ever gets out the hole with a good-size farm, instead of cutting down he'll get him another mule and take on some more. That's what keeps us down.

Such philosophy is for the man who retains some hope for improvement. The most dismal aspect of this situation is the air of resignation everywhere apparent.

If it wasn't the boll weevil it was the drought; if it wasn't the drought it was the rains.

One thing, we ain't got proper tools we ought to have. If you git any good land you have to buy things to make it good, and that takes lots of money, and if we had money to buy these things we wouldn't be so hard up.

What kills us here is that we jest can't make it cause they pay us nothing for what we give them, and they charge us double price when they sell it back to us.

Year after year of this experience for many of them and the hopelessness crystallizes itself at times into despair. "Ain't make nothing, don't speck nothing no more till I die. Eleven bales of cotton and man take it all. We jest work for de other man. He git everything." Mysticism and religion come to the rescue of some who add to hopelessness a fear of the future. "I axed Jesus to let me plant a little more. Every time I plant anything I say, 'Jesus, I ain't planting this for myself; I'm planting this for you to increase.'"

It is evident that all is not exploitation. The high level of illiteracy at times fuses its weight with a diffidence and ignorance which not only invite exploitation but make misunderstandings inevitable. Some families did not know the acreage they were working; the work to be done; the terms under which they accepted the land; the weight of their cotton yield. They were just working; if they came out they would spend the money from the very novelty of having it; if they stayed in the hole, it was only what they expected. "We always owe money and going to owe it, too; jest one month after another always something. That's the way it goes."

The plantation in theory was a capital investment for large-scale production under a continuing routine. Its purpose was not the encouragement of peasant proprietorship. The social relations, labor, mentality, and discipline fostered by it are at the same time reflected in its surviving forms and traditions, and in the continuing selection and molding of its tenant types. It demands an unquestioning obedience to its managerial intelligence; it demands the right to dictate and control every stage of cultivation; it cannot and does not tolerate a suggestion of independent status. Those Negro tenants who have in spirit revolted against its implication, or who have with praiseworthy intent sought to detach themselves from its grip by attaining an independent status, have felt the full force of its remaining strength. Nothing remains but to succumb or to migrate.

I am working myself to death, mighty near; been working mighty hard. I am trying to get straight. I made a bale and a half last year, but never got nothing out of it. I stayed in that little house over there and paid $60 and never got nothing last year, I worked and dug and never got a thing, and when I told him I wasn't making nothing he said, "Well, you are making money for me, ain't you?" And I said, "Well, I can quit." I moved from there, and he didn't know it. Folks went up there looking for Dick Richards and Dick Richards done moved.

Henry Robinson had been living in the same place for nineteen years, paying $105 a year rent for his land. He raises three bales of cotton a year, turns it all over, and continues to go deeper in debt. He said:

I know we been beat out of money direct and indirect. You see, they got a chance to do it all right, 'cause they can overcharge us and I know it being done. I made three bales again last year. He said I owed $400 at the beginning of the year. Now you can't dispute his word. When I said "Suh?" he said "Don't you dispute my word; the book says so." When the book says so and so you better pay it, too, or they will say "So, I'm a liar, eh?" You better take to the bushes too if you dispute him, for he will string you up for that.

I don't want them to hurt my feelings and I just have to take what they say, 'cause I don't want to go to the mines [convict labor] and I do want to live.

Another man complained:

I tried keeping books one year, and the man kept worrying me about it, saying his books was the ones he went by anyhow. And nothing you can do but leave. He said he didn't have no time to fool with no books. He don't ever give us no rent notes all the time. They got you 'cause you have to carry your cotton to his mill to gin and you better not carry your cotton nowhere else. I don't care how good your cotton is, a colored man's cotton is always second- or third-grade cotton if a colored man sells it. The only way you can get first prices for it is to get some white man to sell it for you in his name. A white man sold mine once, and got market price for it.

We haven't paid out to Mr. ——— in twelve years. Been in debt that long. See, when a fella's got a gun in your face you gotter take low or die.

To the Negro tenant the white landlord is the system; to the white landlord the capital of the banks is the system. The land-lord needs credit by which to advance credit to the tenants. The security of the landlord is in the mortgages on his land; the secu-rity of the tenant is the mortgage on the crops which he will raise. Because cotton lends itself best to this arrangement, cotton is over-produced and debts descend to obscure still another year of labor, and the vicious circle continues. In the desperate struggle both may lose, but the advantage is always with the white landlord. He dictates the terms and keeps the books. The demands of the system determine the social and economic relations, the weight of which falls heaviest upon those lowest down. There was a song which old women hummed as they hacked the earth with their hoes. The words were almost always indistinct but the mood of the tune, dreary and listless, fitted as naturally to the movement of their bodies as it did to the slick and swish of the earth under the blows of their hoes. One verse only was remembered by one of them, and it ran so:

> Trouble comes, trouble goes.
> I done had my share of woes.
> Times get better by 'n' by,
> But then my time will come to die.

Chapter IV

THE SCHOOL AND THE PEOPLE

EDUCATION OF PARENTS AND CHILDREN

LITERACY is not an asset in the plantation economy, and it was not only discouraged but usually forbidden. The belief that education spoiled the slave carried over with but little modification for many years into the belief that education spoils a field hand. The oldest members of the community are illiterate, and in those working relations which reveal least change from the past this lack has proved no important handicap. Reading and figuring carry elements of danger to established relations. Since the detailed direction of planting and the handling of accounts are the sphere of the planter, theoretically it is he who can profit most from the technique of literacy. Too much attention to reading about the outside, and particularly to figuring, on the part of Negro tenants, would surely make them less satisfied with their status and bring them into harsh conflict with the system. The need of enough education to read and figure arises largely among those families desirous of escaping from the dependent relationship under the old plantation system.

If figures can make the situation within this group clearer, 113, or 25 per cent, of the 460 male heads of families were illiterate and 113, or slightly less than 20 per cent, of the 579 women who were joint or sole heads of families. For convenience of study a rough division is made of the entire group of families studied into (*a*) illiterates, or persons who can neither read nor write; (*b*) persons who have had from one to five years of elementary education; (*c*) persons who have had five years of elementary training and more. The second category covers bare literates, those who can read a little but cannot write, those who can figure a little but cannot read. The third category seems very broad, but remembering that but few have had more than eighth-grade training, the breadth is only apparent. Of the 460 male heads of families, for example, only 27 had more than eight years of schooling. The group of bare literates contained about half of the male heads of families, and those with five years or more of schooling amounted to 117, or about the same proportion as the illiterates. The women were, on the whole, a trifle more advanced in this respect than the men. Thirty per cent of them fell in the class of bare literates, as compared with 50 per cent of the men, and 35 per cent of them had five years or more of education as compared with 25 per cent of the men. No correlation was observed between the education of husband and wife. In 44 families both were illiterate.

A further measure of the literacy of the group is in the books and periodicals read. There were 452 families, or a little over 73 per cent, in which there were no books of any sort, and 520, or about 85 per cent, in which there was no periodical or newspaper of any type. Where books were found they were, for the most part, a Bible, mail-order catalogues, almanacs, and the type of bright-colored volumes sold by book agents. In 140 homes books of some type were found, and in two of these homes there were as many as 100 volumes. Thirty-six families subscribed to a farm journal, 9 read a daily paper, and 7 received a weekly periodical.

Reading and writing are not a serious part of the routine of daily life for either adults or children. The oldest people easily excuse their illiteracy by explaining that "people didn't go to school in them days like they do now." Many of them have a hard common sense about their work and ordinary relations, and some, though former slaves and illiterate themselves, reveal a firm belief in the mysterious power of education to accomplish fuller freedom for their children. For them writing is a vital symbol, and the ability to write a key to power. Sarah Key was one such person. She was positive that there was good in this form of knowledge, because white folks had been so particular to keep it away from Negroes.

When I come along niggers didn't know nothing 'bout writing. Arch [a fellow-slave] was the only nigger 'round who could write. He done learned carrying the white folks' chillun to school. When Master found Arch could read he fainted. And he didn't find out till after the war. He said, "Arch, you done been to war wid me, slept wid me, and eat wid me. If I'd a knowed you could read I woulda done had your arm tuk off."

When come time to sign warrants to keep on working for Master after 'mancipation, the white folks would write our names down and we would make signs, 'cause we couldn't write. But Arch could write and that was when Master 'scovered it and fainted. He said, "All de niggers done sign to stay dis year, but you git off. You done stayed in war wid me four years and I ain't know that was in you. Now I ain't got no confidence in you."

In the next generation, however, although the tradition that an education was unnecessary persisted strongly, having effect in the failure or inability of many of them to send their children to school, these children on reaching the status of adults reflected a consciousness of the deficiency. A man in his forties confided: "My mother, when I was a baby, didn't seem to think I ought to have an education. I been embarrassed too. I said a many a time, if my mother had sent me to school I would a been a man."

Those persons now in their thirties and forties who went to the schools of the section did so fitfully and during the months when they could be spared from the farming. The fact that women were less useful than men in certain types of cotton cultivation, for example, may account for the larger aggregate of months in school, and their consequent advantage in education.

All that is remembered of this period of schooling is Webster's blue-back speller, used in school; the almanac and Bible; and the crudely severe discipline associated with instruction. "I studied the blue-back speller, too. I can remember just as well when we used to go to school with the almanac. That's all we had to read out of." Some of the regrets of the grown-ups concern their own rather than their parents' early disinclinations toward education.

My folks wanted me to go to school, but I was scared of whuppings so I never would go. I uster hide behind the pines 'stid of going to school.

All the others what went got good learning. Some of them school-teachers. The teacher whupped me once, and I didn't want to go back no more. When my mother found out I wasn't going she whupped me till I like to had spasms. She knocked a hole in my head. After that she kept me home and made me learn to cook, milk the cows, and sew for the other children.

There is a wistfulness about some of the reflections on the lack of education. A tenant from one plantation said: "The world wasn't in light when I was growing up like it is now. Just ignorance. I hated it after the world come into more light." This new desire has come to some late in life, and they have tried vainly and pathetically to do something about it. It is exceedingly difficult to pick up an education outside of the classroom, and there are limits to both the age and the size of pupils in the lowest grades, and to the time for going to school once one has grown up. The sensitiveness to educational deficiencies becomes a fairly reliable index to changing attitudes toward their surroundings, and a desire for general improvement in their status. "I fuss with my people in my sleep now 'cause they didn't give me no schooling. I bought me a book and tried to study but my eyes is getting so bad I can't do nothing like that."

By far the greater number of the middle-aged illiterates and bare literates explain that they did not go to school because they had to work. For some of them it was a matter of pride that they began their working life so early, and their compensation is the possession of a sufficient "mother-wit" for the ordinary problems of their life. "I can't read writing but I got good mother-wit" carries with it little apology for illiteracy. A Negro farmer who operates a small store boasted: "I ain't been to school, but they can't cheat me none figuring." For others this deficiency is important and one for which they are inclined to blame work. "I didn't git nowhere in school. I'm sorry to say I had to work all my life, and I didn't git to go."

The most pronounced change in attitude is now observed among the present parents of the youngest and last generation, who view these values over a wide range. "I tries to send my boy to school 'cause I guess it's your brains now what carries you through this world. . . . . I used to think it was disgraceful for a married woman to taught school. It's not that way now."

One chief element in the zeal for more education for their children is the desire to escape a dismal economic plight. Alvin Boyd, in course of explaining his personal situation, revealed the future plans for his daughter which had been carefully developed by him. He was making a desperate effort to get out of debt and stay out. "We ain't had no advances and I ain't mortgaging nothing this year. Buying my own groceries and feeding ourselves. It ain't much, but I'm tired of mortgaging my family. That's just the reason I'm trying to prepare my little girl."

Of our 612 families, 160 had no children, 146 had children, but none in school, and 276 families had 622 children in school. There were 1,344 whose ages were known among the 412 families with children. Of these, 1,041 were of school age. The 622 in school were 59.7 per cent of the children of school age, somewhat more than half. Some of those out of school are now too old for their grades; some, though still young, were married or unmarried mothers with children of their own to take care of; and still others, also young, were too seriously needed in the field to be spared for school. Large families have on occasion decided arbitrarily to educate two or three of their children and let the others work, attempting thereby to serve at the same time the ends of both work and education.

Although being registered in a school does not mean regular attendance, there were many children who could not go to school at all. Children in the family over eight are considered full farm hands, and only in exceptional cases were they found attending school. Again, children do not begin school until they are six years old. Taking into account the children between six and nineteen who were actually present and living in families, 553 were enrolled and 229 were not enrolled in school. After passing fourteen they began to drop out. In the families generally the youngest school ages were not in school. The figures would run as shown in Table XVII. In the total number of children of school age who

133

should be in school there were four whose grades could not be learned and three who though colored were allowed to attend a white school on one of the plantations. The interruption of school work as well as the character of instruction and for one reason or the other the inability of the children to be advanced in grades are suggested in the grade-standing of 553 children of various ages who are in school.

TABLE XVI

Age	No.
Six-year-olds out of school	48
Seven-year-olds out of school	23
Eight-year-olds out of school	7
Nine-year-olds out of school	10
Ten-year-olds out of school	5
Eleven-year-olds out of school	7
Twelve-year-olds out of school	11
Thirteen-year-olds out of school	5
Fourteen-year-olds out of school	8
Fifteen-year-olds out of school	11
Sixteen-year-olds out of school	24
Seventeen-year-olds out of school	26
Eighteen-year-olds out of school	25
Nineteen-year-olds out of school	19
Total	229

The usual period during which school is kept open is October to May. Attendance fluctuates by months to such an extent as to keep the school work seriously disorganized and render impossible very consistent learning on the part of the children. There is fullest attendance when children are not needed in the field. Other factors, however, enter in to affect school attendance. Lack of sufficient clothing, and in winter particularly the lack of shoes, keeps children away. Distance is another and extremely important factor. They walk usually from one to five miles and back each school day, for there is no service of bus conveyance such as is provided for white children of the county. At one school two children from the same family walked fourteen miles a day. Again, the cost of books, the special fees to supplement the teachers' pay—"for teacher's board," the families explain—keep the numbers down. The teachers, although practically dependent upon

TABLE XVII

Age-Grades of Children of 612 Macon County Families in School

Age	Grade I	Grade II	Grade III	Grade IV	Grade V	Grade VI	Grade VII	Grade VIII	Grade IX	Grade X	Grade XI	Grade XII	Total
6	16	....	....	....	....	....	....	....	....	....	....	....	16
7	42	3	2	....	....	....	....	....	....	....	....	....	47
8	39	14	2	1	....	....	....	....	....	....	....	....	56
9	27	11	3	3	1	1	....	....	....	....	....	....	47
10	19	16	9	5	2	....	....	....	....	....	....	....	51
11	7	11	7	8	5	1	....	....	....	....	....	....	39
12	11	9	14	8	8	2	3	....	....	....	....	....	55
13	7	10	9	9	3	2	2	....	1	....	....	....	43
14	6	3	7	8	5	7	5	1	....	....	....	....	42
15	1	....	5	6	9	11	5	1	1	1	....	....	40
16	....	3	7	8	10	11	5	1	3	3	....	1	53
17	....	1	4	6	4	7	5	4	2	....	2	....	35
18	....	....	....	3	....	5	3	4	1	1	1	....	18
19	1	1	1	3	....	....	....	....	1	....	....	2	9
20	....	....	....	....	....	....	....	....	....	....	....	....	0
21	....	....	....	....	....	....	....	....	....	2	....	....	2
Total...	176	82	71	68	47	48	28	11	9	7	3	3	553
50 per cent..	8.75	10.8	12.78	14.00	14.9	16.0	15.8	17.6	16.8	16.8	17.66	19.3	.....
Per cent over age...	67.1	79.3	88.7	86.7	82.9	91.6	82.1	91.0	77.8	42.9	33.3	66.6	.....
Per cent under age...	0.0	0.0	2.8	1.4	2.1	2.0	0.0	0.0	11.1	0.0	0.0	33.3	.....
Per cent at age.	32.9	20.7	8.4	11.9	14.9	6.2	17.8	9.0	11.1	57.1	66.6	1.0	.....

these fees, do not always feel disposed to insist on them, particularly when it means losing the child because his parents could not provide the sums required. There are other occasions bringing urgent demands for money which the ordinary tenant families do not have. The introduction of sanitation, for example, sometimes means payment by the families for the building of approved toilets. If the schools are fortunate enough to get a competent teacher with ideas and a program, the extra items, such as simple playground equipment, must be privately purchased by the community.

Two of the schools attended by the children of these families were held in a small church. One of the teachers was a young woman of about ninth-grade standing; the other, an older woman, crude but resourceful, was passionately devoted to the education of these children, but handicapped both by her own deficient background and by the lack of physical equipment, including a schoolhouse.

The first Rosenwald School was built in Alabama in an adjoining county, inaugurating a vast school program which eventually included all of the southern states. The extent of schooling possible in Macon County may be roughly indicated by the figures on expenditures for teachers' salaries in the county. In 1930 there were in the entire county 8,580 educables, 1,435 white and 7,145 Negroes. For the 1,435 white children there was expended $57,385 and for the 7,145 Negro children $27,813. Alabama is, of course, one of the states with least ability to support education, and the expenditure for white children is seriously below the standard for the country at large. Moreover, although the ratio of expenditure has remained about the same over the last fifteen years, the amounts spent had been somewhat increased. In 1915 the total amount spent for 9,136 children was $28,792, of which sum $19,247 went for teachers' salaries for 1,283 white children and $9,545 for teachers' salaries for 7,853 Negro children.

THE INFLUENCE OF SCHOOLING ON SOCIAL CHANGES

One of the ways in which isolation is broken down is by literacy. Formal schooling both introduces, and is an evidence of, the influence of the new and presumably higher standards from the outside for the group. In the quite confusing mixture of influences marking the life of the families in this community, it transpires that years of schooling provide an index of a sort for measuring important social differences, as well as changes. It is one of the striking observations of this study that parents' education is correlated with differences among families with respect to (1) size of family, (2) economic self-sufficiency, (3) the numbers of stillbirths and miscarriages, (4) infant mortality, (5) the amount of sickness, and (6) the attitudes of families toward themselves and toward life.

The number of children in the families shows significant variations according to the education of the wife. It appears that the

TABLE XVIII

NUMBER OF FAMILIES WITH SPECIFIED NUMBER OF CHILDREN IN SCHOOL

Education of Mother	Un-known	None	One	Two	Three	Four	Five	Six	Seven	Total
Dead or away.	0	22	3	2	3	0	3	0	0	35
Unknown.....	0	30	8	8	5	1	0	0	0	52
Illiterate......	1	78	15	10	6	0	3	0	0	113
Four years or less........	4	91	42	16	17	8	6	5	0	189
Five years or more.......	4	116	36	25	18	13	9	2	2	225
Total.....	9	337	104	61	49	22	21	7	2	612

educational status of the husband or male head of the house had no appreciable effect on the number of children in the home. In 49, or 43.3 per cent, of the 113 families in which the wife was illiterate, there were no children present. In the 189 families where the mother had a fourth-grade education or less, 49, or 26 per cent, of the families were without children. In the 225 families with mothers or the female heads with a fifth-grade education or more, 25 per cent of the families showed no children present. In families where the wives were illiterate, there was on an average of 1.4 child to a family when all families were considered and 2.4 children when only those with children were considered. In the families where wives had an education of five or more grades, there was on an average of 2.5 children to a family when all families were considered or 3.3 children to a family when only those families with children were used as a basis. The reason for the few children in the illiterate families is apparently the higher death-rate and the number of broken homes among the illiterate families.

Taking into account only those families with children, 29, or 45.3 per cent, of the 64 families in which the wives were illiterate had no children in school; 42, or 30 per cent, of the 140 families with women who had at most a fourth-grade education had no children in school; and 60, or 35 per cent, of the families with the

TABLE XIX

NUMBER OF FAMILIES WITH STATED NUMBERS OF CHILDREN

EDUCATION OF MOTHER	CHILDREN												
	None	One	Two	Three	Four	Five	Six	Seven	Eight	Nine	Ten	Eleven	Total
Dead or away........	18	2	5	3	1	1	0	1	2	0	0	0	33
Unknown...........	17	13	5	6	2	4	1	1	0	0	0	1	52
Illiterate............	49	23	15	13	3	5	3	0	1	0	1	0	113
Four years or less....	49	44	26	18	13	13	10	8	5	3	0	0	189
Five years or more...	58	45	32	22	22	17	12	11	2	3	2	1	225
Total..........	189	127	83	62	41	40	28	21	10	6	3	2	612

most education had no children in school. A better comparison of these three types of families in regard to the schooling of the children is obtained by getting the percentage of all the children in each group in school. There were 165 children in the 64 families with illiterate mothers. Sixty-eight, or 41 per cent, of these children were in school. There were 450 children in the 146 families with female heads who had four years of schooling or less. Two hundred and seventeen, or 48.2 per cent, of these children were in school. There were 562 children in the 169 families in which the female head had a fifth-grade education or more. Two hundred and fifty-three, or 45 per cent, of these children were in school. Further speculation would lead one to conclude that since the rearing of children is chiefly the task of the wife, better education on the

138

part of the mother should insure the child greater care of its physical needs as well as hold the child to the family group.

The number of stillbirths and miscarriages in these families is a significant index to the health of the people as well as to the rate of survival. In the 113 families in which the mother was illiterate, stillbirths and miscarriages occurred in 44.3 per cent of the families. When the wife had a fourth-grade education or less, these accidents occurred in about the same proportion. But when the wife had a fifth-grade or more of education, stillbirths and mis-

TABLE XX

NUMBER OF STILLBIRTHS AND MISCARRIAGES IN RELATION TO
YEARS OF SCHOOLING OF MOTHER

Education of Mother	Un-known	None	One	Two	Three	Four	Five	Six	Seven	Eight	Nine	Ten or More	Total
Dead or away......	4	24	4	1	0	0	0	0	0	0	0	0	33
Unknown..........	1	29	8	7	2	1	0	1	2	0	1	0	52
Illiterate..........	2	63	19	16	6	4	1	2	0	0	0	0	113
Four years or less...	3	104	41	19	10	6	2	1	0	2	1	0	189
Five years or more..	2	148	45	11	7	7	3	1	0	0	0	1	225
Total..........	12	368	117	54	25	18	6	5	2	2	2	1	612

carriages had occurred in only 34 per cent of the families. The average number of stillbirths for the families having had stillbirths showed the same variations for these three classes. The average number of stillbirths and miscarriages for the illiterate mothers was 2.1 children and the same figure for the mothers with a fourth-grade or less education. In the families where the mother had a fifth-grade or more education, the average number of stillbirths and miscarriages was 1.8 children.

In the case of 30 male farm-owners, 7 were illiterate, 11 had four years of schooling or less, and 13 had five years of schooling and more. Once a farmer with children finds himself with a meager surplus, he faces the question of schooling for the children, and if there is some small beginning in education for the parents, the desire is moved to carry it further in the children. One woman said:

My husband make plenty of something to eat all the time. We spend right smart for clothes; I reckon we spent out $40 for clothes and shoes last year. . . . . My daughter takes some magazines, but I read them. My daughter is down in Tuskegee taking college. She teaches down about Uriah and go to college in summer. . . . . My son repeated the six grade 'cause I haven't got him off to high school yet.

There were few farm-owners who either did not have some education themselves or were not attempting to provide it for their children, and with equal frequency it was observed that the beginnings of family life founded upon advanced standards with respect to morals, responsibility, or health were associated with interest in schooling.

It was not surprising that a farm-owner with a family of children, "all mine and my wife's," had learned his trade of carpentry at Tuskegee and had a daughter in school in Montgomery in training for nursing. Said one proud father: "I didn't get the chance to go to school very much, but the chillun dey all fine scholars; can figure and write. Read this from the Bible for 'em, 'Lizabeth. . . . . Waid a minute; I will show you a picture of my gal Mattie Belle. She in school."

The account of one woman who had advanced a full measure beyond her slave parents is a good and full example. Her house, which she had inherited from her father, stood out among her neighbors like something grossly out of place. It was well painted and screened, with a comfortable and well-arranged living-room. She herself was alert and intelligent although there were few congenial families around her.

My father bought this place and left it here for me. We were here when they first began to run cars and they used to mire up right here in front of the house. My father used to make extra money pulling cars out with his mules. . . . . Things certainly change, don't they? He didn't do anything but farm. He came up under the yoke of slavery. I went to Tuskegee and Spelman, too. I have 46 acres here and pay $18.70 taxes. I eat vegetables mostly. I guess that's why I am healthy. I haven't had a doctor in so long I can't remember when it was. My father has been dead eight years now, and I just live here by myself. Perhaps some man would like to have the property but they don't seem to want me, so I just let them alone.

Farm-ownership makes a difference in numbers of children in school and the number of years which these children are retarded. Children of owners make a better showing than the average for the schools. Then there are children who, though in families, are not in normal family units: grandchildren, adopted children, illegitimate children being reared by relations or friends of the mother, children from homes in which one parent is missing. Such children when separated from the totals make a poorer showing than the average.

TABLE XXI

YEARS OVER AGE OF ALL CHILDREN

Years over Age	Grade I	Grade II	Grade III	Grade IV	Grade V	Grade VI	Grade VII	Grade VIII	Grade IX	Grade X	Grade XI	Grade XII	Total
1	39	11	9	8	8	2	5	1	3	0	1	2	89
2	27	16	7	8	3	7	5	1	2	1	....	....	77
3	19	11	14	9	5	11	5	4	1	0	....	....	79
4	7	9	9	8	9	12	5	4	1	0	....	....	64
5	11	10	7	6	10	7	3	0	0	2	....	....	56
6	7	3	5	8	4	5	....	....	....	....	....	....	32
7	6	0	7	6	....	....	....	....	....	....	....	....	19
8	1	3	4	3	....	....	....	....	....	....	....	....	11
9	0	1	0	3	....	....	....	....	....	....	....	....	4
10	0	0	1	....	....	....	....	....	....	....	....	....	1
11	0	1	....	....	....	....	....	....	....	....	....	....	1
12	1	....	....	....	....	....	....	....	....	....	....	....	1
Total...	118	65	63	59	39	44	23	10	7	3	1	2	434
Average.	2.85	3.44	4.07	4.30	3.58	3.68	2.82	3.1	4.0	....	....	....	3.42

Of 37 children of owners between six and nineteen years of age, only 2 were out of school and these 2 were sixteen and seventeen years old. The group of children from the broken or irregular homes totaled 238, and of these 64, or 36 per cent, were out of school, while 46, or about 15 per cent, were normal or above. The striking fact is that when all children are considered, the average child is 3.42 years retarded; when children in broken or irregular families are taken separately, the average is 3.54 years retarded. When children of farm-owners are separately considered, the average is 2.78 years retarded. There is little difference between the

141

TABLE XXII

Years over Age of Farm-Owners' Children

Years over Age	Grade I	Grade II	Grade III	Grade IV	Grade V	Grade VI	Grade VII	Grade VIII	Grade IX	Grade X	Grade XI	Grade XII	Total
1.........	4	3	1	2	3	1	0	0	0	0	0	1	15
2.........	3	2	0	0	1	1	1	0	0	1	.....	.....	9
3.........	0	0	0	0	0	0	0	0	.....	.....	.....	.....	0
4.........	0	1	0	0	0	0	0	1	.....	.....	.....	.....	1
5.........	0	2	1	0	1	1	.....	.....	.....	.....	.....	.....	5
6.........	0	1	1	2	0	1	.....	.....	.....	.....	.....	.....	5
7.........	0	0	1	.....	.....	.....	.....	.....	.....	.....	.....	.....	1
8.........	.....	.....	.....	.....	.....	.....	.....	.....	.....	.....	.....	.....	.....
9.........	.....	.....	.....	.....	.....	.....	.....	.....	.....	.....	.....	.....	.....
10.........	.....	.....	.....	.....	.....	.....	.....	.....	.....	.....	.....	.....	.....
11.........	.....	.....	.....	.....	.....	.....	.....	.....	.....	.....	.....	.....	.....
12.........	.....	.....	.....	.....	.....	.....	.....	.....	.....	.....	.....	.....	.....
Total...	10	27	19	14	10	14	.....	.....	.....	.....	.....	.....	37
Average.	1.42	3.0	4.72	3.5	2.0	3.5	.....	.....	.....	.....	.....	.....	2.78

TABLE XXIII

Years over Age of Children for Broken and Irregular Homes

Years over Age	Grade I	Grade II	Grade III	Grade IV	Grade V	Grade VI	Grade VII	Grade VIII	Grade IX	Grade X	Grade XI	Grade XII	Total
1.........	9	2	2	1	2	0	4	0	1	0	1	1	23
2.........	8	5	7	0	0	2	1	0	2	1	.....	.....	25
3.........	4	4	2	0	0	4	2	2	0	0	.....	.....	18
4.........	1	4	2	3	3	5	0	1	1	1	.....	.....	20
5.........	1	9	2	4	1	2	2	.....	.....	.....	.....	.....	21
6.........	2	2	2	3	3	.....	.....	.....	.....	.....	.....	.....	12
7.........	0	0	3	1	1	.....	.....	.....	.....	.....	.....	.....	5
8.........	0	0	2	1	.....	.....	.....	.....	.....	.....	.....	.....	3
9.........	0	0	0	1	.....	.....	.....	.....	.....	.....	.....	.....	1
10.........	.....	.....	.....	.....	.....	.....	.....	.....	.....	.....	.....	.....	.....
11.........	.....	.....	.....	.....	.....	.....	.....	.....	.....	.....	.....	.....	.....
12.........	.....	.....	.....	.....	.....	.....	.....	.....	.....	.....	.....	.....	.....
Total...	25	26	22	14	10	13	9	3	.....	.....	.....	.....	128
Average.	2.32	3.73	4.04	5.35	4.4	3.53	2.44	3.33	.....	.....	.....	.....	3.53

average-family children and the broken-family children so far as the record of these children is concerned—a fact which seems to be supported by the similarity of both of these groups under the identical pressure of the prevailing economic system. The difference becomes notable between the owners and the other groups with an advantage of about eight months of schooling in favor of children of owners. It is consistent with this trend that the child most advanced for age (a thirteen-year-old in the ninth grade) came from a family with the highest recorded family income for the year.

The irony of the situation seems to be in the fact that the life of a tenant in the economic system under which they live is not always congenial when he begins to broaden his horizon. The more alert and ambitious of the men seem to drift away to southern or northern cities. A few of the women also leave. This may explain why the women still living in the county represent a level of education slightly above the men. Curiously, when income of families is divided according to the grades—illiterate, little education, education above the fifth grade—the illiterates were at the bottom of the scale, those with more than fifth-grade education ranked next, and those with little education ranked highest. For example, in the four highest-income brackets—$200–$299, $300–$399, $400–$499, $500 and over—there were 19 illiterates, 26 with five years or less of schooling, and 24 with more than five years of schooling. In the highest of these, $500 and over, there was a practical advantage for those with five and six years of schooling but a pronounced falling-off of those with eight years and more. If the logic of these figures is to be followed, it appears that the environment is less hostile to men with little education than to men with enough to read and write easily. Practically considered, the most successful families financially are those who are neither too illiterate to take advantage of their surroundings nor have more schooling than is demanded by their dependent economic situation. They would be expected to thrive best in an environment that bred few landowners, tolerated few innovations, and placed a penalty upon too much book-learning.

Occasionally a tragedy gives dramatic vividness to the conflict arising under the system. Henry Harding had tried for eighteen years to get somewhere. He studied and read and tried to apply his knowledge, but without effect. Every time he tried to help himself his situation tightened. But a tenant trying to support a family on fifteen acres and send some of his children to school has a small chance. He began to brood. His wife, Mary Harding, told briefly his story:

My husband was an intelligent man. He nearly finished Tuskegee. He had worked hard but we had lost all we had. On his fiftieth birthday, the twenty-fourth of November, we worked in the field all day and he kept saying he wouldn't be here long, and he wanted us to hurry up and get the cotton picked. It made me nervous. Every time he'd come home I'd send the boy behind him 'cause I didn't know what he might do. We took some potash from him one night. He wouldn't eat no supper. When I got through supper I was reading a "true story." I likes to read *True Stories* and he knowed so much he took it from me and told me ter stop reading that junk. Hit was on Thanksgiving Day and they was bringing my girl home from Tuskegee School to visit. I always will believe that he lost his mind, for he got outta bed and wandered out dere in the field. Then he got holt of some more potash and et it, and died and never said what he lost hisself fer. He just suicided and killed hisself.

The influence of Tuskegee extended into the community and in an interesting manner. In point of distance this institution was from ten to twenty miles removed from the families of this study. There was also a cultural and social distance. There were members of the community who had attended school, learned trades, and returned. Booker T. Washington was remembered and liked by some of the older individuals. He was twice referred to in course of comment upon themselves and their interests. In Sambo the cabins had been whitewashed in preparation for a visit from him about twenty years ago. He came—a great man with a personality which took them in, which understood them, and which they could understand. On another occasion an old woman had remembered an antipathy which he expressed toward fishing as a recreation. He had said that it was a lazy man's sport, and she confessed to having adopted his prejudice. The extension program of the institution had registered at points, particularly around Shorter. The wife of a farmer in Shorter was just coming home on one of our visits. She had been out on one of the canning-club meetings. Said she: "You just come in time or I wouldn't be here. I just come from the Farmers' Canning Club. We sure had good eatin's today. We done stuffed salads with beets, raw cabbage, and made this here mayonnaise to go on it. You know Miss D——, I reckon?

In one instance there was reference to an association which existed with the purpose of aiding Negroes in the purchase of farms. This association was not active now. One Negro had taken in a considerable amount of land on default, and was attempting to manage his tenants under more approved regulations. He had many complaints about the reaction of the Negro tenants to the relaxed discipline and was then very discouraged with prospects generally. There were two teachers in the community who had studied at Tuskegee.

Beyond this touch of intimacy there were those who "went up to commencement." Some of them had relatives in the school; others went to see. The town of Tuskegee, which is the county seat, shared interest to some extent with the school. It is for the horse-and-wagon travelers a good day's journey, and few of them have animals of their own or conveyances of any sort.

Students from this section who had come back to live apparently found it extremely difficult to escape the main currents of life in the community. But most often they were to be found among that small group that aimed at self-improvement and economic independence, although against manifest odds. Ralph Roy went out from the community to Tuskegee, where he learned the trade of blacksmithing. He belonged to a family in which five grown brothers and four sisters lived together in one house. Each son cultivated a stipulated amount of land on a co-operative basis. The farm was left to them by the father, since dead. The home of the Roys was one of the few places where the kitchen was not used as a bedroom. In the kitchen there was a crudely boxed-off space between the stove and a table which was intended as a dining compartment. The table inside was neatly covered with red oil-

145

cloth. But the five sons and four daughters slept in the two rooms. When Ralph came back from school he courted a young girl, and after a period a child was born. The young woman said nothing of marriage. She says it did not occur to her at the time. He was having some difficulty getting established in his trade. But it disturbed Ralph, and he urged her to marry him and she did. They have been living together pleasantly since. He has his blacksmith shop on the place and spends most of his time in it, although work is slow. Blacksmithing has been steadily declining and he has found it necessary to follow the pattern of the community in its economic life, by renting a plot of farm land, and for this he pays a rental of fifty dollars annually.

Thomas Woods "left off in Junior class in Tuskegee way back when it wasn't but four or five buildings there." His father had begun buying their present farm in 1890, and had paid a considerable amount on it. When the father died the son continued the payments, but they lost the property without ever knowing how much money had been paid. He still lives on the place, however. Thomas Woods had learned carpentry at Tuskegee. Although he had lost his home, he had retained certain new desires and interests acquired through contact with the institution. He rented land instead of working on shares. The year before he made eight bales of cotton which sold for $40 a bale, but when he had paid his debts he was $140 "in the hole." However, instead of getting advances from a planter he borrowed the money from the bank. This proved rather expensive because "the interest eats you up." He had painted and "rehauled" his home; they have an automobile—though it does not run. Unlike the mass of tenants he knew what was wrong, although he could not do very much about it. He knew that in order to raise more from the soil it would be necessary to put more labor, tools, fertilizer, and work animals into cultivation, and that one had to have money for these instruments of production; that if everyone did this there would be a surplus crop which would put all these at naught. "A poor colored person," he said, "just got to come up by the hardest." He and his wife are not only legally married, but have not been separated

146

from each other for more than a month during their entire married life of thirty years, for any reason. The wife said: "Only time I ever stayed away from my husband was a month I was in Dayton, Ohio. I just stayed that long 'cause they all said I wouldn't stay."

Moses Green learned the trade of carpentry and bricklaying at Tuskegee, over twenty years ago. This is what he said about himself:

I got seven children and they're all mine and my wife's.

Pretty big family now since times are so hard, but I manage to get along. I do little carpenter work for the white and colored folks out here whenever there is any to be done. Didn't get much work last year 'cause people ain't building no houses. I guess I did 'bout $100 worth of carpenter work last year. I learned my trade at Tuskegee, carpentry and bricklaying. Don't get much bricklaying to do.

It's hard to say just how much money I spend for clothes. Got such a big family. Last year I bought a suit for $50, so I won't have to buy none this year. My wife bought a suit last year for $15, and my daughter bought one for $40. That's the one I told you goes to school in Montgomery. Come here, Marguerite, and tell about your school.

MARGUERITE: I've been going to school in Montgomery for three years, taking nurse training. Ain't had but six months' training. The first year I was sick and had to come home; the second year I was sick and stayed there in the hospital; and this year I didn't get but six months' training. I stay sick all the time, but I'm determined to be a nurse. I don't know just what my trouble is; the doctor calls it some kind of funny name. [Girl tried to think for fully ten minutes but could not give the name. She didn't mention how the illness affected her.]

MOTHER: I think they done worked her too hard.

FATHER: I didn't make much of a crop last year. I made a bale of cotton and got enough to pay back the $40 on the government loan. The government loan works this way: The government man comes out to see you and he takes a synopsis of what you have. The owner then waives the rent until the government is paid, then he has to put in for his part afterwards. If you don't make anything the government carries it over. They [the government] deal with the man straight, not the landlord. They leave a government man who comes around and notifies each man when the money is due.

I worked with the Bradley Lumber Company from November to June of this year. Got $60 every two weeks. Worked till the company went busted, but I've got to do a cash business this year 'cause I made enough money when I was working.

Beyond the sense of sharing the new values of the Institute, there is indication of further social distance. The spirit of race consciousness has entered and identifies itself with color consciousness in a manner that places the Tuskegee school in a different world of relations. A man who hopes to send his son to school expressed some apprehensions about his ability to fit into the color scheme.

I wants to send my son to school as far as he can go, but somebody's got to speak a word for him up there at Tuskegee. That school ain't got no race pride. They ain't so much on the black ones. All them black men up to Tuskegee marries yellow women, if they're able to keep 'em. You know yellow women want more than black ones. That's the reason me and my wife ain't never separated—she's good and black. . . . . I suppose if I'd a gone to Tuskegee and had schooling I'd a married a yellow woman too. . . . . So many colored folks only want to be with white folks. All of them Tuskegee people is like that.

It was evident in this case that there was some confusion between color and culture, and a conviction that to get along one must "either look like white or act like white." The same man, when talking to a Negro visitor of his own complexion but of considerably different education and cultural background, asked, "What nationality is you? You looks colored, but you don't talk like it, so I ain't sure. Do you love colored folks?" Then ruminating further on the question of color he confided: "I got a cousin. Her pappy is white. Old Dr. ———. Everybody knows that. Well, he sent her off to school. Now she's married some white-looking nigger and teaches school. She warn't no better'n me but just 'cause she's white-skinned she got ahead. I ain't never done nothing in my life but I've tried to live right and do good."

The Education of Parents by Children

Children of parents who are zealous to have the mystery of letters mastered have a new sentimental value for their parents. They have the key to power, and the great pride of these parents is to hear them read, not so much because they are interested in what is read as in the demonstrated ability to understand a printed

148

page. "Come here, Markus," a parent shouted, "and let the man hear how you can read." It is the children who are now intrusted by their families to keep the ages, because "their minds are stronger." They read the letters that occasionally come in from relatives in distant parts of the country, and bring home the gossip from the school. The children become, thus, a link with the new culture. New notions of sanitation and hygiene percolate into the old homes: the value of screening, the dangers of infection from careless and ignorant habits, the hazard of open wells and careless waste disposal. The slow rate of transition, generally, through this medium appears to be due quite as much to the inadequacy of the present local elementary schools as to the inability or unwillingness of the older members of the group to abandon their traditional ways.

Chapter V

RELIGION AND THE CHURCH

THE CHURCH AS A SOCIAL INSTITUTION

THE church is the one outstanding institution of the community over which the Negroes themselves exercise control, and because it stands so alone in administering to their own conception of their needs, its function is varied. The religious emotions of the people demand some channel of formal expression, and find it in the church. But more than this, the church is the most important center for face-to-face relations. It is in a very real sense a social institution. It provides a large measure of the recreation and relaxation from the physical stress of life. It is the agency looked to for aid when misfortune overtakes a person. It offers the medium for a community feeling, singing together, eating together, praying together, and indulging in the formal expressions of fellowship. Above this it holds out a world of escape from the hard experiences of life common to all. It is the agency which holds together the subcommunities and families physically scattered over a wide area. It exercises some influence over social relations, setting up certain regulations for behavior, passing judgments which represent community opinion, censuring and penalizing improper conduct by expulsion.

The authority of the church here does not appear to be as strong as in certain other Negro communities, nor does it seem to have, in its disciplinary restraints, that immediacy which could make it most effective in controlling conduct.

The notable distinction in growths is between the church as a social center, the church as an agency of social control, and the church as the medium of spiritual expansion. With respect to the first, there has been a pronounced development; with respect to the second, the church is less effective than in other communities with a different organization of Negro life; with respect to the last, there is a widening gap between doctrine and behavior which leaves the traditional doctrine empty and unconvincing in relation to the normal currents of life.

It is respectable to belong to church, and practically all families retain some degree of connection with it. Only 17 of the 612 families had no church connection. The pattern of religious observance was borrowed, like many of their other cultural traits, from their earlier associations with whites under slavery. Despite the fact that they now control very largely their own religious organizations, there have been few adaptations to the changing exigencies of their own life. The satisfactions derived from this institution, apart from such objective indications of social response as could be observed, are questions related to the character of the religious experiences of the group with which this account does not presume to deal.

The community is predominantly Baptist. Methodists rank next in point of numbers. In 612 families, 439 were Baptists and 147 Methodists (86 A.M.E. and 61 M.E.). These two denominations from the beginning of their influence in America made a pronounced "evangelical appeal to the untutored mind," and in time, although not at first especially interested in the Negro, they drew into their fold most of the Christianized Negro slaves. A feature of evangelical programs of these two sects was the camp meetings of the Methodists and the protracted meetings of the Baptists. What the church is now to the Negro the camp meeting was for the whites of the same section as late as a generation ago. It was the chief social and religious event of the season, a festive occasion to some, an intensely religious experience for others. Negro slaves were allowed to attend them, usually after the white people had had their session of religious enthusiasm and demonstration. It was during the heyday of their camp meetings and revivals at the beginning of the nineteenth century that patterns of religious expression were established. It was at this time that the ecstatic shouting, screaming, falling, rolling, laughing, jerking, and even barking of mass hysteria under the stress of religious enthusiasm, now most commonly regarded as characteristically Negro emotionalism, came into vogue. Likewise, during this early period the sermon patterns of exhorting, with accompanying mannerisms, were first noted. Many of the stereotyped expressions which go to make up the common prayers may be traced to the vivid language of these early evangelists. These expressions, based largely upon scriptural language, are common to many parts of the country and are as fixed as ritual. Faris suggests the influence of these patterns on the Negro slave as a possible explanation of patterns of their own emotionalism in religion:

The social situation in which the American Negro found himself, in all probability, furnished the pattern by means of which he was guided in his religious life. Extravagant as these reactions are, they can all be matched by others just as remarkable in the white race that was the teacher of the black. . . . . Until the last twenty-five years one could be pretty sure of seeing someone "shout" at the revivals of the white people, but it has practically died out at present.[1]

Andrew Polk Watson gathered a group of religious experiences of Negro former slaves, some of whom recalled their first contact with these camp meetings: "When the white folks had revivals the niggers from all around would gather on the outside and listen at them sing and pray."[2] The present forms of religious observance by Negroes in this section may reasonably be assumed to be survivals of the patterns now largely discarded by whites, and discarded by many Negroes as well, as they advance from one level of culture to another. Even more obvious survivals are such outmoded doctrinary restrictions as the ban upon card-playing, social dancing, and baseball which, in the present situation of greatly changed attitudes toward these harmless diversions, have become so highly artificial in the relationship of the church to the community. These restrictions, as elsewhere noted, are en-

[1] Ellsworth Faris, "The Mental Capacity of Savages," *American Journal of Sociology*, XXIII, 603.

[2] *Primitive Religion among Negroes in Tennessee* (M.A. dissertation; Fisk University, 1932), p. 26.

forced in a relentless and more insistent manner than perhaps any others, and by their very strength and sanctity make difficult the development of new and more fitting controls. For example, venereal clinics[3] have been established in several of the churches because they were the natural social centers, but the social implication of these clinics was nowhere recognized. This was important to the successful operation of the clinic, but a situation which would have been socially impossible where there was greater sophistication or where the church had translated this health problem in terms of social relations.

The independence and consequent lack of organization and regulation of the Baptist organization probably account for its vogue in this section as well as in other rural sections. An individual of strong personality may become a leader and minister even if illiterate, provided he knows well the accepted forms of worship and response. He is required to have a good voice, a power of imagery, and ability to control his people. To this might be added the ability to raise money. There is little formal ritual. Such is not called for in so intimate a community. There are ceremonies, however. The Methodists are not very different in their modes of worship, but there is the advantage of a changing ministry, which permits exposure to new experiences from the outside.

The Church in Action

The Damascus Baptist Church stands at a far junction of the dusty and tortuous road leading out from Hardaway, with no other building within sight, or in fact within miles, save an old and sagging school building close by it. The church is a small, painfully conventional boxlike structure with gabled roof and a small bell tower over the entrance. It has once or twice been whitewashed but is now gray under the long assault of time and the elements. Two giant oaks at the rear, dripping with a Spanish trailing moss, give shelter for the horses and mules of the communicants. Back of the schoolhouse with its broken windows and

[3] A phase of the Rosenwald Fund demonstration in the mass control of syphilis.

sagging shutters is a small cemetery with boards and short tomb-
stones jutting up at odd angles to mark the mounds of departed
members. Twelve mules and a horse are hitched to the oak trees,
and farm wagons, still holding empty chairs and baskets, are scattered about the green. Besides these conveyances are fully a dozen
Ford automobiles, worn and plastered with dry mud, and, loung-
ing in these cars, engaged in conversation are men, young and old,
carefree and serious. The principal cluster of women and small
children is around a pump which stands midway between the
church and the school. They are drinking with an easy leisure.

Inside the church there are three rows of plain wooden benches.
The walls of the interior are of white, painted, horizontal boards,
and the ceiling, as far up as could be reached, is painted a vivid
green. At the end of the room is a very cluttered rostrum. The
inclined pedestal has the center; the pastor's seat is directly behind. Then there are three small benches for the choir, two hat
racks, and an old clock which is out of order. On the wall back of
the rostrum is a large calendar with a picture of Lincoln, an even
larger placard announcing a "drive" for $225,000 on behalf of
Selma University in 1927, a framed crayon portrait of a former
pastor, a placard warning in red letters of the danger of malaria,
and two framed certificates. Beside the rostrum is a coal stove.

There is a cheerful bustling among the two hundred and fifty or
more persons in the building as they fan themselves and accommodate their natural flow of conversation and gossip to the novelty of church clothes. From one corner of the room a voice is heard
above the hum of conversation, trailing tentatively into a long-
meter hymn. It is the beginning of the preparation for the mood
of worship. The noise of the congregation dies down as the voice
gains in volume and certainty, and others take up the lines. Finally, the congregation is singing lustily. A deacon of the church rises
and in loud supplication raises a prayer:

Lord our Father who art in Heaven, let your will be done on earth as
it is in Heaven. Give us this day our daily bread and forgive our debts
as we forgive those who debt against us, for thine is the Kingdom. Heavenly Father, we feel thankful this morning and ask you to send the Holy

Ghost for Jesus' sake. Bless these our sisters and brethren, O Lord, our Heavenly Father, and we want dying men and women to know that besides you there is no other God before you, and they must know that they got to give account of all the deeds done in this body.

The audience has been only politely restrained during this part of his prayer, and the younger members are frankly whispering and continuing their greetings. There is need of more warmth in his address to God, and he forsakes the repetition of one set of stereotypes drawn from lines of scripture for another which has a more certain response value:

I'm talking about that same God who bled and was crucified and died on Calvary's hill; [*almost angrily*] talking about that same God John saw.

There were scattered "Amens."

Behold the Lamb of God who take away the sins of the world. Have mercy on us, Lord.

(More "Amens.")

Father, bless the church, bless the sick and 'flicted; remember the minister, remember the members, and when we done going up and down the road be with us and stand by us and the praise will be "Thanks for Christ our Redeemer's sake. AMEN."

Before his voice is still a song is raised, a formal hymn:

> My soul be on thy guard, ten thousand foes arise
> The hosts of sin are pressing
> To draw thee from the skies.

Another member, who has stood up in readiness during the last verses of the hymn, intones:

Lord, our Father, some have gone to the left and some have gone to the right; O Lord, bless those who stick close to the cross; throw around them your strong arm of protection; help our dark days, O Lord. You know you said you would protect us and stand by us. Bless the sick; bless the Pastor; bless the Deacon Board; help them to lead us and guide us. Heavenly Father, help us to grow stronger in the faith; be with us and stand by us. You said a long time ago that if I pray and pray hard you would hear me again. Bless my sister's children; bless my mother who has gone before me. If I don't ever meet her in this world let me meet her when we have done done with this old world. AMEN.

There is now a more fitting mood for the minister. During the singing and praying he has been detached, sometimes rapt in abstraction, sometimes leaning over to whisper matters of practical concern over the business of the church. He is a stocky, dark, elderly man, well aware of his rank as a preacher. Now he is all attention, and with a heavy solemnity he approaches the pedestal.

My friends, we are very glad to meet you here this morning. [*Don't talk, don't talk.*] Everybody ought to be happy today. I am going to ask Deacon Brown to take all these baskets and carry them right back yonder, out of the way. Some of us could be in our sick rooms, and some of us could be in our liquish graves, but we are here, and we wants to ask you for your prayers. 'Tis good to pray. Prayers of the righteous prevaileth much. Sisters and brothers, God done set time to make things known to us, and I'm not satisfied unless I'm preaching the word of God.

He is reminding his audience of his obligation to preach, of the unquenchable instinct to evangelism on which a large part of his authority rests.

The Gospel is the bread of life and it must be preached throughout the world. One morning this week I felt like preaching. I was jest thirsty ter preach. You know if you is praying and someone slips up on you, you gits shame, so I choosed my wife and told her ter watch, and I stood before the mirrow till my soul was satisfied, and one time I heard her tipping round by the side of the house ter hear me. Her soul was hungry too, sisters and brothers. These words were spoken by Paul. Paul was a great man, you know.

He is a minister who has not lived always in the community, and he has some basis in his experience for a comparison of his people with others. He can hold out a light. This is one of the social functions of the church.

Paul studied education; he didn't mind going to school. Lots of our boys and girls don't lak ter go ter school. We laks ter play hookie. We turn our back on learnings, but Paul wan't lak that, and after he educated he turned himself as who we call a sheriff terday. You know, sisters and brothers, after you get an education there is a chance fer you, you can git a position. You know Paul didn't know anything 'bout Jesus. He ain't come in contact wid Jesus yet. The other day a lady was coming through the community. Dr. C—— and I was passing down the highway, and she greeted us wid a smile, and as far down the road as I saw

156

her I could see the intelligence in her, and later when I talked wid her, I got acquainted wid her through her smile. That's the way wid Jesus.

Paul was lak you and I. He was choosen among one hundred and one thousand men and told "As you go, go and preach the Gospel." Before we seek our soul salvation we could go ter the dancing room, and after the dungeon shuk and chains fell off, we could have a vision wid God.

Instruction is not, however, the main function of the sermon. There must be enthusiasm, even ecstasy, and the minister who is incapable of stimulating this is soon out. The reference to education is brief, but it is possible to wax eloquent over the horrible sin of dancing. This is a part of the dogma of the church which affects only the younger members, but which is clung to tenaciously as an element of the respectability of church membership. Other more serious forms of social behavior prevailing in the community are not often touched upon, or if referred to at all it is done in a spirit of great daring.

Paul ain't no Christian now; ever'where he would hear the Gospel preached he would go and bring the news back ter Jerusalem. Sisters and brothers, you know ever'where the Gospel is preached the devil is there to 'sturb the souls of Christians; ain't many been really borned again, you know. Them's that done been borned again is a few. Ananias done been down ter Damascus, and he said, "I'll go down ter Damascus," oh, yes, my sisters and brothers, he said, "I'll go down and preach until they come off the dancing floor and till the dancing mistress pulls off her dancing shoes; till she change her soul and seeing Jesus is near ter my soul." I can see Ananias preaching. He was afraid of Paul. I can see Paul, oh, yes, I can see him when he got the news that Paul was down in Damascus, and the devil tuk the British soil, and Paul decided he would put a stumblingblock in this preacher's way. Then I can see him when he went ter Jerusalem ter git his letter and saying, "I want ter go down ter Damascus where Ananias is preaching, and find him and bring him back ter Jerusalem." I can see when the devil began ter write the letter. Then I kin see him when he went ter the brothers ter go on their wicked journey.

The words of the minister are not so impressive as the manner in which he intones them, in an excited singsong. Once well launched, the audience gives encouragement in their responses: "Amen"; "Yes, Lord"; "Preach it, boy"; "Uh huh!"; "Have mercy, Jesus";

"Come, Holy Spirit, we need you now"; "Jesus comes by." The imagery, which is most effective, is that which is enshrouded in the most impenetrable cloud of mystery.

Sisters and brothers, you know God is so high you can't go over him, and so wide you can't go 'round him, and so low you can't go under him. Jesus says yer got ter come in by the door. Jesus went down ter Damascus and saw the people shaking and shouting in glory. He told Ananias that Paul was riding. Ain't nobody never heard no voice lak dat before. Brothers, help me, help me preach this Gospel now.

A point of enthusiastic departure is that of some great conflict of the soul. This can be made more realistic by sudden allusions to well-known experiences.

When Paul got 'way down the road on his journey he fell down prostrate on the ground three days. *Hallelujah!* No doubt the birds was singing sweet songs. He got hungry; hungry for bread; thirsty fer water. "Stay, stay there," God said; "lay right there three days." Finally God tempted him wid his Godlike power. O Paul, O Paul, O, O Paul, did the Gospel call you one morning wid his still voice? Oh, yes, sisters and brothers, and he said, "Saul, Saul," and Paul answered, "Here am I, Lord. I know I been against thy work; what wilt thou have me ter do?" He looked at his hands and his hands looked new; looked at his feet and his feet looked new; and, O sisters and brothers, he said, "Git on your journey, Saul, and keep on down ter Damascus. Don't go back ter Jerusalem." Oh, no, I'm not afraid of praying. I can see Jesus going down ter Damascus. The people was sick and he opened the door and said ter Ananias, "Don't be afraid of Paul. Paul is coming in the morning. If you get tired of setting, go right in the house of Judea." God done told Paul that Ananias would meet him, and he tell one that the child of God done tuk his feet out of the miry clay and waited for Ananias. I'm talking wid my God, sisters and brothers, and that makes everything all right, and soon that morning Ananias made an address ter Paul; the greatest ever been made in the world. Paul go on back ter Jerusalem. God done purged Paul wid the Holy Ghost on high. Paul said, "I'm gonna preach from on high." Brothers and sisters, they was standing on the highway. I can see them now. The world was waiting. I can see the children bound by the hands of the devil standing by the wayside. Look at him; jest listen how he preached. *Hallelujah!* He jest wanted ter join Christ's men. The people done heard so much bout Paul some of them was so 'fraid, some started to murder him. But somebody tuk him from the mob crowd by the wall. Sisters and brothers, that was the

Holy Ghost. Chillen, if you pray the world can't do you no harm. The first morning Paul went out he 'sulted wid God. He met my friend, O God! Preached until men believed. When Paul started on his second missionary journey he said, "O God, who must I git ter go wid me?" and Jesus said, "Go on the outskirts of the city of Philippi. Believe I am the Son of God. A woman stays there; she is a po' woman, but she will give you room in her home. You stay there." I can see, brothers— I can see, brothers—he began preaching the Gospel. I believe that Jesus Christ is the Son of God. People begin ter git on easy, but he preached on and on till they began ter believe and thirst for the word of God. But soon they tuk Paul and Silas and bound 'em in the jail.

The dramatization of incidents of the New Testament constitutes a large part of the sermon, but the experiences are so related as to make it possible for his people to identify themselves with the characters in this great struggle. All that God asks either of ancient and eminent Saul or of modern and humble Susie Keys is faith and prayer.

I can see when they began ter put them in the Philippi jail. Children, have you prayed? I done prayed. Silas asked, "What will we do?" Paul said, "I want ter have a little talk wid God." Chillen, I tell you a child of God has a hard time in this world.

Preacher sits down, still speaking:

Night come and the roosters didn't crow. Birds wan't singing no sweet songs. Cows wan't chewing no cuds. Way, way in the night—chillen, do you ever pray in the night? I heard old Saul singing, "Amazin' grace, how sweet the sound that saved a wretch like me." 'Bout that time old Paul said, "Lord, O Lord, you promised good ter me. You is my sword and shield, and you got my portion due." Then Paul said, "Jesus, I am your child." Then Jesus told his angel to "git two wings ter cover your head, two ter cover your feet, go down ter Jerusalem and shake jail, and buckle loose the jail and let my chillen free." "Take this key of gold." Looka yonder, looka yonder, chillen.
[*Getting up.*] 'Fore day Paul on one side an Silas on the other. Silas said, "Lord, Lord, what will you have me ter do?" He said ter him, "Stand right there; don't move a step."

The shouting has begun with sudden sharp groans of spiritual torture, then screams of exultation. Three or four persons are expressing themselves with shouts accompanied by a variety of physical demonstrations, while most of the audience responds in low accents. There is a phase of worship referred to as "helpin' out" the preacher, in which a line will be repeated several times by the minister or even a leader from the floor, and the audience joins in with a low moan. "The mountain so high, but I'm coming on"; "Lord, I done started and I can't turn back"; "Lord, I didn't come here for to do no harm"; "Trouble done been here, calling us a long ways"; "Well, you talk about Jesus; he's a friend of mine"; "Well, it's all night long I'm on my knees"; "I jest come here, Lord, for to sing and pray"; "Well, I feel like moaning. . . . ." The preacher continues:

When the clouds swing high over your head say, "World, World, O World, I done fought a good fight. Sometimes my heart was bleeding, sometimes runned over and called ever'thing 'cept a child God." Sisters, is you on the right track? Is all your tickets been signed and your chains fell off? Did you tell ever'body, the white, the colored, the po', the sick? Is you got a letter written in your heart? Makes your heart burn, makes you cry, makes you laugh. Is you done told ever'body? Oh, yes, ever'-body! AMEN, AMEN.

Song: "Long Ago."

I think somebody oughta get 'quainted wid Jesus. We gonna sing while the doors of the church be open.

> My soul, be on thy guard,
> Ten thousand foes arise.
> The hosts of sin are pressing hard
> To draw me from the skies.

Someone wid de spirit please come ter the altar and pray.

An old man arises and grips the bench ahead, with heavy, gnarled hands:

O my Heavenly Father, hit is again I done bowed on my knees ter give thanks fer thy holy name. Nothing we feel worthy ter offer Thee but a sinful heart fer your judgment. We bow not fer show ter the world, and not ter be well spoke of but because we know we got ter die. You done lent us this life and, Heavenly Father, we got a duty ter perform. We come first thanking Thee for this guidance. Help us ter rastle wid the combats of the world. Don't let us get weak on the way. In acts of confusion guide us and we will follow. Lord, lead us we ask Thee. We thank

Thee that we is working for a Kingdom not made wid hands. We are following you, Captain Jesus, 'cause you said your Kingdom last always. Sometimes, Jesus, you know the devil gits us by the hand, but we want you ter catch us by the hand and lead us out. AMEN.

The song which follows is one of humble triumph:

My Lord done been here, blessed my soul, and gone away.
I wouldn't be a sinner, I'll tell you the reason why—
    If my Lord God would come here I wouldn't be ready to die.
My Lord done been here, blessed my soul, and gone away.
I wouldn't be a gambler, I'll tell you the reason why—
    If my good Lord would come here I wouldn't be ready to die.

The preacher has done his duty in arousing the audience. He turns again to the problem of behavior.

My friends, we done sung the songs of Zion; done broke ter you the bread of life; done opened ter you de doors of de church; and done prayed these 'firmed prayers; and still there's more. You know I thinks 'bout the people in the community; how can you dance when there's a starvin' family over there? When you been dancing all Saturday night you ain't a fit subject fer the Lord. You gotta cut the dancing out. If you go up there ter the graveyard you'll see just as many short graves as long un's. You oughta quit dancing. You say you is a Christian; if you is a Christian you better show some signs. If you don't quit you're on the road to hell; talkin' 'bout you 'blige ter dance and you can't help it. 'Member in Noah's time, when the world was 'stroyed? Last night me and my wife was settin' outside the house and we heard singing and dancing, and here starvation is in your meal barrel. The old folks talking 'bout chillen young gotta have some fun, but they just stumblingblocks in their way. I laks ball games well as you, but I don't lak ter hear my members down there cussin'. Then you don't 'speck your pastor when you see him in all places. Me and my wife sets out ever' Saturday instead and reads God's word. You ought not ter do things 'gainst the plans of salvation. You ought ter show some signs of Christians down there. If you can act it at the church and on the roads and in the fields you can act it down there. Chillen, you better quit dancing. Now next month when the convention meets in Birmingham, I wants you sisters and brothers ter git around and git your pastor a seersucker suit, some socks, and some shirts. And I need shoes too. I gotta go down there and represent you, and I wanta do hit right.

The collection is lifted. Four young men stand before the pulpit and begin to sing, while two deacons stand by the table and persuade the members to come up and contribute.

The Funeral of Brother Jesse Harding

This funeral ceremony is reproduced in its entirety because it reflects many facets of community life. There is evident in the behavior of the people the conflict of certain new notions from the outside with their own traditional modes of life. The deceased represented standards and ideals out of relation to the common exigencies of life in the community. Moreover, the church, while attempting to defend the deceased's right to proper burial based upon his successful career as a business man, was itself aggrieved over his indifference to the institution. Finally, there is indicated in the physical features of the ceremony the manner in which new articles of material culture are introduced into the group. There is a tacit questioning of the authority of the church to exact ceremonial observance where group sanctions have been disregarded by the deceased.

Jesse Harding, although a landowner, was not well liked in the community. He belonged to a family of landowners founded by his father many years ago. There are a few others in the community who own land, but Jesse Harding was a fairly successful farmer and above all a good business man. He did not share the spirit of the community in which, even in the aggregate, there was little property. He was honest, straightforward, paying his own debts and exacting payment of debts to him. During the war he had been drafted and carried to France. It gave him a chance to get away from the community and observe how things were done. Under different circumstances, perhaps, his life would have been considered worthy of emulation for his thrift and foresight. But not in this community. The people came to the funeral, but there was neither praise of his life nor sorrow over his passing. All the devices of the preacher failed to stir them to any of the usual demonstrations of grief which even strangers may command, or to participate in the ceremony with any sort of unction.

At about three o'clock on Sunday the bell began to toll. It was the signal that the procession was moving to the church. The crowd that had been sitting around since the morning service, chatting and eating, jumped up and crowded around the windows and doors to watch the approach of the body and the mourners. Those who had been waiting outside began pushing in for seats, and there was much talking and gossiping, most of which was about the deceased. The preacher came in, showing traces of both excitement and anger. Mounting the rostrum, he raised his hands, but the tumult continued. Then he spoke: "Everybody hush your mouths. You ain't at no frolic; you're at a funeral. Now don't nobody talk. We ain't at no corn-shucking. You all talk like you at a moving-picture show." His remarks had been ill chosen, for there was tittering over his reference to frolics and picture shows. He tried another appeal. "Be quiet, please. Don't talk. Sh . . . . Who's that talking over there, and I told them to stop talking? If white folks had a been in here you could a heard a pin drop." This was not only a warning by suggestion; it was a confession. The shadow of the plantation extended even into their most intimate institutions.

Quiet followed, but whether from fear or shame or satiety was not clear. The preacher continued: "Now you know we will have to have two or three seats here for the family. You all [*pointing to a group before him*] just move out, please, and let the family have these front seats." Having settled his audience, he picked up his Bible swiftly and stumbled down the aisle to meet the family and the corpse, now waiting at the door. He found them and started back with hardly a pause, leading them to the front, chanting solemnly:

Man that is born of a woman is few days and full of trouble. He cometh forth like a flower . . . . [*everybody stand up*] . . . . and is cut down. He fleeth also as a shadow and continueth not, etc. . . . .

The choir sang:

> There is rest for the weary
> On the other side of Jordan,
> There is rest for me.

The preacher spoke again. "I'm going to ask you all once more to please give the family all the front seats. . . . ."

When I come to die. . . . .

He carried these last words smoothly into a spiritual:

> I want to be ready, I want to be ready,
> To walk in Jerusalem just like John.

A deacon offered up a perfunctory and almost completely stereotyped prayer, during which the pastor shouted several times, "You better pray," and the audience responded with low and doleful moans, more like a learned song than the spontaneous expression of feeling. Another song, "Beautiful land of God," and the preacher announced: "We are going to spend about ten minutes to have Brother Wiley and Brother Saunders to say a few words. The family has asked that they say a few words, and I will give them just about three minutes each." Brother Saunders arose briskly. He was one of the few persons of the community who had known the deceased well and could appreciate his curious objectives in life.

PASTOR, MEMBERS, AND FRIENDS OF DAMASCUS BAPTIST CHURCH: I have known this young man practically all his life. He stayed right here and was with us all the time. I can say this young man was a real man; you know you can't say this about all men and women, but he was a real man; a man that was worth while. He served his country and that was the cause of his death. Mr. Harding was a real business man; he didn't play; he didn't believe in no foolishness. If you want to do business with him it was all right, but if you went for foolishness he didn't have no time for you, and everything he said was just about true. You could believe him if you wanted to, but what he said was so. I come to see him last Wednesday a week ago, and we set down on the porch and talked; I with him and him with me. He started to talk about death, and I told him that death would take care of itself, and I started talking about something else. He said "Let's talk about death, because you know I got to go 'cording to the Scripture. I got to go to another building, and you know I got to go." I want to say to you all, be you a man or a woman, if you live for something you will die for something.

The audience had listened only half-heartedly, restlessly, and with none of the emotions which a funeral is expected to evoke. Brother

Wiley sensed this, and, after a brief allusion to the coldness, made a very perfunctory remark and sat down without further endangering his standing with the audience. He said: "This seems to be a mighty quiet funeral. You don't find many of our funerals so quiet. We are here on a very sad occasion. I been knowing Brother Jesse for a long time, and we thought a lot of him in this community." The preacher felt a challenge to his greatest skill in arousing this audience to the appropriate feeling for such an occasion. But he had great difficulty in finding words. His sermon offers a remarkable example of forced movement, from the platitudes of the beginning to the artificial "rousements." "Friends, this is a very sad occasion," he reminded them again. "Brother Jesse was converted under Rev. Dr. Banks, who has gone on to heaven." Still getting his bearings: "Brother Wiley and Brother Saunders has given you some very good talks." The chill of the audience bore down upon him, and he admitted, almost bargainwise: "Brother Jesse had his faults, like you and me. I talked with him at home and at the hospital." He excused himself for not visiting him at the hospital oftener: "They had to ask me to not come to the hospital so much, 'cause there was so many sick folks just like Brother Jesse." Everybody knew the deceased's forthrightness and it could be mentioned again.

Brother Jesse was the business man of the Harding family. The old man was lucky before them; all of that family has been lucky. He was a keen business man. If you went to ask him about a certain thing, and he tell you ain't nothing to it, it wasn't nothing to it, and that's all there is to it.

Then, reading the faces of his audience, he faced the issue squarely:

I know you all waiting to see what I'm going to say. Brother Jesse told me, and not only me but others, that he didn't go to church as often as he ought to have. But God has forgive him for that. I'm saying this for the other young men here that ain't been to church before this year. God ain't gonna love you. Jesse didn't go to church as he ought to have, but I tell you one thing he did do. He would pay what he owed and he would give a receipt for everything, and he would give a receipt when you did business with him. *He was a business man, somehow or other.*

There are other virtues implied in his life which came closer to the general community notions of respectability. "He died and left his wife in good shape. Left her his home; left her not begging; left her with something around her. She's crying now but she ain't crying 'cause she ain't got nothing to eat." It was this thrust by the preacher which brought the first response. The audience quieted for a while as if stunned, and the preacher indulged in a few easy personal reminiscences.

He always made me welcome in his home. He not only invited me there to breakfast or dinner one time, but all the time whenever he would see me he would ask me if I wouldn't have something to eat with them. He didn't talk no foolishness, but he was a business colored man; he had sho-enough visible long eyes.

Then, addressing the corpse, he said: "Jesse, we are going to talk from the text we used to talk about. 'For we know this is a building of God not made with hands eternal in the heavens.' " At this point the sermon was interrupted by the singing of an old hymn. The widow arose and walked around the casket, waving her hand in farewell at the remains and crying, "Goodbye, goodbye, I am all by myself now; aint' got nobody, Lord, nobody but me and myself." A friend came up and began fanning her. By the end of the song the preacher had better command of himself, and launched into his sermon, deliberately and with determination.

When we are about to build a house the architect makes out all the plans and states the number of things it takes to go into the making of this building. We go according to the directions that he gives us. Bad disaster of a serious kind, rainstorms, and what not comes along and destroys it, and it goes back to the dust from whence it came. The upkeep is always more expensive than the building. To build a building and not have the upkeep is a waste of time, material, and money. Time after time somebody had to go around to look after the building to keep it up. Brother Harding had to go make preparations for another building. When God created heaven and earth he had nothing to start with; he had no material. He planted the world while the world was dark. He didn't have nobody to pull up by, nobody but himself. That is the kind of protection Jesse had. When you got your hands in God's hand you don't need to worry. In Indiana once I went down to visit a building that took ninety-nine years to finish—just lack one year of taking a hundred years to build. But that building is going to rot down; time is going to wear it out. Storms and rains is going to tear it down after a while. Jesse's government sent him over in France. He got gassed and gas got all through his body, but he done it for me and you. He is saying, "All you can do for me, Mr. Hoover, now is give me a home over yonder. Got to go back and have a home when the government done signed up. Gonna need one after a while."

The creation of the world by God out of nothing is one of the most powerfully dramatic incidents in time and space. It provides an opportunity for imagery of the most effective sort, and is colored with a deep and eternal mystery. It was this picturization that the preacher resorted to by way of awakening his audience.

God talked, and one thousand birds came from nowhere. He talked and the waters of the deep come gushing up. [*I got to hurry on now.*] Jesse begin to breathe the breath of life. When God breathe the breath of life in you, you are going to know it. Noah built the ark, but I'm talking about this house not made with hands. Old house built upon the sand give away some time. You can't live in a house when it gets too shaky. Old disease got in Jesse's house and he couldn't live. Brother Jesse's heart can't move no longer 'cause disease got in it. Mrs. Jesse heard Jesse talking to someone but she couldn't see who it was. God was telling him to come on in. Jesse said, "Take me and keep me out of my misery." He was talking to someone but none could see who it was but Jesse could see. When T.B. get into your body you can't stand it. All right, Jesse, all right, all right, boy, do the best you can; I ain't gonna cry no more. Don't cry, everybody has done all they could. Jesse gone and left us all. He said, "I am fixing for another world; the things of this world won't do me no good. I will meet you over yonder after a while." They tell me that if you believe in the word of God, he will save you in the dying hour. When he was converted he asked what they meant when they said, "Believe on God and keep his commandments." Brother Tate told him to just believe in the word of God, and trust him and turn loose and a power from on high would do the rest. O man, O man, after a while the old Kaiser said, "I believe I will go down here in France and play the old devil with the young boys." Jesse went over there with a bunch of boys from here; some was with the mechanics and some was on the firing line. The old Kaiser played the devil with our boys. I can imagine I can hear Jesse praying to come back home. He didn't have no wife then. O Lord, O Lord, O, it got so dark then in France, they say one time they was digging graves 138 hours, burying men who had fallen in

France. Brother Jesse didn't happen to fall in that crowd, but he had to stand in water up to his knees. He told me once he didn't see how he got that disease, and I told him that he brought it back from France; that he caught it over there. I told him not only him but there was thousands of other boys in the came condition. He went in there one evening and got on the scales and he had lost seven or eight pounds, and the next week they put him on the scales again and he had lost about eight and a half pounds, and he said, "I can't stay here long going away like this." After a while he got to meet that monster Death. At the hospital they weigh you to see how you are getting along. All that is over with you now, boy. You ain't gonna stand in line no more. We won't see him no more going to see after the stock in the barn. O man, I will meet you after a while. I fancy Jesse talking to his father, and him asking about all of the children down here. O wife, you won't have to walk around the bed giving him medicine no more. O Lord, O Lord! O Jesus, take care of us! I imagine I can see Jesse walking in Jerusalem just like John. Ain't got on no soldier's clothing, ain't got on no gas mask; but he's got on the helmet of salvation, sitting around God's throne.

The congregation was now partially aroused. They began humming and moaning loud enough at times to cross the words of the minister, but without force or spontaneity. "You all sing mighty sorry," the preacher chided. "You act like you can't sing." Then noticing some of the members stealing out, he shouted: "Don't nobody go out. Don't nobody go out over the corpse." Another song was started and four women accommodatingly shouted "Lordy, Lordy" and ceased promptly with the music. Once more the preacher attempted a figure: "Jesse, you are not over the council of Daniel, of John, of Amos. We will meet again. We will meet over yonder. Jesse's wife comes first." At mention of her name, the wife began crying aloud again, "O Lord, I ain't got nobody; Lord, nobody but me now, Lord."
The preacher observed, sadly:

Jesse can't say nothing, Lord.

I imagine I can hear Amos and John say, "I wonder where my mother is." Jesse will see them soon, and say, "I'm troubled, Lord; I'm troubled." Jesse ain't going to cry no more; he ain't going to tell me about being motherless and fatherless. Don't give up sisters, brothers, and wife. Love each other and live at peace with one another. AMEN.

Don't nobody go out. The undertaker will tell you which way to come up and see the body. This body has been embalmed so there ain't nothing to be afraid of. We got a little debt on the pump, so you all put a nickel on the table as you pass to look at the body. Don't talk. Pass quietly, please. Don't talk. Don't go outdoors. Go out behind the body.

> O Lordy, let your will be done.
> O Lordy, let your will be done.
> Says, O Lordy, let your will be done.
>
> If it takes my mother,
> Let your will be done.
>
> If it takes my mother,
> Let your will be done.
>
> O Lordy, let your will be done.
> O Lordy, let your will be done.
> O Lordy, let your will be done.

You all ain't dropping no nickels on the table.

On the third Sunday our anniversary will be completed. Every member of this church ought to be registered. Seems like you all forgetting to honor the older members of this church. Now listen here: Sister Harding has lost her husband, and we realize that, and I want every brother and sister to console her. Go and throw your arms about her and help that wife and comfort her. Go over there tomorrow morning and help her clean up everything. . . . . The family will go down the same aisle they come up.

At the graveyard the Negro undertaker who had come up from Montgomery was introducing a new device, an automatic lowering apparatus. The pall-bearers were temporarily nonplused, and were lost for something to do until they were permitted to fill in the grave. The preacher sang, "I want to walk in Jerusalem just like John," and at the end of the song announced that he wanted to take the occasion to speak of the fact that the funeral had been conducted from the house to the grave by a "member of our race." He called the undertaker, who promptly stepped forward to acknowledge this recognition. Said the minister:

You can see for yourself he's a shore-enough member of the race; he's like Brother Thomas over there and we all agree that he is real dark.

I want to remind you also how necessary it is to keep up insurances so that you won't be a burden on other people when you come down to die.

As the body was lowered into the grave a brother of the deceased man leaned upon a woman mourner and wept aloud. Others waved their hands at the corpse crying, "Goodbye." A woman standing back from the group of mourners screamed, "You said you wanted rest and now you got rest."

THE CHANGING CHURCH

The sixtieth anniversary of the Macedonia Baptist Church was the occasion for a retrospective comparison of the church since slavery. Although not a regular service, it afforded interesting documentation of the changing mores. There was a program with announced papers, but the older members who took part in the celebration simply accepted the stilted announcement of a paper to be presented as an opportunity to talk. The minister had tried hard to introduce a note of formality into the ceremonies, with indifferent success. It was an artificial performance challenged by one exasperated old member who frankly stated her fear of the disintegration of the institution as a force in the life of the community. She was realistic and accurate in her appraisal, which provoked general irritation. The chairman made her sit down.

We are celebrating our sixtieth anniversary today. . . . . Don't talk. Some of you school girls back there are talking. . . . . We are celebrating. . . . . We asked all of you ladies to dress in white. Some of you all had old white dresses and some of you all coulda got them. Of course all of them didn't know about it is excused. All you members who wore white dresses take the front seat. We going to be hard on them that knowed and didn't. You could take thirty cents and buy one. You can make a dress out of three yards, and you can get goods for ten a yard. . . . . All the members take the middle aisle. We are asking everybody to write your name on an envelope. There will be a secretary to take it 'cause everybody can't read everybody's writing. . . . . Everybody haven't got sixty cents put in a quarter or dime, and if you ain't got one borrow one. We are going to be hard. We can't whip you but we can make you feel mighty bad.

We are going to have two subjects today. The first one is going to be delivered by one I have known all my days. He's been our superintendent of Sunday school for years. His subject is "Difference in Spiritual Progress in the Church Now and Twenty-five Years Ago."

The superintendent arose and put on his glasses to speak. He said:

I can't say so much about the difference in the church twenty-five or thirty years ago but I know it is a big difference. My mother used to take me by the hand and lead me to church and Sunday school. They used to have midweek meetings and Saturday-night meetings, and men and women was converted by prayer meetings. We don't take the time now to have meetings like they used to have twenty-five or thirty years ago. I believe, though, that times will be better to come. Used to be my mother and your mother would start shouting soon as they got in the door of the church. Now you might think it a little different, but we are serving the same God today as we did thirty years ago. Everything in the world has changed. In those days people had to go to the graveyard, and 'less'n you told a great long tale about a dog or something else you couldn't be let in. We don't do that now. We know that Jesus Christ is right here and you can get him anywhere if you got the love of God in your heart. Now let us try to serve God pure and honest; let us begin singing, preaching, or whatever we do—serve him with a pure heart.

> Lordy, won't you hear me pray;
> I want to be holy every day.
> Lordy, won't you hear me pray;
> I want to be more holy every day.

The minister proceeded with the program:

Next subject on hand to be delivered [*under his breath he muttered*] ain't but one thing 'bout it he is able to do and I want to ask him to cut it sorta short. His subject is: "My Vision of the Future Church," by Deacon A. M. Turner.

Deacon Turner strove to be correct in every detail:

MASTER OF CEREMONIES, MEMBERS, PASTOR, AND FRIENDS: One way we will have a future church will be the way we lead our lives daily and give the folks what they need. I am not a preacher; I was only called to be a deacon. Ain't very much work I can do. I might say something here he wouldn't like, yet he and I work together; if we fall out nobody won't know it but us. Every church that ever been organized or come up rested on that Book there. If we ever be anything in the future we got to come out to church; that is our only hope. People that got children ought to bring them to the Sabbath school or send them. When you fail to bring your child up in the Sunday school you have just failed. Train your child in the way you would have it to go; when it get old it won't depart from you. Young people is our only hope. You try to break a old dried-up stick and it will break every time. I am scared of the man or woman who won't let their children be brought up in the Sunday school. I mean from the Deacon Board on down. You can't just turn them loose. If we never have no prayer service here we don't know whether our boys can sing or not. We got to quit so much frolicking. Your son and daughter gonna do and say just what you do. You want your child to be able to say, "I want to be like mother or father." Our only hope is to bring them to the Sabbath school, have prayer services so that child will be able to take care of the future church.

> Look 'way down that lonesome road,
> Look 'way down that lonesome road,
> Look 'way down that lonesome road.
> I see trouble down that road,
> I see trouble down that road,
> I see trouble down that road.
> Lord been here and blessed my soul,
> Lord been here and blessed my soul,
> Lord been here and blessed my soul.
>
> I ain't gonna lay my religion down,
> I ain't gonna lay my religion down,
> I ain't gonna lay my religion down.
> Look 'way down that lonesome road.
> Look 'way down that lonesome road,
> Look 'way down that lonesome road.

AMEN, AMEN.

At this point one of the older members of the church, a woman, got up and began talking, even though she was not on the program. "The future church gonna be worser than that what is past. Now all the chillun think 'bout learning is the 'black bottom' and all other devilment." The master of ceremonies began to ring the bell for her to sit down, but she was indifferent to it.

We was scared to do anything. Just much difference in Sunday school now and then as day and night. Everybody is learning things now what they ain't got no business. They won't even go to school. I am the mother of this church, and I will say what I please. This is my old stand and I'll say what I please. Boy come long and say he believe the Lord done pardoned his sins and if you don't watch him he will be back in thirty days saying he needs 'ligion. If you don't change the church is lost. Listen, I'm gonna talk but I ain't gonna say nothing out of school. They must be educated in the heart first. Look up and love God in his heart. "Seek ye first the Kingdom of Heaven and all these things will be added." You got to move, you can't do nothing with a educated heart only, you got to be educated in your hands next, then you must be educated in your feet and in your eyes. That's what it takes for the future church.

The master of ceremonies began tapping the bell with force, and continued until she finally sat down. He said in apology:

Brothers, I know you all honor Sister Moore. Course our time is short but she has acted as a mother to me when I used to go to school here. Any time old folks get up I give way to them. I'm 'fraid of old folks till today. If we had space we would have some more. I am satisfied our boys can put it over.

The chief sermon was to be delivered by the pastor. He came forward bustling and earnest giving orders to the congregation between the lines of the introduction to the sermon.

My friends, we are happy to be here. Come on to the front, ladies. You all must take turn about and help find these ladies seats, and you all must help keep order. Now we are praising God today and in our praises don't forget the sixty years God has been with us. I must mention here, before I forget it, that Brother Boyd has asked for our prayers, and when you all pass there go and ask how he is getting along, but don't go in and talk to him for he is mighty sick and don't have strength to talk. Come right on down to the front, ladies. Bring them right on down this way, brother. Make believe you love them; that's the way to do. When you go to First Baptist they always make you welcome, and they make you feel at home. I am glad to have our members and friends here, and I wish we had time to hear them all. Ladies are not wearing the short dresses now and they can take the front seats. Thank the Lord they are letting them down and they won't have to be ashamed to take the front seats. Don't talk, don't talk, please.

There is quite a change in now and years ago. There is quite a change in everything. I want my son to be a partner with me. I want to take him along by my side and let him tell me what he thinks. When you knock them down now you may not get off so light. You know folks used to knock and beat their children around, but you can't do it so well now. Our old folks got afraid from slavery. I want my boy to talk to me and not feel like he is afraid of me. He talked to me not long ago. He said, "Papa, I believe the Lord got something to do with this thing." He wanted a job and couldn't get it, and wanted a new suit; that was why he was talking so to me. Whatever my business may be I want my son to know about it. If I got a dollar I want him to have one, but let him work for it, and get it like I did. A man that haven't got a dollar and

173

can't get one ain't much of a man. It takes a hustler to get one. If I couldn't get a dollar I would go to Europe or somewhere else and get one. I ain't gonna stay no where I can't get a dollar. Some of us ain't got nothing and don't want nothing. When he gets to the place where he doesn't want nothing he is in a bad fix.

I want to preach thirty minutes, and want to be through in that time. I believe I want to hear you all sing a verse, just a verse:

> I heard the voice of Jesus saying,
> "Come unto me and rest.
> Lie down, thy weary one, lie down,
> Thy head upon my breast."

I been here twenty years, going on twenty-one, and I never smelt a drop of whiskey on one of my deacons' breath, and they ain't never offered me one. I ain't never told them to tell a woman no secret and they ain't never told me one. If they ever had any bad tricks they never told me. We have been straight and fair with each other these twenty-one years. You ought to say "Amen." They treat me with the highest respect; yes, they have. They must be all right, ain't they? I am going to give them credit.

The text I am gonna take is just two sentences. The first is "I have fought a good fight"; second, "I have kept the faith."

I have fought a good fight; I have kept the faith. The Scripture designates just as our leader, as our captain of soldiers; before a man or woman can make a good soldier he must realize that life in this battle cannot be lost; he must believe that he is gonna win. We lost soldiers in France but the United States conquered. Jesus Christ died but he brought life by dying. Some people think the church is something to be played with. A man goes out on the battlefield and goes out there to win. It takes a brave person to be a good soldier. That is why they give so much praise to the man who volunteers to go to the army. We had boys in the last war to volunteer; and that's what we want in the church. I am ready to serve, not have to persuade folks to do anything. That's the kind of religion we ought to have. I never give a dime for a man who never do nothing in the church. A man that won't do nothing in the church ain't much to him. You say "Amen" mighty dry. Any man that won't serve needs a changed heart. When a man's heart is changed he is willing to serve. You don't have to ask if he belongs to church; you know it by how he goes about his work.

Any attack on the traditional ways is hazardous, and this minister approached the issue with some misgivings.

You can't hardly change an old man from his ways; he is stubborn as the devil. You can change young folks. An old man is set in his ways. Brother, I am preaching now; you all better say "AMEN." I been talking this way for twenty years and I ain't been put out yet. They might cuss me out, but they ain't put me out. I will be like the monkey—"ain't gwine nowhere." I'm telling you now I ain't gwine nowhere. Get this rich thought I am giving you this morning. It isn't money—any fool know money will last only a short time. In his soul religion ought to be the strongest thing. Get love in your hearts. Wake up, Brother Swenny, you know you can't sleep over me. You got to go somewhere else to sleep, 'cause I'm gonna wake you up. A man who can serve and won't serve just needs to be born again, that's all.

The illuminating byways of the sermon illustrate the manner in which new ideas enter. He is bringing to them new ideas about education, consolidation of effort for efficiency, race spirit, and he is well aware that his high mission of instruction is encountering the doubt and dismal conversation of the group.

We don't want no deacons on the board who won't serve. I am thinking the time is gonna come when these churches have got to double up. Ain't no need of all these churches around here. Railroads are going together and banks are going together. A colored man don't like to think; a white man thinks in terms of millions; not only the white man but the intelligent Negro. You just as well get ready to think. You fool around and don't educate your girls and boys, but he got to pay for it. I had rather be dead and in my grave than have my children come up ignorant. If I had a child and couldn't school him, I had rather go somewhere and fight. Some of you say you can't do without them, but you would do without them if they would die. You can get along without them all right if you just try sending them away to school. O Lord, everything is all right, ain't it? I know you all don't like it, but I don't care if you don't. Don't talk, don't talk. Christ shed much blood and had great suffering. You all haven't suffered. You are getting along fine. A man that is a good Christian don't have a hard time. I tell you, my friends, we can say I have fought a good fight and I have kept the faith. Let us go on. I told you the church back yonder had to face a terrible crisis but we have to die to conquer. What does it mean to die? If a man got to die to win, let him die. The boys over in France brought the bacon home and Uncle Sam is doing what he can for them now. Our girls have got to have courage to go on. Matthew was put to death by the point of a sword; next Mark was tied to a wild beast and drug through the streets of Alexander. Preachers used to wear long-tailcoats and beaver hats, but now they wear whatever they want. I am going to wear the kind of hat and shoes, too, I want to wear. There ain't no need to be dead. I wouldn't give a dime for a teacher who come to class all drawn and dead. We want plenty of pep in them. I believe that teachers who teach our children ought to be Christians. I believe a man teaching Sunday school ought to be a Christian and a man teaching psychology or anything else ought to be a Christian. About sixty-some-odd years ago we didn't have teachers like we do now. You folks back there will have to be still and quit getting up and going out. . . . . I can't preach with all that noise.

James was crucified with his heels up and head down. Luke was hanged to an olive tree. You can't mean much unless you suffer for the church. We have as much devilment as white folks; it's tit for tat. I have often heard it said, "Be careful how you promote a colored man, because after you promote him he goes crazy." He got crazy 'bout automobiles but he done quit; now they all standing under sheds. You used to be able to hear a "chuck, chuck, chuck" everywhere. But they are driving wagons now. Every man that don't volunteer in the army ain't a coward, but if he enters he can be helped and can be made strong where he is weak. I am preaching now; you ought to be up shouting. My daddy was a soldier in the Revolutionary [Confederate] Army. As long as the drums tapped he was encouraged to go. You can say, "I will love Jesus"; you ought to be encouraged to go on. There is somebody crying for the word of God; you ought to be willing to go.

I have fought a good fight. I am nearly through, my friends. Be a soldier in the army. Well, what you gonna fight this army with? Prayer is the first weapon; a man that won't pray won't make a good soldier. The man who won't love the church is not a good soldier. A man that is born again will be brave; a man can't mean much in the army if he ain't got that weapon. I don't care what you do, but pray. God Almighty will hear your prayers if you just call him right. Joshua was in a mighty battle and he called on God, and he reached out his mighty hand and stopped the sun. . . . . Wake up, sister!

My friends, by faith the children walked down in the Red Sea on dry ground. Any man won't hear him ain't got faith. God called Abraham to offer his son Isaac on the altar as a sacrifice. He just went right on and obeyed God. He told his son to get ready to go on over to the mountain. He was obeying God. My friends, don't set down; go to work and God will make you well. You quarrel about what you can't do; nothing is impossible with God. Get prepared. When Abraham was about to kill his son God sent a message to him not to strike. God can do anything. Adam just done what God told him not to do. After a while, my friends,

God will come back. I want to ride up one of these mornings; I want to say I've kept the faith. I wonder if the church will meet me on that morning? Since that time sixty years ago somebody has said, "I have kept the faith." I got a mother over yonder, and I hope to meet her some day.

> Father, I stretch my hands to Thee,
> No other help I know, etc.

There began a low moaning all over the church at this point, and it was impossible to hear everything the preacher was saying at the time; but it lasted only a few minutes.

We thank thee, our Heavenly Father, for sparing us. We are glad to meet at church one more time again on this side of death. Many who started with us is deprived of this privilege of being here this morning. You being God, you know the secret of every man and woman's heart. We know that you know all about us, Heavenly Father. You know every turn we make and kept our bed from being a cooling-board this morning, and we was able to look upon a day that we never will forget as long as we live. We have kept our feet in the paths of righteousness. I once was lost but now I'm found, was blind but now I see. Bless the people of this congregation. When we stack up our books and Bible; got to stoop down and unlace our shoes, take us home in thy Kingdom, for Christ's sake. AMEN.

> What kind shoes I'm gonna wear? Golden slippers.
> What kind shoes I'm gonna wear? Golden slippers.
> Golden slippers I'm bound to wear.
> Yes, yes, yes, my Lord, I'm a soldier of the cross.
> Yes, yes, yes, my Lord, I'm a soldier of the cross. [Repeat.]
>
> What kind crown I'm gonna wear? Starry crown.
> What kind crown I'm gonna wear? Starry crown.
> Starry crown I'm bound to wear.
> Yes, yes, yes, my Lord, I'm a soldier of the cross.
> Yes, yes, yes, my Lord, I'm a soldier of the cross. [Repeat.]

Now we are going to open the doors of the church. If anyone like to join the church, come right on up.

> This heart of mine, this heart of mine,
> When Jesus fixed, when Jesus fixed this heart of mine.
>
> One day, one day I was walking along
> When Jesus fixed, when Jesus fixed this heart of mine.
>
> All night long, down on my knees,
> When Jesus fixed, when Jesus fixed this heart of mine.

I haven't got time to tell you what I want to tell you; seem like you all are in a hurry. I hope the rain will run you all back in. Don't nobody leave till we show them what Macedonia folks can do.

The connection between the ceremonial function of the church and the basic religious sentiments of the people is not clear. Nor is it apparent how closely these religious sentiments apart from the church are related to individual social conduct. Not all religious sentiment was related to the church, and not all reactive church members gave expression to religious sentiments. A woman who felt a friendlessness for which the social church was responsible could say: "I ain't got nobody, nobody but Jesus. I know I got Jesus." A man who acknowledged profound belief in God said: "But I ain't got time to be going to all these here church processions." There is, moreover, a pervasive skepticism of the pretensiveness of the church which has little relation to religion.

They turn you out sometimes for playing ball. They don't want you to play cards either. They don't want you to do nothing but work and give them money to set down on in this county.

The church don't give you nothing; but they rob you, though. They come after every chicken you got.

There were persons who disliked the church, and those who merely disregarded all its attempted regulations, but nowhere was there observed anything approaching religious skepticism. Imperfect understanding of the Bible extended at times to the ludicrous, as, for example, in the serious expostulation of one man: "Cain found his wife in the land of Nod, and she was a monkey." The dominant attitude was one of unquestioning belief in and re-reliance upon God as a protection against everything that was feared, and an answer to everything that could not be understood.

In so simple a society the range of the unknown fell far into the field of ordinary experience. Just as God brought droughts, rain, pestilence, disease for a purpose both local and inscrutable, there was no appeal from his elections, whether with respect to the incidence of contagion or the exigencies of the cotton crop. All is mystery colored by a faith and fatalism which tended to dull both striving and desire. The conventional response to a death in the

178

family, to the acuteness of hard times, to tragedy, and to the prospect of personal death and damnation is "seeking." And such seeking partakes of all the fears which make up life. It probably accounts for the frequent "visions" and dreams so colored by the workaday world, and for the ecstasies of the release. It seems just as true of the religious experiences of this group as of other similarly naïve Negro groups of which it has been observed that they were not converted to God, but converted God to themselves.

Chapter VI

PLAY LIFE

The deadening routine of the daily labor and the seasonal stress in farming lend high importance to the leisure time. There are few who do not in course of the year have periods free from work. The community had provided for itself certain forms of diversion, as follows:

The Church

Regular Sunday services, camp meetings and revivals, funerals, wakes, prayer meetings, are definite recreations, particularly for the older people. These pleasures are occasionally combined with more secular fun: "Church is all the entertainment I has; every meeting Sunday"; "I go to church jest a little; hunting is 'ginst the law."

The Saturday Trip to Town

This is the occasion for a good time. It is sometimes combined with a certain amount of marketing. Old friends meet in town, gossip, eat peanuts, and drink soda pop and not infrequently corn whiskey, shop about, and, if they have any money, buy things for the family. There is a moving-picture show for Negroes in Tuskegee which some of them attend. Once a month is the usual frequency of visits of this sort. It sometimes affords recreation for older men to go down to the country store, or to the highway, or to the small railway station, to sit and talk, on the chance of some excitement.

Sports

There are notable conflicts in the community with respect to certain sports. The most common diversions like ball-playing, frolics,

THE YOUNG PEOPLE GO TO TOWN

and cards, being under the ban of the church, can be indulged in only by defying the regulations of the community's strongest institution. This happens, nevertheless, on a large scale. The Saturday ball game during the summer is one of the most popular diversions. Next in importance is fishing. Men and women, young and old, find this a sport both pleasant and useful since it also provides a meal for the family. Fishing, however, has been condemned as a lazy man's sport and likewise requires a license. Still another form of recreation is hunting. This could be as useful as fishing, but hunting comes under the regulation of the state. There is a hunting season and the requirement of a license. The possession of guns by the Negroes is not looked upon favorably by the white community. As a result, most of the hunting is done covertly. The people are aware of the law, but violate it occasionally, as much for food as for sport. "I had 'chicken' for supper today. I have to call it 'chicken' 'cause it's 'g'inst the law to hunt rabbits now."

Church Suppers

Church suppers are both the answer of the church to the secular parties and a means of indirect taxation of members. A favorite form of entertainment is the box supper and picnic, in which each family brings its own basic food while they purchase lighter refreshments; and the old folks' parties—"tackie parties," they are sometimes called—where the fun consists in seeing how ludicrously one can dress himself. "The folks all dress up and looks ugly, puts moss all on they heads and paint they faces, and then charge five cents for you to come up and look. That's how I raised three dollars for my church last year. I put on the concert all by myself." These parties, however, have taken on many of the features of a secular frolic, and older members have been discouraged from attending, quite as much out of fear of getting hurt as of dissatisfaction with the secular trend of the proceedings.

The Frolic

This is the great feature of the rural recreation. These affairs begin as dances where refreshments are sold and wind up, frequently, in the most wanton merrymaking. In this respect they are characteristic of all peasant merrymaking, a reaction to, and escape from, the other extreme of their life-cycle. The frolics and "parties," held on Saturday nights, were mentioned by practically all the younger members of the community. The churches inveighed against them as an incident of the evil of dancing. They are held from house to house; there is usually an abundance of corn whiskey available, and they not infrequently end in violence. The houses are small and ill lighted and couples make little secret of the character and intensity of their love-making under the wide-flung blanket of darkness. One old woman referred thus to these affairs: "Now my son, he has lots of entertainment. He goes to all dem dances on Saturday nights. I ain't feeling so favorable to that. Dere's so much cutting and killing going on, but he's got to look out for hisself now; he's a man like everybody else, I 'spects." Church members are not expected to attend these affairs on penalty of expulsion, but many of them do, and in listing their recreations included frolics along with the church.

The murder of the young woman at one of the frolics, which was mentioned during the early period of this study, was not wholly surprising. At that affair the drinking had reached the point of an orgy. "They was all so drunk they spit all on the bed. Then they got tired and run around spitting up and down the mantel. . . . . What I likes most is to drink a little corn but you can't find none now. The sheriff's been here so much folks is scared to keep it, but they brings it up from Montgomery."

There was, occasionally, the franker listing by individual men of sexual intercourse as their relaxation. Two unmarried women said that they liked to "pleasure themselves with men" when they were not too tired. A more polite way of referring to this form of entertainment by men was "setting around playing with womens."

Aside from the conventional outlets there are other means of using leisure time which, while perhaps less harmful than the frolics and parties, yet contributed little to the cultural development of the community. There is practically no reading and no concerts or lectures, apart from those offered in connection with church

182

programs. Those who do not like what is offered by the community may "piddle around the house," "set on the porch and rock," "lay down and sleep," "wallow around the house," "play with the cat," "walk about and visit," or "jest set down."

The winter period, which is free from active outside farming, offers miscellaneous duties for the men: chopping wood and "fixing things." The women sew and quilt, and this is sometimes listed as recreation. Changes in the material culture of the community have brought new, though somewhat limited, forms of diversion. One of these is automobile riding. A few families possessed automobiles, but joy rides, interestingly enough, encountered conservative opposition on the part of the community. Men objected to having their women ride in automobiles and quite serious results have followed the indulgence.

Lodges and Societies

The tradition of the burial society hangs on in the mutual organization which, though concerned chiefly with death benefits, build up and hold their membership on the strength of the social features. In a situation under which families were losing such insurance as they had, the burial societies were gaining in strength.[4]

I belong to the Burial Union. That ain't the same as the Union Aid. We pays only when a member dies. We got 'bout 400 members and each pay 20 cents. I'm carrying a Burial Union and when I die the money goes to whoever I willed it to. We have several branches in different locations, one in Liverpool, one in Hardaway, and one in Shady Grove. The difference in this and the Union Aid, it pays when you're sick and you pays every month. Ours is a co-operative business. The nation is too divided now and we people is trying to get together. We come together every month for a meeting.

Some of the insurance companies operating in the neighborhood have adjusted their methods to community habits, and instead of collectors they attempt to organize the people into lodges. Of these there is a considerable variety, from the "Love and Do

4 There were 224 of the 612 families who now have, or have had, insurance, and 170 of these paid premiums of 25 cents a week or less. Twenty-one companies and lodges were represented in these numbers.

Wells" to the "Sons and Daughters of I Will Arise." There has been a loss of confidence in most of these recently, owing to frequent financial failures, the inability to meet sickness and death payments, and the widespread exploitation by both whites and Negroes from the outside. One man said: "I was in the American ——— and the American ———. It went down. When they first come around they made out like it was colored but we found out it was white. I had paid about $15 in it when it went down." A woman gave a similar experience: "I couldn't tell you how much money I didn't lose in dese societies. Paid whole lot a money and de society break down."

Mother: I put 'bout $500 in dem; I can't tell 'xactly how much, but I wisht I had it.

Another person said:

Yes, we lost money in the American ———. All three of us were in there for over five years. He had to pay $1.10 a month and $1.00 each for me and grandmother. The next year it was raised to $1.20 a month each. They just kept raising on us so we got out, and it soon went down here. They claim to be colored but I thinks it's white. After we got out they decided they couldn't carry us less we reinstate and we all decided to stop. We tried to get our money back, but they said we'd have to see the deputy that set me up, and he was dead then.

Actually these companies were at times within the law in their refusal to pay certain benefits, but it was as hard to convince their policyholders that they were within their rights in refusing payment as it was easy to sell them a policy which they could not read and which actually promised them nothing. Some of the stipulations made it impossible to pay unless there was illness or death from diseases which were as rare in Macon County as Asiatic cholera.

There are no radios, but 76 families had victrolas, bought on the instalment plan from agents in the community. There was but one banjo in the entire 612 families. This musical instrument is never so invariably associated with the Negro in actual life as it is on the stage. There were twenty-one organs and three pianos in the families, and most of these were out of repair; but playing provided some amusement. Both the organs and the pianos were in the homes of owners.

There is being introduced, with some prospect of better control, a new form of recreation centering around the schools, where these are at all active. School closings with commencements, school parties, and festivals offer perhaps the most wholesome forms of recreation now obtainable in the community for children and adults.

Chapter VII

SURVIVAL

MACON COUNTY ranked third in Negro mortality in a list of 67 rural Alabama counties, according to the 1929 mortality census. There were 406 deaths and these gave a rate of 18.4. This rate was exactly the same as that for the white population in this county. There is, however, something unexplained about the figures. Just one year before the Negro mortality was 22.1 and in 1925 it was 22.2 and second highest in the state. The ratio between white and Negro deaths has remained approximately the same, and the mortality of the white population of this county has exceeded that of Negroes in the majority of counties of the state. This may indeed be a reflection of the hard life of the northern section of the county where most of the white residents live (in the shadow of their own past).

One of the unexplained circumstances in the number of Negro deaths for 1929 may possibly be connected with the discrepancy between the numbers of Negroes dying as reported by the federal census, on the one hand, and the county health officer, on the other. The records of the latter show 60 white and 154 Negro death certificates while the census shows 87 whites and 406 Negroes, residents and nonresidents. This would presumably include deaths at the Negro Veterans Hospital located in the county near Tuskegee. During the same year 119 white and 574 Negro babies were added to the population. The white population, thus, it seems, had 98 per cent more birth survivals than deaths and the Negroes about 3.6 per cent more. The extent to which the lower Negro rates of survival are related to inadequate birth registration is not evident in the figures alone, nor does the county health officer know what proportion of the total was registered. There is some evidence that the number of Negro births registered is less than the actual number of births. In our 612 families, which might be taken as an average, there were 69 children under one year of age. These were 2.7 of the total population. If this rate may be assumed for the entire population, it would be expected that 600 of the children born during a given twelve months' period would be alive. Such an estimate, however, would not take into account those who were born and died during the first few months of the year. If these were included it would point to a somewhat greater discrepancy. Since the fecundity rate is known to be high, a situation exists which emphasizes the high infant mortality rate as well as the rate for stillbirths and nonviable abortions.

In order of numerical importance the chief causes of death, as listed by the county health officer, were violence, heart disease, stillbirths, tuberculosis, influenza, nephritis, cancer, pellagra, and malaria. The distribution is unusual. Little confidence can be placed in the figures available on this mortality. In the first place, diseases are not adequately diagnosed because of the uncertain relation of doctors to sick persons, the rather general ignorance of disease, the reliance upon folk diagnosis and cures, and the exceedingly high rate of venereal infection in the population. The relative inaccessibility of many of the families leaves them very largely to the informal agencies of the community for handling both sickness and death. When violence is responsible for death it becomes a matter of both health and crime registration, and the state steps in with considerably more determination and insists on greater accuracy in the record.

The only index to sickness among the families studied was the non-technical one of persons being treated for malaria, pellagra, and syphilis, the latter under a special demonstration instituted as an experiment by the Rosenwald Fund. The county health service provided some mass treatment for persons with malaria. In 100 of the 612 families, or 16.3 per cent, all members of the family had been treated for malaria; in 194, or 31.6 per cent of the families, one or both of the parents had been treated; and in 50 more families, or about 5 per cent of them, some of the children and one or both parents had been treated. Twenty-eight of the families, or 4 per cent, reported that some of the children had been treated. In 212 families, or 43.6 per cent, there was no record of treatment for malaria. This does not measure the extent of malarial infection. Pellagra is similarly a common malady as indicated by the scaly, cracking skins, but there was no medical appraisal of the extent, since this would have required professional examination. Forty-one families were receiving, or had received, some treatment for pellagra. With respect to syphilis, however, the opportunity for determining the extent was unparalleled for studies of this type.

The Julius Rosenwald Fund, in co-operation with the United States Public Health Service, had undertaken a study of the prevalence of syphilis among Negroes in selected areas of the South. The health officers of six southern states were brought in co-operation with the Fund, through the Public Health Service and demonstrations were set up in six areas. The purpose of the demonstration was to provide a basis for determining the practicability and effectiveness of measures for the mass control of syphilis. Macon County was selected as one of these areas because of the proximity of Tuskegee Institute, the John A. Andrews Hospital, and the United States War Veterans Hospital, and because the administrative controls of the county and state, particularly in the health and welfare divisions, were co-operative. A thorough campaign was made to include as large a number of families as possible within a limited section of the county, in examinations which included Wassermann tests. All ages of both sexes were examined, and as many treated as would accept. The results of the medical examinations provide perhaps one of the most complete samples of a total population anywhere available. In this county 3,684 Wassermanns were taken, of which 1,474, or 35 per cent, were positive. This rate, incidentally, was the highest of the six demonstrations. A county in Georgia stood next with 26 per cent, on the basis of 5,775 tests; a county in Mississippi was next in order with 20 per cent on 9,753 tests; a county in North Carolina ranked fourth with only 12 per cent positives on a basis of 10,196 examinations. The average for the 30,000 serological examinations was 20 per cent positives.

In Macon County the large number of positive Wassermanns for children pointed to heridito-syphilis. The large number of positive reactions in men and women of advanced ages presented a problem for the medical men, since it is usually expected that the disease would have manifested itself in the advanced ages in other and more violent results.

The highest positive rates for men were found in the age group twenty-five to twenty-nine, with 32 per cent of their cases, and the women in the age group twenty to twenty-four, with 34 per cent of the cases.

Most of these families were not burdened by defectives so far as it was possible to ascertain. In 588 families, or 96 per cent of the total, there were no defectives. There was a blind child in 2 of the families. Two families had what appeared to be an imbecile, and 5 families had a person subject to "spells." A crippled person was found in 13 families, while 1 family had a ten-year-old child that had been crippled and an imbecile because of infantile paralysis since he was two or three years old.

The number of stillbirths and miscarriages in these families also served as an index to the health of the people in these communities. In the 612 families there were 490 known stillbirths. Less than half of the wives were responsible for the 490 stillbirths and miscarriages. There were 368 families in which none was reported.

To understand the somewhat unusual incidence of certain diseases and causes of death it is necessary to go back again to the life of the families.

Violent Deaths

There is a tradition of violence which seems to mark personal relations to a high degree. Although strictly speaking not a matter of health, reference to the setting in which these violent deaths take place is important as a phase of the social life as well as the mortality. They include accidents of various sorts as well as homicides. The violence of life was an inescapable fact in a large number of families of the county. In another connection reference has been made to the violence attending jealousy in sex relations, but violence is not confined to love affairs. The large amount resulting in death in this group of 612 families may be considered simply another index to its cultural status. A woman who was asked about sleeping with her windows open replied that "people do's so much killin' round here, I'se scared to leave 'em open." Another, referring to their recreation, explained why they stopped attending the dances: "Dere's so much cutting and killing going on." One notes either casualness or fatalism in recounting deaths in the family by violence.

My little grandchild what dead got a grain of corn down her throat, I think. She was shelling corn when she started coughing and she look jest like she had whooping cough, and never did get well. My other boy got kilt. He was jest stabbed to death. Oh, they sent the boy what done it to the reformatory.

Playing with Weapons

My brother wuz killed accidentally by his wife. He had gone to see 'bout my oldest sister who had gone crazy. He took my brother-in-law's automatic pistol back to Birmingham with him 'cause he was 'fraid my sister would get holt to it and hurt somebody. He had promised to teach his wife to shoot it, so one mornin' he was learnin' her. He took all the cartridges out and give it to her to shoot but he had left one in. He didn't know one wuz in the barrel. She took the pistol and 'cose she wuz scared to shoot it, and she throw her head on the side and her hand out and shot it and it hit my brother right in the head.

Juvenile Murders

My brother got killed out there by the creek. He was coming home from a ball game one evening and two boys grabbed him. I spose they got to fussing and the boys got mad and kilt him. We found him dead over there. They caught the boys. . . . . One was a little boy 'bout twelve. They sent him to the 'formatory. The other one they sent to the mines for seven years.

Absent Sons

My boy got killed in Birmingham. They say he got shot—I don' know.

A White Gentleman Shot Him

My boy dead now. A white gentleman shot him. He went to his house to see his sister working there, and the gentleman told him to stay 'way. 'Twas his fault, I reckon. The man said, "Stay 'way."

A Baseball Bat

Our preacher's brother just got killed. He was at a ball game and a boy was batting and instead of hitting the ball he turned the bat loose and it went and struck him. The boy batting musta had something in him [corn whiskey].

All of this suggests the rough-handed closeness of a frontier community before adequate control of personal relations have been developed. There is the significant difference that social control in this community is related only vaguely to law. The courts are outside of the scheme of life; adjustment of relations in the past has been very largely the province of the white planter. Such unanimity of sentiment on law as exists is a common disposition to remain as far as possible out of contact with the courts whether as plaintiff or accused. Where these traditional forms of control over all phases of Negro social life by the white proprietor are weakening, as is apparent in the younger generation, or where there are no protectors available, the adjustment of disputes becomes a matter of the individuals involved. Instead of providing security as the arbitrator of personal differences, the courts are an institution to be feared, a medium through which justice is to be secured only by recourse to some individual white protector. Thus, differences tend to be settled on a personal and face-to-face basis. This sentiment helps further to account for the prevalence of weapons of defense.

One of the most frequently asserted evidences of respectability is that "we ain't been in no trouble yet." It is sufficiently difficult to avoid, in the community setting, to make avoidance a virtue.

Woofter reports an interesting situation among St. Helena Negroes, who live relatively isolated but very largely under their own social controls. There is similar attitude toward the "law," which they refer as to "the unjust law," in contradistinction to their own extra-legal machinery centered largely in the church. The local magistrates, recognizing this, encourage settlements through their own agencies. Cases of violence are thus very often avoided. A consequence is that there is very little crime and extremely few civil suits. Out of a population of about five thousand there were only about thirty-five cases annually brought before the local magistrate and most of these were cases of nonresidents.

Folk Knowledge of Disease

Except on the basis of a general health examination it would be impossible to estimate the extent of sickness from various diseases. Complaints are generalized into merely "feelin' kinda poorly" or "I ain't no good," and generalized complaints call for the generalized measures of patent medicines, or home herb remedies. "Black Draught," "666," salts, and castor oil make up a large part of the treatment of disease. Other standard remedies are "White Wonder Salve," calomel, and quinine.

Unless there is some folk pattern of treatment, death may result from sickness which in all probability could be avoided or intelligently treated. As one illiterate mother stated: "I had one child to die when it was just three days old, but I ain't never knowed what the trouble was. It just cried an' cried for three days and nights and then died."

Children die in great numbers and mothers accept their death with a dull and uninquiring fatalism. Some of the expressions back of the infant mortality rates are thus most casual and uninformed: The mother of eleven children sighed when she recalled "I don' had lots of chillun to die. I don't know what ailed them." Another, referring to her stillbirths, said, "I birthed eleven chillun. I got two living, six was born dead, and three lived a little while. That boy that died when he was three days old bled to death at the navel."

All that another mother knew about her infant's death was that "he just keep on spitting up blood and then died." "The granny" explained that "strainers" [meaning constipation] killed one infant, and eating too much dirt while carrying twins killed both of them for another of her patients. Then came this accident, which left a heavy memory for the mother:

I was washing and my little baby asked for some water. I said, "Wait, honey; mammy busy," and I plumb forgot him till he scream. He done drunk my lye. He die so pitiful and hard I wisht I'da stop and give him a drink.

By some good fortune there are those who survive serious attacks without the aid of physicians. A man and his wife, aged fifty-three and forty-six respectively, live alone and pay $65 for rent of their farm. One daughter of the husband died of tuberculosis. The husband said:

Don't ask me if we've been sick; that's all we bees. Last year I paid nigh over one hundred dollars for my sickness alone, and then my old lady there she's all time sick. Got so once we thought we was losing her for fair. All one side was paralyzed. She didn't speak for twenty-four hours. All the church folks come. Some give money, some give food, and she just lay there and hold 'em. Didn't know who gie'd 'em. She don't know yet. Well, I got busy. God and myself worked, rubbed, and twisted her till she finally come 'round. I tell you I believe in the Lord. He just didn't mean for me to lose her. . . . . I has all kinds of trouble with my stomach. That's why I'm sick.

The following is an account of one woman's "miseries" as she described them. She had been sick for three years.

I was in the field plowing one day and I felt something jerkin' my head around. Then I tried to spit and I couldn't. I said to my sister, "Can yo spit?" And she did, but I couldn't. I been sick and not able to work for three years. I has miseries in my stomach.

Indigestion ("indijestus") is a frequent complaint among the families, and this is a description of it:

My boy's out there is sick. He got indijestus. It jest takes him that way every time he gets a little cold in him. He'll start coughing and it hurts him all in there [lungs and chest], and you kin hear him trying to git his breath and he just has that indijestus with it every time.

My girl is sick too. The boy ain't sick as the girl. He only gits that way when he takes cold, but she dat way all the time.

193

This mother had thirteen children, and most of them had had trouble with "indijestus." The family gave evidence of being wracked with tuberculosis without the least suspicion of the lethal character of the ailment. Each successive death was an accidentally ill effect of "indijestus." Other descriptions of ailments suggest serious maladies, but in the absence of both diagnosing physicians or adequate treatment of these disorders they usually take this fatal issue, and perhaps affect others through contagion.

My husband he got sores all over him and I ain't got but one sore.

This child takes fits after his daddy. He ain' long stopped having them.

All my chillen is fond of having fevers.

They tell me its "two bumps" [tuberculosis]; anyhow he keep a terrible misery in his throat so he can't swallow water.

Two of my chillen die with "yellow thrash." I gived them thread salve made from yellow berries but they die right on.

I been sick a year going on two months. I ain't nobody, honey. See all these here sores on my legs [*pointing to open sores as large as one's hand*], water runs out of my legs there like that all the time. I can't lay down. I have to set up all the time. I can't lay down. If I lay down this here water you see running out will overflow my heart. I ain't nobody to be depended on. Liable to be dead tomorrow. I jest set here all day and fan flies. All this begin when I was four years old; now I'm at changing life. Sometimes I'm so hot look like I'm gonna run out of my skin, but in the evenings I get jest as cold as ice.

My wife here she out of her mind; jest come and go you know. She been sick so long.

My boy there [aged eleven] he had tumors—you know, a risin' come out on his head. In three weeks them doctors got sixty dollars but they saved him. For myself you see I ain't got no teeth. I tooks a dose of calomy and 'fore I know it my teeth all start dropping out. I has the ear run, too, but that ain't so bad. Now my wife she died 'cause she had some tumors in her stomach. Them folks at the hospital [in Montgomery] just killed her. How I knows 'cause one of them nurses is my friend and she tole me herself they jest feeled around and couldn't find the tumor so they jest out and out and cut the wrong vescicule.

I been sick about four years. I have shortness of the breath and fulness of the chest.

I got plenty chillen dead. One eleven months old died with fever; one the thrase run over him and one girl sixteen died in 1915. She got wet the wrong time. Doctor claim she had pellagacy. She said she could hear something inside her head, and she break out with great big old red bumps. Then they went in an' where they left was just as black. She didn't live no time. She was sick four weeks to the day she died.

I been so sick with my back and running bladder.

My daughter died with the fever. I don't know 'zackly what kind of fever it was. Dr. ———— say it was swamp fever, but Dr. ———— say it was malaria. My son die with heart trouble. That what Dr. ———— say, but Dr. ———— say it was bad blood. Dr. ————'s father was my husband's father's master. That's wha' he gets the same name.

That child there has spells since she was a little baby. Jest one right after another from eight to four o'clock every day for two years. I dosed her with calomel and I sent to Montgomery and got some worm powder and got nineteen worms from her in one day. But she can't learn nothing in school now. She jest sets with her mouth open and her tongue doubled back most of the time.

The heavy fall of death prompts to reliance upon both herbs and something akin to magic, in the attempt to bring about cures. The little granddaughter of one of the older women became ill.

I done all I could. Then one of them nurses in Tuskegee says to me I weren't doing the right thing by the child. Honey, I sho' was hurted so much 'cause I done everything for the little motherless thing. So I got me a bottle of castoria and fed it to her but hit didn't help her none. By and by I was told to wash her in dish water, so I done that every night for a long time. Then when I fear'd it warn't no use, my dead friend she come to me in a dream. She and me was dear friends together. She stood right there at the bed like real and she washed up a big sheet till hit was pure white. She ain't never spoke till she got done. Then she hung it up and spoke for the first time. She said, "Dat child ain't gonna die; she gwine live and grow up from there restrenkened." I got some more castoria and worked on the baby and here she am—well and healthy. It sho' was a miraculous sent from God.

Whooping cough is treated by tying a leather string around the child's neck. A necklace of cork and moles' feet is used to make teething easy. "White Wonder Salve" softens up old injuries; "Thread Salve" cures "yellow thrash." A woman said: "Papa died with pneumonia. He wouldn't use nothing but rubbing medicine, and wouldn't never call no doctor." Another woman, with enormous sores of long standing on her arm and breast, was trying to nurse her baby. "Dese boils hurt so bad," she complained. "Dey's sore from de kernel. I been so sick I could hardly stand up." She put sulphur and vaseline on these sores. There was, however, a sense of the possibility of contagion. She talked of weaning the baby "so de boils won't turn on it." Still another woman kept a string around the children's necks to keep off disease. Pomegranate hull tea and broom-straw root tea are used for "back weakness." Peach-tree leaves and elephant tongue are good for fever. The woman who gave this formula said "doctor ain't no good when it comes to fevers." Boiled fireweed and lard make an excellent salve for burns. Sheep-nanny tea, kerosene, and sugar may be used for whooping cough, or red onions alone. If swollen feet are sweated first in pine top and mullen, then in cedar water, they will give no more trouble. Pepper and salt will cure spasms.

Use of Physicians

Rural calls are expensive and time consuming to make, whether the physicians take into account the ability of patients to pay or not. During the past year 258 of the 612 Negro families used the professional services of physicians, 322 did not use them, and in 32 cases the information could not be secured.

The expenditures for health as nearly as they could be estimated were as shown in Table XXV.

The fee for an office consultation is $2.50 and $3.00. Fees for rural calls appear to vary according to distance and accessibility,

196

sometimes amounting to $12. A curious practice of using proxies in the diagnosis of disease is noted in the following case:

I fell mighty low sick. I don't know exactly what the trouble. Think the doctor says it was an abscess on my bladder and it busted. The doctor didn't come to see me 'cause he was busy wid a label case, but he sent Mr. ———— over to see me and he took down my complaint and written up my case. No, Mr. ———— ain't no doctor but he writes up my case and takes it back to Dr. ———— and he sent me some medicine.

All of the physicians serving the Negroes of this part of the country are white, save one who lives in the town of Greenwood. Some of the physicians are also landowners. One doctor, in par-

TABLE XXIV

HEALTH EXPENDITURES

None	248	$30–$34	1
Amount unknown	115	35– 39	0
Under $5	112	40– 44	5
$ 5–$ 9	45	45– 49	1
10– 14	33	50 and over	17
15– 19	17		
20– 24	13	Total	612
25– 29	5		

ticular, seems to be greatly liked and admired by the Negroes. He extends them credit, does not exact exorbitant fees, and is sympathetic with their complaints. A few of the plantation-owners will send doctors to their good workers when they are ill, or guarantee the payment of their bills. This is sufficient security since the doctor's bill can be taken out of the crop. For the most part, however, the doctors insist upon some security for the debt before calling. Ownership of a cow, or mule, or other property will suffice, and these are taken in if the bills are not paid within a reasonable time. Some of the objection to doctors was based upon their insistence upon prompt payment in cash.

They just gets all our money when we is sick. A poor nigger has a hard time. You phones them and they say, "Is you got the money?" If you ain't, you need not 'spect them. You gotta have that money right on the table or you just lies here and dies.

197

Adjustments are made around the necessity for doctors. One woman, in speaking of her husband, said:

When I get sick, he don't take me to no doctor. He'll buy medicine and bring it to me. He'll go to the doctor hisself, but he won't take me. Last time I was sick I had stomach trouble and he kept getting me medicine and I got worse, so he got a midwife and she said my womb had fallen. She fixed it up and I got all right. He had been giving me "666" and castor oil.

As serious as any other factor, however, in the attitude toward and frequently fatal result of disease is the air of resignation toward sickness when it comes. It explains to some extent the frequent lack of faith in doctors and the diffidence about certain public health measures.

Old man B—— took dropsy. His legs bust open and his feet bust open. He had money enough to buy fifty-cent socks, but he ruint so many they had to put ten-cent socks on him. They take him to springs but it didn't do no good. When God get hold of you, you can go to any kind of springs but it won't help you none.

An old man and his wife, both devoutly religious, sat waiting for death. Said the husband:

The Marster [God] give me notice about six months ago for me to wind up my portion of this world's goods and to go in secret prayer. I was in the room and he come in too and just look like I could shake hands with him. I don't feel sick but I'm painful.

Said the wife:

The Lord come to me about three or four weeks ago. I was in bed and I look up and saw him just like I'm seeing you, and he was in a book. I got up and put on my burial clothes and he was waiting for me. I called my son to come in there and look at him but couldn't nobody see him but me. I kept waiting all day dressed for I thought he done come to take me. I'm prepared to die when he do come to get me. I ain't dead yet and I thought good God done come after me long time ago.

Midwives

The rôle of the midwife and her method can be best understood in the account of one of the best-known "grannies" of the county:

How Training Was Acquired

These old people 'round here learned me how to deliver babies. Long before I ever thought 'bout it we was at Mr. ———'s sister's house and she got confined and they sent for the granny and she didn't come. I didn't know and mammy didn't know what to do. So I measured the baby's navel and cut it off and I cut it off too much and that baby died, but the doctor didn't do nothing about it but he said that old granny ought to be stopped for not coming to see about her and I couldn't help it 'cause I was doing the best I could. Then after that, when I was living down on the hill a girl got confined and her brothers got on the horses and started for the granny and 'fore she could get there the baby begin to come on and I told her I wan't gonna let it drap, to let it come on that I wan't gonna let it hit the floor. I put the girl to bed good as I could, and I didn't put a cloth to her but I seed after the baby.

Treatment of the Mother

You know you don't put a cloth to a woman till after three days; it is best to let it drain for that long. It will kill her if you bound her up before that time. I don't like to have a crowd around when I am bringing a baby; somebody might go out and say one thing and some will go out and say another. Some of them will go out and talk about how the woman carried on and I just don't like to have them around. You turn the baby on the right side so as to give the blood chance to go all through his body. Then you turn the mother on her right side and let her lay on her right side for 'bout a hour.

A Knife To Cut the Pains

I usually put a sharp knife under the pillow; they say that cuts the pain, but I don't know whether it do or not. Some people say they can tell how many children you gonna have by the number of rings on the cord, but I don't believe that's so 'cause the old granny told me I was gonna have 'bout ten chillen and I ain't never had but one. After that I said I was done with that saying.

Mighty few of the chillen glad to see you come, for they 'fraid they will have to give you a little bread. Now when I lived in Birmingham all the little chillen used to see me coming and holler, "Yon come my mammy," and they all say, "Don't you stay down there and suffer for nothing to eat."

Cutting the Cord with Scissors

I always cut the cord with scissors and when I get through I just slip them under the pillow. They tells us you ought to get hold of what you charge before you hit a lick of work. These folks don't want to pay you for nothing. I heard that Mrs. F—— was telling all the women to use G——. G—— is a right nice seamstress and I reckon she do sewing for Mrs. F—— and Mrs. F—— tell the women to use her, but I reckon the Lord will straighten things out. I loses more than I make trying to get my money.

Causes of Deformity

Plenty women's chillen is deformed 'cause its the way they do in carrying them and they always trying to lay it on the fever, 'cause fever don't cause you to be deformed 'cause I try to hold the jints together so close so that they won't be deformed. I had a brother who was deformed; he was marked by a turtle. My mamma was plowing one day and plowed up a turtle and she stuck a plow in the back of his head. He sets his feet out like a turtle and walks and slides them back like one. I got one of his shoes in here now and it don't look like it was ever straight. I was a plow hand when my first child was born and I plowed up to the time and it didn't hurt it none; its just all right if you don't let the plow kick you. That woman over yonder plows all the time and it don't hurt her, and that other woman said she went over to her mama's and picked a bag of peas and carried them home and that's what caused her to have him deformed.

Dirt-Dauber Tea for Labor Pains

Some folks say if you pick the dirt out of dirt-dauber holes and make tea out of it, it will cut the pains, but I don't know whether that will do any good or not. I sometimes give them a little weak camphor to force the pains and that is mighty weak too. Sometimes when folks eat dirt and when the baby comes its a whole lot of dirt on his back where they have been eating too much. I don't believe in using so many of these old things 'cause I believe some of them is pizen.

White-Flannel Weed for "Whites"

There is a weed grows out here called "white flannel" that is mighty good for whites [leucorrhea]. A woman asked me once, "Ain't you a doctor woman?" And I told her yes, and she told me her daughter don't never have no health and said she can't hardly get over the floor, and I told her to go get her some white flannel and make her a tea off it; and she wanted to know if a yard would be enough to get and I told her it wasn't no cloth but a weed. So I went up on the hill and found her some and give it to her. That woman got all right. Her husband had to stop work every week one day and stay home with her and help her scrub, but after she started taking the white-flannel tea she got all right. That white flannel sho' is good.

How To Reduce Water

Another thing, some women when they has babies they drink so much water that their stomach's get large and poke way out and get pot-gutted; well, if you fix up some corn bread with a heap of salt in it and put it on the fire and let it burn right black and then split it open and put it in a bucket and let her drink off that, her stomach will come down jest as nice.

Hot Ginger Tea for Retarded Menstruation

Heap of them come to me for female trouble but I tell them to go on to the doctor 'cause I'm 'fraid to fool with so many things. When the flowers is clogged I give them hot ginger tea.

Bad Blood and Corn Bread

When I went to the clinic they said my blood was good, but I told the doctor my blood might be good but there was something the matter with my body 'cause I can't eat corn bread no more. I used to eat corn bread all the time and I believe I eat too much 'cause one day something come and said to me just like somebody talking, "That corn bread is killing you." It done that twice and I quit eating it 'cause I didn't want it to kill me, and I told the doctor about it and told him to give me some medicine for it.

The county has been attempting to give some instruction to the Negro midwives, recognizing that most of the deliveries are made by them. The health officer has corralled sixty-seven of these midwives and has been talking to them about cleanliness and essential though elementary hygiene for mother and child, and about the necessity of records, although most of the midwives are illiterate. From the record of the health officer's work it appears that each midwife had been talked to once in individual conference.

Attitude toward Syphilis

In the entire 612 families interviewed there was not a single expression which seemed to connect syphilis with the sexual act. The fact of "bad blood" carried little social stigma and was spoken of in about the same manner as one speaks of having a "bad heart" or "bad teeth." The violent expressions of jealousy, manifested toward women suspected of transferring affections to other men, reflected no relation to transmitted infection. In one instance only was "bad blood" associated with heredity. "I knowed I had bad blood 'cause my mamma had scrofula when I was born." In but few instances was "bad blood" associated with syphilis as a venereal disease. Where there were obvious physical manifestations of the disease the persons were referred to as being afflicted, but this was generalized. Often no distinction was made between complaints and the symptoms of "bad blood." Accordingly, treatments for bad blood were expected to cure headaches, indigestion, pellagra, sterility, sores of various sorts, and general run-down condition.

Attitude toward the Health Demonstration

The Rosenwald Fund experiment in mass control of syphilis was probably more successful in bringing a large number of persons to have blood tests made than any similar venture. The reasons for this lie in the character and habits of the population. There was a lack of social embarrassment in being examined and treated for syphilis. The directors of the experiment succeeding in giving a medical rather than a social stress to the connotation of "bad blood."

My blood was drawed twice but they never sent me no invitation about it. I bet my blood ain't good 'cause I hear everybody say they blood is bad. I think mine ought to be bad too. I just went down there one day and said I wanted shots and they shot me.

The tradition of dependence and obedience to the orders of authority, whether these were mandatory or not, helps to explain the questionless response to the invitation to examination and treatment. In the conduct of the demonstration, however, the greatest kindliness was shown the patients, and the invitations were in no sense supported by force, either direct or implied.

The extent of sickness among the Negro families and the hope of relief without cost were means of drawing and holding them. "Me and my wife went over to the schoolhouse and they drawed our blood and say it was good, but I can't understand why we are always so painful." The familiarity of some of the Negro families with the method of giving "shots" by physicians for which comparatively large sums were paid had given them a "set" for the demonstration. Free "shots" were taken as a boon. The fitting of "salves" and red medicine of the old clinic into old habits of getting relief gave confidence. Some of the persons attempted to get the salves for general complaints, even though their blood was reported "good." "They said my blood was good. You don't get no treatment if your blood is good, but sometimes I wish it was bad 'cause they gives away a salve up there and I wanted some of it so bad." The "shots" were indeed expected to cure all complaints.

They drawed my blood twice last year but I never did get no hearing from it. Look like mine ought to be bad 'cause I was bothered with pellagacy sometime ago.

I goes down to the clinic last Wednesday for the doctor to give me a shot but he didn't give me none. I had a roaring in my head for four or five years.

Good effects observed prompted many to continue treatment and others to seek examination and treatment.

I never knowed women to have babies like they do this year. Them shots is making them have babies. I knowed women who been married a long time and this year they are all poking out. There is K—— W——; she about thirty-odd years old and been all about different places too and she been taking them shots and now she is 'way out yonder. You reckon them shots make you have babies? I sho' don't want no more and if they do I rather have bad blood.

Just think of Sister S—— up there. Her husband was as raw as a piece of meat the first of this year, but he done got better since he been taking these shots.

The medicine I took helped me 50 per cent. I had a terrible misery in my throat. I was sorry for the time to come to drink water, it hurt me so bad. I have taken twenty shots and it certainly has helped me.

The cost of doctors has helped attendance at the clinics:

I tell you dem doctors done de people a whole lot of good 'cause heap of people wan't able to pay a doctor. They have done this country good 'cause heaps of dem was in a bad fix. The doctors done git tight on de people since dese clinics been through here. They won't come to see you less you got the money or will pay something. See these folks is knocking them. They charge seven, eight, nine, and ten dollars 'cording how far they have to come.

Finally there was the attitude of appreciation for the gesture of helpfulness which the demonstration represented, and a response on that basis. Many of the families are enthusiastic in their praise of the work being done by the clinic. The wife in a family consisting of mother and father and ten children said:

Them shots really hoped me. 'Til last May I ain't layed down a night the whole night and slept without getting up and staying wake in twenty years. I can lay down and go to sleep with the chickens and never wake up. When I got so I could rest, I got scared. I used to get up and not feel like working, but now I can get up and feel good. . . . . This baby [a little girl five years old] has taken twenty and she don't cry none hardly. That little boy [aged seven] was born sick, and he has taken all his shots and he is so much better. He used to get off and hide and never did run and play like the rest of the children. We would have to hunt for him all the time. I was jest expecting to find him dead any time 'cause he would go 'way off somewhere and hide all the time. Now he runs round jest like the rest of them. [The mother and father and eight of the ten children gave positive Wassermanns.]

The figures for mortality, morbidity, illegitimacy, illiteracy, poverty, insufficiency of food and clothing, are barren records for an understanding of the human struggle behind them. They all come to a focus in the story of Mary Hardy, a very sad and very bewildered woman, whose career follows the pattern of life around her, because she could not understand how or why her children continued to die from some strange, persistent malady. She was not married but had wanted the security of a husband and a family.

The first man I liked real well give me a baby. My grandmother made me leave home, and I went and lived with another woman till the baby came, then grandma let me come back home, but he stole me again one night. I had to wait till my grandmother was sleep, so it was about nine o'clock and I slipped out of the window and he was down in the woods waiting for me. I went with him to his people and I stayed with his sister. I never did stay with him, but my grandmother would not let me come back home after I'd done run away and he kept putting me off. He promised to marry me the next morning. I never would a run off with him if he hadn't promised to marry me, but kept putting me off and I wanted to go back to grandma, but she told me not to come back there less she tell me, so I just had to stay. I stayed there with his sister three years and got these other two chillen. His mother kept the oldest boy and raised him.

When my third baby was coming, his father jumped up and married another girl. She was in a family way and I wondered why he married her 'cause she was in a family way and he didn't marry me when I was in a family way too. This girl was a school teacher and he married her one month before she got down. Then when he started coming back 'round, I told him, "I ain't going to fool with you no more; you done fooled me enough." I got real mad. I got mad about him, so I told him to stay away 'cause I felt bad about it . . . . and I was 'specting to marry him.

He left here and went to Montgomery. Then he sent me money to come to him but I was so hungry that I took the money and bought us something t'eat. I guess I'd a went if we hadn't been so hungry. After he married, he would give me rice and things for the chillen every time he saw me in town. He just seemed to be in love with the chillen. They say now that he is living with another woman. His wife died when she was getting down the second time. He had left and went to Montgomery to work but they wasn't separated. It was after she died that he sent for me to come to him.

Now my youngest boy is sickly and got bumps breaking out on his face—you know, fever blisters, but big ones, and when they burst they leave a sore. The sore leaves a black place when it dries up. I took him to the doctor once and he said he charged $2.50. I didn't have but $2.00, so he said he would charge me that. Then we had to send for him once and I ain't never paid him for that. He usually charge $12.50 to come out here.

Just when I thought I got my chillen well, my oldest boy died. He just rotted to death. This is how he got sick. He started with a headache. He said his head nearly bust open and Br'er [brother] got some salts and give him and he didn't complain no more for about two weeks; then he went to school one morning and the next morning they didn't have no school and he got up and it started with a hurting right here [just inside the elbow bend]. He said it was itching first, then hurting, and he just started running 'round having fits. He just went crazy. We rubbed and greased his arms and we rubbed him good, but he just went crazy and tore up the things in the house. The doctor give him some medicine when we took him to him and he said it was pellagacy but I ain't seed where it done him a bit of good. He told one man down here that it was the curriest pellagacy he ever seed in his life, and he told somebody up there that he didn't know what it was; but he told me it was pellagacy. Well, that boy would run away and I'd hear him calling way up on the hill. He just come unjointed. It all just rotted off—all his hands and arms. He bit one of his fingers off and he never was in his right mind after he first went crazy. He would take the bed down and when you ask him what he was doing it for, he's say he wanted to put it up on a hill. He swold up and just come in two. He died in two weeks.

When I got sick I went to Dr. ——— and he told me I needed shots but that he couldn't give them to me 'cause I wasn't able to pay. He asked me if I had any property and I told him no. He said he just couldn't give 'em to me then. He said, "If you just had a cow to put up against it!"

The experimental health demonstration set up by the Rosenwald Fund in a portion of the county in 1930 has made certain social discoveries vital to other than the venereal problem. The adequate treatment of specific luetic conditions demanded preliminary general physical examinations and these laid bare an extravagant incidence of other disabilities. Some 7,500 blood examinations and 3,200 urine analyses were made on those under treatment, and a total of 2,042 prescriptions dispensed during the first year. Apart from this, however, 3,500 typhoid inoculations were given, and 600 children immunized against diphtheria, and 200 vaccinated against smallpox. This altogether, with the Red Cross distribution of seeds for gardens and yeast to be used in combating pellagra, constituted one of the most intense concentrations upon a reconstructive health campaign of any rural section in the South.

It was evident, however, that the dependent relationship of the Negro tenants to white landowners called for education of the landowner as well as the tenant. And although this has not yet become common in either direction, there are indications that some of the white planters are recognizing time off for health as profitable in the end. One of them commented thus to an official of the demonstration: "The year before this demonstration was put on I paid out over fifteen hundred dollars to doctors for medical service. This year I have had a doctor on the place only twice and those were for new babies. The men work better. . . . ."

The startling inbreeding of disease among the Negroes, the violent eruption of nutritional disorders, and the rapid contagion of infectious diseases are intricately bound up with their isolation, their low literacy, and their cultural backwardness. They have little or no knowledge of the diseases responsible for their excessive deaths, and little access to physicians when the seriousness of ailments exceeds their simple folk remedies. With these, however, goes a life-organization which permits neither the full responsibility of the planter for their troubles nor the free development among and for themselves of controls over their most common disabilities. The situation has fostered a striking disorganization.

As in other respects, the most far-reaching changes in habits are proceeding at most rapid pace in the work done with and through the children. This suggests that along with the programs of adult education, social work, and compulsory health regulations, the elementary schools demand foremost attention if these changes are to be given permanence and significance.

Chapter VIII

CONCLUSION

THE basic assumption of much of the literature regarding Negroes in America, scientific and otherwise, is that they represent a culture which is, in itself, widely different from that of the Euro-American culture in which they live. This is implicit in the frequent and serious references to the success, or failure, or ineptness of the members of this group in taking on the white man's civilization. The unique situation of the Negroes and their relationship to the American culture, however, raise questions of considerably wider range than this local and racial relationship. For it is possible to observe in the adjustment experience of this group, under well-defined conditions, something of the process by which individual and group behavior patterns themselves are conditioned.

It has been impossible to escape the force of tradition, as represented in the customs established under the institution of slavery, and adhered to, by the white population in their relation to the Negroes, and by the Negroes in relation to themselves. What has resulted is an inevitable outcome of these traditions as expressed in the life of the subjects of this study. The community studied reflects a static economics not unlike the Mexican *hacienda*, or the condition of the Polish peasant—a situation in which the members of a group are "muffled with a vast apathy." It is unquestionably the economic system in which they live, quite as much or even more than the landlords, that is responsible for their plight. These fine distinctions, however, are not usually made by the Negroes; and to them the system is the government, and the government is the landlord.

208

The social results of the economic system in this area, past and present, have been positive and unmistakable. The tradition, supported by what remains of the plantation structure, has given a measure of equilibrium to the social relations existing within the structure. From the nature of the external conditions determining the early social organization of this group it has taken form, naturally, outside the dominant current of the American culture. At the same time, and unfortunately, the very fact of this cultural difference presents the danger of social disorganization in any sudden attempt to introduce new modes of living and conceptions of values. The situation is one clearly of isolation and cultural lag. Changes are occurring slowly, however, and it is possible to observe and to measure them.

Strangely enough, the changes appear to have come in this setting least rapidly through the introduction of machinery. Farming implements are practically the same as they were three or four generations ago. On the other hand, however, there has been definite cultural penetration through the medium of the school, the church, the influence of persons educated outside the community, the exposure to demonstrations in health and agriculture, and through returned migrants. Throughout, the weight of tradition, as would be expected, has resisted these changes.

It seems warrantable to suggest that slavery was an incidental product of the plantation and that the habits and customs of the Negroes, in so far as they are peculiar, were both shaped and preserved by the conditions inherent in the plantation system itself. The high point in the development of the plantation was the high point in the development of the institution of slavery. There were plantations in America before there was slavery. Indeed, the Virginia colony was first a plantation. It is essentially a frontier device. Thompson has described the plantation as being characterized by forced labor, open resources, and concentration upon a staple crop. The passing of the frontier could have no other effect than to render the plantation, in its institutionalized form, archaic.

There is strong indication that the social relations which evolved under this structure, largely as a phase of control, are responsible for both the cultural backwardness of the labor force and the romantic efforts, against the logic of economics, to preserve the structure itself. The feature of the plantation development in this country, which had most persistent and compelling influence upon the social life of the Negroes, probably began with the requirement of mobility in the labor, as a result of the vicissitudes of the first staple crop. The cultivation of tobacco resulted in such rapid and wasteful exhaustion of the soil as to require constant movement in search of new lands. Such mobility demanded attachment to the person rather than to the soil. It is obvious that a contingency of this character would favor slavery over the status of simple serfdom, as the old world knew it. Moreover, there was the problem of property inheritance which, in the new world, was more conspicuously and profitably a matter of labor than of land. These factors in themselves helped to fix the logic of slavery, and to fix it within the plantation economy. And, although the industrial system itself might be considered, in a sense, a plantation economy, it has never invoked, as did slavery, the complete dependence of labor upon the proprietor of the plantation. The plantation technique, on the side of administration, was most efficient in respect to discipline and policing, and this technique has survived, more or less, despite the formal abolition of the institution of slavery.

The objective of this study has been, so far as possible, to portray realistically the life of a rural Negro community under the influence of a plantation economy. It is not possible or desirable to formulate from these observations general conclusions regarding the Negro rural community as a whole. There are, however, certain inescapable characteristics of this agricultural economy: The plantation communities in which Negroes live, in so far as they are areas of highest population concentration for this group, are also likely to be areas of greatest cultural isolation. In such communities will be found, with but few exceptions, similar situations measurable in terms of illiteracy, mobility, schooling, tenantry, and like factors.

In 1930 there were 164 counties with preponderant Negro populations. The number of such counties after 1860 first increased then slowly declined, and not until 1920 did the number fall below the level of 1860. In that year there were 244 counties in which half or more of the population was Negro, and in 1880 there were 300. Throughout this period of seventy years since slavery the areas of heaviest Negro population concentration have remained practically the same.

Not all tenant areas, however, are areas of heaviest Negro concentration, and, similarly, there are other types of agricultural areas with Negro populations which do reveal striking contrasts. There are at hand certain comparative data from other southern counties with different Negro population proportions, and different historical backgrounds. Gibson County, in Tennessee, referred to earlier, is a diversified farming area, with only 23 per cent of its total population and 18.8 per cent of its rural farm population Negro. Within the minor civil divisions of the county the Negro proportions fluctuate in numerical importance from no Negroes to as much as 41.3 per cent of the population. This suggests, in the first place, a greatly modified isolation, and a wider current of communication with the outside. In Macon County the smallest Negro proportion in a civil district is 58 per cent and the largest 97 per cent. In Gibson County there is greater and longer-range migration, a more pronounced interest in education, more property ownership, and more clearly recognizable affectional ties within the families.

The lack of dependence upon a staple crop and the absence of a plantation economy may be pointed to as being, in part at least, responsible for the higher home-ownership proportions. Differences in customs follow closely these statistical differences, and suggest very clearly the different standards and codes under which the two types of rural areas operate. There is more money in circulation in the farm-owning areas, and this is an aid both to domestic planning and to the development of independence.

The frequency of active affectional relations between parents and children creates a distinctly different picture of the dominant pattern of family life. Moreover, in these landowning areas the fathers play a stronger rôle in the family, and the children away from home more often maintain contact and remain a functioning part of the social unit of the family.

Staple crops are a mixed blessing. The economic advantage of the old pattern of cotton cultivation has disappeared in the face of the challenge of world-competition to the crop itself. When at the high noon of its power, profit, and glamor, the southern states were supplying the raw materials for a large part of the world. There are today over fifty cotton-growing countries. But despite the evident decadence of a once flourishing institution, the social habits inherent in the system hang on little challenged and even less changed. Soil exhaustion and abandonment go on despite the fact that the limit of the frontier has been reached. A natural response to this has been the constant and determined movement away of both Negro and white populations to the city and its industries in so far as these industries could absorb them.

The romantic personalities of the past who dominated the plantation are rapidly passing. Control becomes increasingly impersonal. Large areas of Mississippi, Alabama, Louisiana, and Georgia are already in the possession of banks or insurance companies in satisfaction of mortgage defaults. The situation suggests the need of a complete reorganization of agriculture, and particularly in the Cotton Belt, in respect to both production and distribution.

The surplus of cotton grown in the South has already forced the desperate expedient of attempting to reduce the cotton acreage. The first attempt at reduction, however, merely served to intensify the limited cultivation, with the result that more cotton was grown on smaller acreage by fewer persons. The greatest pressure is being felt at present by the tenants, dulled and blocked in by a backwardness which is a fatal heritage of the system itself. But the fate of the tenant is but an aspect of the fate of the southern farmer generally, and the plight of all of these awaits a comprehensive planning, which affects not merely the South but the nation.

INDEX

PHOENIX BOOKS
in History

PHOENIX BOOKS
Sociology, Anthropology, and Archeology